Christoph David Gladisch

Verification-based Software-fault Detection

Verification-based Software-fault Detection

by
Christoph David Gladisch

Dissertation, Karlsruher Institut für Technologie
Fakultät für Informatik
Tag der mündlichen Prüfung: 8. Februar 2011

Impressum

Karlsruher Institut für Technologie (KIT)
KIT Scientific Publishing
Straße am Forum 2
D-76131 Karlsruhe
www.ksp.kit.edu

KIT – Universität des Landes Baden-Württemberg und nationales
Forschungszentrum in der Helmholtz-Gemeinschaft

KIT Scientific Publishing 2011
Print on Demand

ISBN 978-3-86644-676-2

Verification-based Software-fault Detection

zur Erlangung des akademischen Grades eines

Doktors der Naturwissenschaften

der Fakultät für Informatik
des Karlsruher Instituts für Technologie (KIT)

genehmigte

Dissertation

von

Christoph David Gladisch

aus Tichau

Tag der mündlichen Prüfung: 8. Februar 2011

Erster Gutachter: Prof. Dr. Bernhard Beckert,
KIT - Karlsruher Institut für
Technologie

Zweiter Gutachter: Prof. Dr. Peter Müller,
ETH Zürich - Eidgenössische
Technische Hochschule Zürich

Zusammenfassung (German Summary)

Motivation und Überblick

Software wird in vielen sicherheitskritischen Systemen verwendet. Bei der Softwareentwicklung können jedoch Fehler entstehen, da der Softwareentwickler versucht seine unpräzise Vorstellung von einem Programm präzise in einer Programmiersprache zu formalisieren. Mit formalen Methoden kann dieses Problem reduziert werden. Formale Methoden fügen zur Softwareentwicklung eine zusätzliche Schicht hinzu, welche es erlaubt gewünschte Programmeigenschaften zu formalisieren und zu überprüfen. Deduktive Softwareverifikation ist eine formale Methode mit deren Hilfe die Korrektheit eines Programms bezüglich einer formalen Anforderungsspezifikation bewiesen werden kann. Programme sind jedoch oft fehlerbehaftet, d.h., sie erfüllen ihre Anforderungsspezifikation nicht, und somit gelingen Korrektheitsbeweise oft nicht. Die Möglichkeit Softwarefehler zu entdecken ist daher wichtig um die Effizienz der Softwareverifikation zu erhöhen. Eine weitere Einschränkung der Softwareverifikation ist, dass es oft nicht praktikabel ist Softwareverifikation rigoros auf das Programm und alle anderen Komponenten anzuwenden, welche für das korrekte Verhalten des Programms verantwortlich sind. Eine Kombination aus Softwareverifikation und Softwaretesten ist daher selbst dann wichtig, wenn die Korrektheit des (Teil-) Programms bewiesen wurde.

In dieser Dissertation werden neue Techniken für die Detektion von Softwarefehlern (auch bekannt als Softwarebugs) entwickelt, welche auf einer formalen deduktiven Verifikationstechnologie basieren. Der Ansatz dabei ist mit einem Verifikationsversuch Informationen aus dem betrachteten Programm zu extrahieren und diese anschließend für die Fehlerdetektion zu verwenden. Die Techniken sind in zwei Kategorien aufgeteilt. Die erste Kategorie besteht aus rein deduktiven Techniken, welche spezifische Probleme der deduktiven Fehlerdetektion lösen. Dabei sind die wichtigsten wissenschaftlichen Beiträge (a) eine Technik zur Generierung von Gegenbeispielen (counterexamples), bzw. Gegenmodellen, aus Formeln der Prädikatenlogik erster Ordnung mit Quantoren und (b) eine Technik zum Deduzieren der Existenz von Softwarefehlern aus offenen Beweisverpflichtungen, welche unter Verwendung von Schleifeninvarianten und Methodenkontrakten entstanden sind. In der zweiten Kategorie sind Techniken für die Generierung von Softwaretests enthalten, welche auf den Techniken aus der ersten Kategorie aufbauen. Dabei erweitern wir existierende Arbeiten zur Generierung von Testfällen aus Beweisstrukturen und beschreiben neue Werkzeugketten (tool-chains), welche die verifikations-basierte Testgenerierung mit traditionellen Techniken zur Testgenerierung kombinieren. Die vorgestellten Ansätze nutzen die Informationen, die bei der Softwareverifikation berechnet werden, wodurch eine homogene Kombination aus Softwareverifikation, deduktiver Fehlerdetektion und Testgenerierung entsteht.

Teil I

Diese Arbeit wurde im Rahmen des KeY Projekts[1] durchgeführt. KeY [Beckert et al., 2007] ist ein Softwareverifikationssystem, welches am Karlsruher Institut für Technologie (KIT)[2], an der Universität Koblenz-Landau und an der Chalmers University in Göteborg (Schweden) entwickelt wurde. Im Teil I der Dissertation werden der Formalismus und der Verifikationsansatz von KeY erklärt. Diese bestehen aus einer Instanz von Dynamischer Logik [Harel, 1984] und einem Sequenzenkalkül, welcher klassisches Theorembeweisen und Programmverifikation für JAVA kombiniert. Die in dieser Dissertation vorgestellten Techniken basieren auf dem KeY System und dessen Formalismen. Wir nehmen jedoch an, dass die hier präsentierten Techniken auch als Erweiterungen für andere Verifikationswerkzeuge geeignet sind, welche im Ansatz dem KeY System ähnlich sind. Solche Werkzeuge sind zum Beispiel VCC [Cohen et al., 2009], Spec# [Barnett et al., 2005], Why/-Krakatoa/Caduceus [Filliâtre and Marché, 2007], ESC/Java2 [Chalin et al., 2005], sowie die Beweisassistenten Isabelle/HOL [Wenzel et al., 2008] und PVS [Owre et al., 1996] in einigen ihrer Anwendungen in der Softwareverifikation. Solche Werkzeuge verifizieren ein Programm auf einer quellcode-nahen Ebene anstatt eine abstrakte Repräsentation des Programms zu verifizieren. Programmeigenschaften werden im Stil von Hoare-Logik [Hoare, 1969] und Design-by-Contract [Meyer, 1997] mit prädikatenlogischen Formeln als Vor- und Nachbedingungen von Programmcode repräsentiert. Des Weiteren verwenden diese Ansätze die wohlbekannten Konzepte, Methodenkontrakte, Klasseninvarianten und Schleifeninvarianten. Die Analyse des Programms erfolgt mittels symbolischer Programmausführung [King, 1976] oder Berechnung der

---

[1] www.key-project.org
[2] KIT – Universität des Landes Baden-Württemberg und nationales Forschungszentrum in der Helmholtz-Gemeinschaft

II

schwächsten Vorbedingung [Dijkstra, 1976]. Die durch die Programmanalyse gewonnen Beweisverpflichtungen sind prädikatenlogische Formeln, welche anschließend mit Hilfe eines Theorembeweisers oder eines Satisfiability Modulo Theories (SMT) Solvers, wie zum Beispiel Z3
[de Moura and Bjørner, 2008], auf Gültigkeit überprüft werden. Ein
Verifikationsversuch mit solchen Techniken ist die Ausgangsbasis für
unsere Techniken, auf die wir im folgenden kurz eingehen.

Teil II

Wenn ein Programm bezüglich seiner formalen Spezifikation korrekt
ist und zusätzliche Programmannotationen, wie Methodenkontrakte,
Klasseninvarianten und Schleifeninvarianten, hinreichend ausdrucksstark sind, dann können moderne Verifikationswerkzeuge die Korrektheit des Programms meistens automatisch Beweisen. Das Problem ist
jedoch diese Vorbedingungen zu erfüllen. Programme und Spezifikatio-
nen enthalten oft Fehler und die zusätzlichen Programmannotationen
sind oft nicht hinreichend ausdrucksstark um einen Verifikationsbeweis
zu schließen. Aufgrund der Semi-Entscheidbarkeit der Prädikatenlogik
erster Stufe ist es oft unklar, ob ein Verifikationsversuch fortgeführt
oder abgebrochen werden soll. Eine offene Beweisverpflichtung bedeu-
tet nicht zwingend, dass ein Fehler im Programm oder dessen Spezifikation (kurz Softwarefehler) existiert, da eine Fortführung des Verifikationsversuchs eventuell zum Beweis führen kann. Die Techniken im
Teil II dieser Dissertation helfen Softwarefehler zu entdecken und daher Verifikationsversuche abzubrechen die nicht gelingen können. Das
Besondere an diesen Techniken ist, dass sie die gewonnen Informationen aus dem Verifikationsversuch wiederverwenden und dadurch den
Berechnungsaufwand für die Fehlerdetektion reduzieren. Da die Fehlerdetektion deduktiv funktioniert, wird vom technischen Standpunkt
betrachtet auch die deduktive Verifikationstechnologie wiederverwen-
det. Das Resultat ist eine Symbiose aus deduktiver Softwareverifikation
und Fehlerdetektion.

Um einen Softwarefehler basierend auf einer offenen Beweisverpflichtung zu detektieren werden in unserem Ansatz zwei Bedingungen ge-
prüft: (1) ein offener Beweisast muss gültigkeitserhaltend sein und (2)
die Beweisverpflichtung im Blatt dieses Astes muss ein Gegenmodell
haben. Diese Bedingungen zu prüfen ist schwierig. Um Bedingung (1)
zu prüfen, muss mit Programmabstraktionen wie Methodenkontrakten, Klasseninvarianten und Schleifeninvarianten umgegangen werden.

Gegenmodelle für offene Beweisverpflichtungen implizieren nicht, dass die betrachtete Software einen Fehler hat, weil das Problem darin liegen kann, dass ungeeignete Programmabstraktionen verwendet wurden. Wir lösen das Problem durch Prüfung der Bedingung (1), wofür wir ein sehr effizientes Verfahren entwickelt haben. Um Bedingung (2) zu prüfen, werden in der Regel SMT-Solver eingesetzt. In unseren Experimenten haben wird jedoch festgestellt, dass SMT-Solver schnell an ihre Grenzen stoßen, wenn (Gegen-)Modelle für quantifizierten Formeln gefunden werden sollen. Modellgenerierung für quantifizierte Formeln ist ein lang erforschtes Problem, für das wir eine neue Technik vorstellen. In unseren Experimenten konnte diese Technik Modelle für Formeln generieren, welche SMT-Solver nicht lösen konnten.

Teil III

Der vorgestellte Ansatz kann nicht nur Fehler entdecken, sondern er liefert auch unterschiedliche Informationen, welche dem Benutzer helfen die Fehler zu finden. Zu den Informationen gehört der Anfangszustand des Programms, der zum fehlerhaften Programmverhalten führt. Im Teil III der Dissertation werden diese Informationen zur Generierung ausführbarer Tests genutzt. Fallunterscheidungen, welche sonst bei der Programmausführung gemacht werden, führen zu Fallunterscheidungen in der Beweisstruktur während des Verifikationsversuchs. Die Beweisstruktur enthält die Pfadbedingungen zur Ausführung der unterschiedlichen Programmpfade. Die verifikations-basierte Testfallgenerierung (VBT) erzeugt Testfälle aus einer solchen Beweisstruktur. Dadurch kann eine hohe Testfallabdeckung erreichen werden was zum höheren Vertrauen des Benutzers in das korrekte Funktionieren der Software führt. Mit Hilfe der Techniken aus Teil II können auch Testfälle generiert werden, welche garantiert Fehler in der Software entdecken. Die Tests können in Kombination mit einem Programmdebugger genutzt werden, um den Fehler zu lokalisieren.

Die Dissertation beschreibt auch neue Ansätze, welche VBT mit traditionellen Testwerkzeugen kombinieren, wie zum Beispiel Black-box Testwerkzeuge und Capture & Replay (CaR) Werkzeuge. Der erste dieser Ansätze verwendet die Pfadbedingungen, welche zuvor aus einer Beweisstruktur extrahiert wurden, um die Anforderungsspezifikation der betrachteten Software strukturell zu erweitern. Verwendet man diese erweiterte Spezifikation als Eingabe in ein Black-box Testwerkzeug, welches eine Testabdeckung der Spezifikation sicherstellt, so führt das effektiv zum White-box Testen. Ein Vorteil dieses Ansatzes ist die Trennung von Zuständigkeiten. Ein weiterer Vorteil ist, dass das Black-box- und das Verifikationswerkzeug die technischen Fähigkeiten des jeweils anderen Werkzeugs nutzen können. Diese Vorteile treffen auch zu, wenn VBT mit CaR Werkzeugen kombiniert wird. Wir haben eine Werkzeugkette bestehend aus KeY und dem CaR Werkzeug GenUTest [Pasternak et al., 2009] implementiert. GenUTest führt dynamische Programmanalyse durch und generiert aus beobachteten Programmausführungen isolierte Unittests mit Testorakeln, welche neue Programmausführungen mit der alten Programmausführung vergleichen. KeY auf der anderen Seite generiert Tests, welche eine hohe Testfallabdeckung erreichen, und es kann korrekte Programmausführung sicherstellen, wenn das Programm zuvor verifiziert wurde. Die resultierende Werkzeugkette aus KeY und GenUTest erzeugt isolierte Unittests mit einer hohen Testfallabdeckung, welche für Unit Regressiontesting geeignet sind.

Die Verfahren und wissenschaftlichen Ergebnisse, welche in dieser Dissertation beschrieben sind, wurden auf internationalen wissenschaftlichen Konferenzen vorgestellt und publiziert. Folgende Publikationen des Autors haben zu dieser Dissertation beigetragen: [Gladisch, 2010a], [Gladisch, 2010b], [Gladisch et al., 2010], [Gladisch, 2009], [Gladisch, 2008a], [Engel et al., 2008] und [Beckert and Gladisch, 2007].

Acknowledgements

This thesis was realized thanks to the support and encouragement from many people to whom I would like to express my gratitude here.

First and foremost, I would like to thank my supervisor Prof. Dr. Bernhard Beckert for his excellent guidance and support – financial, personal, and technical. I'm grateful for the freedom he gave me in research and the opportunity to participate at numerous workshops, symposia, conferences, and at a summer school, a winter school, and a research stay abroad. I appreciate the opportunity to work with him and the research positions he offered me at Universität Koblenz-Landau and at Karlsruher Institut für Technologie (KIT). He has been a rule model for me in many respects. Discussions with him and his comments to this thesis were very helpful and further improved the quality of this thesis.

Prof. Dr. Peter Müller from ETH Zürich enjoys a high reputation in the software verification community. I'm grateful to him for accepting the role of the second reviewer of this thesis.

My great gratitude goes also to Prof. Dr. Ulrich Furbach from Universität Koblenz-Landau. I enjoyed working at his research group for 7 years since the beginning of my Studienarbeit (minor thesis). I'm grateful that I was able to use the facilities at his research group (AGKI), for being able to participate at social events, and for his guidance when I applied for the extension of my fellowship. I would like to thank him for the research position in the iCity project at the time when Prof. Dr. Beckert moved to KIT.

I would like to thank Prof. Dr. Peter Schmitt and Prof. Dr. Dr. h.c. Ludwig Tavernier for their letters of support which helped me to receive the single university-wide *Landesgraduiertenförderungsgesetz*-fellowship at Universität Koblenz-Landau. I would like to thank the university for receiving this grant for 2 years and 9 months as well as for additional research positions.

I'm thankful to my former colleges for a friendly atmosphere and enjoyable work together in the research group of Prof. Dr. Furbach at Universität Koblenz-Landau: Markus Maron, Dr. Ammar Mohammed, Ekaterina Pek, Björn Pelzer, Claudia Schon, Christian Schwarz. My special thanks goes to Markus Bender who was working as a student assistant for several years and helped implementing and maintaining the verification-based testing techniques described in Chapter 7.

I would like to thank my colleges at the KIT and members and former members of the KeY-project for collaboration, for discussions, or for help: Dr. Wolfgang Ahrendt, Thorsten Bormer, Daniel Bruns, Dr. Richard Bubel, Dr. Christian Engel, David Farago, Prof. Dr. Reiner Hähnle, Dr. Vladimir Klebanov, Dr. Philpp Rümmer, Christoph Scheben, Prof. Dr. Peter Schmitt, Mattias Ulbrich, and Dr. Benjamin Weiß.

In March 2009 I went on a *Short Term Scientific Mission* to the University of Tel Aviv where I stayed at the research group of Prof. Dr. Amiram Yehudai. I would like to thank Prof. Dr. Yehudai and Dr. Shmuel Tyszberowicz for their great help and support during my stay and for our long collaboration. I'm grateful to Benny Pasternak for modifying the tool GenUTest as needed to combine it with KeY during my stay in Tel Aviv. I would like to thank the COST Action IC0701 of the *European Science Foundation* for this funding.

Jean-Louis Lanet provided the banking application that served as a source for examples and experiments in several chapters of this thesis and I would like to thank him for that.

Several people helped to proofread parts of this thesis. I would like to thank: Thorsten Bormer, Daniel Bruns, Christian Dietz, Dr. Shmuel Tyszberowicz, Markus Wagner, Dr. Benjamin Weiß, and Paul.

I owe my deepest gratitude to my parents and grandparents for their love, support, encouragement, and discussions. They helped me in many ways. Writing this thesis would not have been possible without their support.

Zutiefst danke ich meinen Eltern und Großeltern für ihre Liebe, Unterstützung, Ermutigung und Gespräche. Sie haben mir in vielen Weisen geholfen. Diese Dissertation hätte ohne ihre Unterstützung nicht entstehen können.

Karlsruhe, Dezember 2010
Dr. Christoph D. Gladisch

Contents

List of Tables

List of Figures

Abstract

Software is used in many safety- and security-critical systems. Software development is, however, an error-prone task where a software developer tries to precisely formalize in a programming language their imprecise ideas about a program. Formal methods help to reduce this problem. These methods add another layer to the software development allowing to formalize and to check desired properties of a program. Deductive software verification is a formal method for proving the correctness of a program with respect to a requirement specification. However, since programs often have faults, i.e., they do not satisfy the required program properties, program correctness proofs often do not succeed. The ability to detect software faults is therefore important to increase the efficiency of software verification. Another deficiency of software verification is that it is often not practical to apply software verification rigorously to a program and all other components that are critical for the the correct behavior of the program. The combination of software verification with software testing is therefore important even if a correctness proof for a program (subset) has been established.

In this dissertation new techniques for the detection of software faults (or software "bugs") are developed which are based on a formal deductive verification technology. The general approach is to start with a verification attempt in order to gain information about the respective program and then to use this information for software fault detection. The techniques are divided into two categories. The first category consists of purely deductive techniques that solve specific problems for detecting software faults if a verification attempt is not successful. The most significant contributions are (a) a technique for counterexample generation from first-order logic formulas with quantifiers, and (b) a technique for deducing the existence of software faults from a failed verification attempt when loop invariants and method contracts are used. The second category consists of test case generation techniques that are based on the techniques from the first category. We extend existing work for the generation of test cases from proof structures and describe tool-chains that combine verification-based test generation with more traditional test generation approaches. The described approaches take advantage of information obtained during verification and in this way combine verification technology with deductive fault detection and test generation in a very unified way.

This research was carried out in the scope of the KeY project [KeY-Home]. KeY is a software verification system developed at Karlsruhe Institute of Technology (KIT)[3] (Germany), Universität Koblenz-Landau (Germany), and the Chalmers University in Gothenburg (Sweden). The main scientific results underlying the proposed dissertation have been published at international conferences.

In this thesis the pronoun "we" refers to the author of this thesis. The pronoun "they" is frequently used as an epicene, i.e. gender-neutral, pronoun according to The Cambridge Guide to English Usage (2004).

---

[3] KIT – University of the State of Baden-Württemberg and National Research Center of the Helmholtz Association

1

Introduction

Software is used in many safety and security critical systems. While it may be forgivable when a text editor crashes, software faults in vehicles, airplanes, heart pace-makers, radiation therapy machines, or banking applications can have catastrophic impact on finance and human lives. In traditional engineering domains mathematical models are developed and verified before devices, machines, or buildings are built. Formal methods in software engineering follow a similar idea and are increasingly encouraged in the development of software systems. The development of formal methods for software development is an active research area. Due to their recent gain in maturity, these methods are also repeatedly applied in industrial context.

Deductive verification is a formal method that allows proving the correctness of a program with respect to a requirement specification. A verification proof is valid for all input- and output-situations of a program. We regard Hoare-style [Hoare, 1969] and design-by-contract [Meyer, 1997] oriented verification approaches that verify programs on the source code level. The requirement specification is usually written for each program method using a variant of first-order logic as the specification language. The specification describes the expected behavior of the method via pre- and postconditions. The meaning of such a specification is that if the program method is executed in a state where the precondition holds, then after the execution of the method the postcondition must hold as well. A verification tool then generates verification conditions by analysing the program source code and the specification. If these verification conditions can be proven, e.g. by utilizing first-order theorem proving, then it is ensured that the program satisfies its requirement specification.

In practice, however, programs usually have faults (also known as software bugs). In general, the search for the correctness proof of a faulty program does not terminate because such a proof does not exist in a correct verification system. Yet, when the proof search is terminated, e.g. by timeout, then it remains unclear if the program is correct or not. In practice, verification tools usually terminate after a few seconds or hours. If in such cases a proof is not found, then the reason is usually that not all possible rule applications like quantifier instantiations and program abstractions were enumerated. Thus, as long as a proof has not been found, the user does not know if they should continue searching for a proof or if they should search for a fault in the program or its requirement specification. This problem results from the semi-decidability of first-order logic. The detection of software faults, which is the subject of this dissertation, plays therefore a major role for deductive software verification.

The detection of software faults is, however, not only important during the verification process, but also after the correctness of the program has been proven. In practice it is often very hard or even not practical to apply a formal verification process completely to the program, the compiler, and its environment consisting of software and hardware. In contrast to verification, these components are engaged when software testing is applied. Software testing is not capable of showing the correctness of programs for infinitely many input- and output-situations but it allows the user a degree of confidence that the program behaves as expected in its environment. The degree of confidence in the correct behavior depends on how well the program is tested or, in other words, how high the test coverage is. In contrast to verification, tests do not attempt to formally verify a program, but instead, they try to reveal software faults. Thus, the higher the test coverage of the program is, the higher is the confidence of the user about the correct functioning of the program.

In this dissertation new techniques for software fault detection are described and investigated that are based on verification technology. The general approach followed in this dissertation is to start with a verification attempt in order to gain information about the regarded program and then to use this information for software fault detection. The techniques are divided into two categories. The first category consists of purely deductive techniques that solve specific problems for detecting software faults if a verification attempt is not successful. The

4

second category consists of test generation techniques that are based on the techniques from the first category. The described approaches take advantage of information obtained during verification and in this way combine verification technology with deductive fault detection and test generation in a very unified way.

The research was carried out in the scope of the KeY-project [KeY-Home]. KeY is a software verification system developed at Karlsruhe Institute of Technology (KIT)[1] (Germany), Universität Koblenz-Landau (Germany), and Chalmers University in Gothenburg (Sweden). The main scientific results underlying the proposed dissertation have been published at international conferences.

1.1 State of the Art and Challenges

This section is devoted to give a high-level overview on the state-of-the-art and challenges that are related to the approach described in this thesis. A more detailed description of related techniques and references is given in the respective chapters.

The novel techniques described in this thesis are extensions of verification technology. Therefore the state-of-the-art and challenges in verification technology are relevant for our contributions. We restrict our view on verification techniques for the verification of programs on the source-code level. Those techniques differ from approaches which use more abstract representations of the program and specification such as the B approach [Abrial, 1996], Alloy [Jackson, 2002], Abstract State Machines [Börger and Stärk, 2003], or Z [Spivey, 1992].

State-of-the-art deductive verification systems for source-code level verification are for instance VCC [Cohen et al., 2009], Spec# [Barnett et al., 2005], Why/Krakatoa/Caduceus [Filliâtre and Marché, 2007], ESC/Java2 [Chalin et al., 2005], and KeY [Beckert et al., 2007], as well as the proof assistants PVS [Owre et al., 1996] and Isabelle/HOL [Wenzel et al., 2008]. Most of these tools take a two step approach. In the first step, symbolic execution or predicate transformation is used in order to transform a program method and its specification into a set of first-order logic formulas which are called verification conditions. In the second step, the verification conditions are forwarded to theorem provers or to SMT solvers such as Simplify [Detlefs et al., 2005], Z3

---

[1] KIT – University of the State of Baden-Württemberg and National Research Center of the Helmholtz Association

[de Moura and Bjørner, 2008], CVC3 [Barrett and Tinelli, 2007], or Yices [Dutertre and de Moura, 2006a]. If all verification conditions are proven, then the correctness of the program method with respect to its specification is formally verified.

Software verification is an active international research area. For instance, the COST Action IC 0701, which is funded by the European Science Foundation (ESF), consists of members from research groups in deductive verification located in 17 European countries. Due to an increasing maturity level of verification techniques and tools, they can be applied to increasingly realistic programs. For example, in the Mondex case study a JAVA CARD implementation of an electronic purse has been verified with the KeY tool [Tonin, 2007]. In the project Verisoft[2] a complete software and hardware system consisting of a CPU, an operating system, and applications running on the operating system were verified using primarily Isabelle/HOL [Paul, 2005]. In the following project, VerisoftXT[3], software verification was applied among others to Microsoft's Hypervisor which is a layer of software located between the hardware and one or more operating systems [Leinenbach and Santen, 2009]. In the L4.verified project[4] the operating system kernel seL4 consisting of 8,700 lines of C code has been verified [Klein et al., 2010].

Yet, software verification is an iterative and time-consuming task. In practice, most of the time verification attempts fail during a software verification process, which is a major factor that makes the verification process expensive. For some of the state-of-the-art verification tools an unsuccessful verification attempt is, however, not a useless effort. From a failed or interrupted verification attempt a rich set of information is available that has been computed during the analysis of the program and specification. The above-mentioned verification tools utilize this information in order to help the user determine why the verification proof does not succeed. For this purpose these tools provide means to generate counterexamples from verification conditions that cannot be proven. If a counterexample can be found, then it is clear that the verification condition cannot be proven and the counterexample helps the user to understand the problem. In some cases the counterexamples can be regarded as program inputs that reveal software faults. In such cases the counterexample can be used to generate a test that ex-

---

[2] http://www.verisoft.de
[3] http://www.verisoftxt.de
[4] http://ertos.nicta.com.au/research/l4.verified/

ecutes the program in a manner revealing the fault. The user can then use an ordinary program debugger in order to locate the fault. However, an unprovable verification condition does not necessarily imply the existence of a software fault, and counterexamples of such verification conditions are not necessarily valid program inputs that reveal faults. The problem occurs when program abstractions in form of, e.g., loop invariants and method contracts are used during verification. If a program abstraction, i.e. a loop invariant or method contract, is used and a verification condition has a counterexample, then the user does not know if (a) they should fix the program abstraction or (b) if they should fix the program or its requirement specification. This is a problem in state-of-the-art deductive software verification systems that we address.

A theoretical framework for static program analysis with abstractions is abstract interpretation [Cousot and Cousot, 1992]. In the abstract interpretation approach, the domain of program variables is abstracted and the program is symbolically executed with abstractions of values. Automatically generated abstractions differ, however, from user-provided abstractions which are given in form of loop invariants and method contracts. The difference is that user-provided loop invariants and method contract often express properties which are semantically more complex. A variant of abstract interpretation is predicate abstraction [Graf and Saïdi, 1997] where abstractions are constructed from a finite set of predicates. In this way, also more complex semantic properties can be expressed by providing semantically complex predicates. A technique for automatically generating abstractions which are under- or over-approximations of program states is *counterexample guided abstraction refinement* (CEGAR) [Clarke et al., 2000]. Depending on the particular setting one approximation is sound for proving validity, i.e. correctness of the program, and the other is sound for showing the existence of a fault in the program. Abstract interpretation and predicate abstraction are integrated in variants of the KeY tool in [Bubel et al., 2009] and [Weiß, 2009], respectively. The focus of our work is, however, not the generation of abstractions. We assume that verification conditions are already generated using, e.g. user-provided, loop invariants and method contracts. We propose a technique that investigates under what conditions the counterexamples of verification conditions are valid program inputs that reveal software faults. In this way, the technique helps to disambiguate the reason for verification failure when

7

using loop invariants and method contracts extending the current state of the art.

Some state-of-the-art techniques for the generation of counterexamples from verification conditions, which are first-order logic formulas, are satisfiability modulo theory (SMT) solvers, e.g. [de Moura and Bjørner, 2008; Barrett and Tinelli, 2007; Dutertre and de Moura, 2006a; Detlefs et al., 2005]. These tools can check if first-order logic formulas are satisfiable or unsatisfiable. By negating the input formula SMT, solvers check if the original formula is valid or if it is falsifiable, i.e., if it has a counterexample. SMT solvers combine the advantages of fast SAT solvers, of decision procedures for theories that are used in verification, and of theory or decision procedure combination methods. However, since first-order logic is only semi-decidable, SMT solvers cannot always decide whether a verification condition is valid or if it has a counterexample. This is especially the case if the input formula contains quantifiers. For proving the validity of a quantified formula the problem is to find an instantiation of the quantifier(s). Quantifier instantiations can be enumerated for arbitrary formulas, which may not terminate, but a proof exists for any valid first-order logic formula.[5] On the other hand, for proving the existence of a counterexample the formula must be in a decidable fragment of the decision procedure. The problem, when generating counterexamples, is that formulas outside the fragment cannot be handled by the decision procedure. Decidable fragments of decision procedures are, for instance, the Bernays-Schönfinkel class [Ge and de Moura, 2009], the array property fragment [Bradley et al., 2006], and rational or Presburger arithmetic for which quantifier elimination techniques exist [Ghilardi, 2003]. If quantified formulas use symbols from different theories, which is often the case with verification conditions, then these formulas do not *fit* in the decidable fragments of the procedures. Consequently, satisfiability of these formulas usually cannot be decided. We present a novel technique to address this challenge.

Formal software verification and software testing are the two major approaches to ensure the correct functioning of programs. Software verification is the only means to guarantee that a program is correctly implemented. However, due to its cost, software verification is restricted to safety critical software and special application domains, in practice. Software testing, on the other hand, is commonly used in industry and

---

[5] The background theory must also be representable as a first-order logic formula.

is applied to software projects of arbitrary size. Yet, software testing is not capable of showing the correctness of programs for infinitely many input- and output-situations. Because of the complementary strengths of verification and testing, an increasing interest in the combination of the two approaches can be observed. In recent years, several international conferences have adapted to accept contributions from both fields. The convergence of both approaches is especially encouraged by the international conference series *Tests and Proofs* which started in 2007. Several contributions of this dissertation were published at those conferences.

Test suites that provide a high code coverage can be generated, e.g., by combining the well-known techniques symbolic execution and model generation, as it was already proposed in the 1970s [King, 1974, 1976; Clarke, 1976]. This approach has gained much attraction in the last decade [Meudec, 2001; Zhang et al., 2004; Xie et al., 2005; Sen et al., 2005; Deng et al., 2006b; Cadar et al., 2008; Tillmann and de Halleux, 2008; Pasareanu et al., 2008]. The gain in maturity of symbolic execution has been largely influenced by the advancements of verification technology. Symbolic execution alone, however, cannot guarantee the analysis of all execution paths. In verification approaches, program abstractions, such as loop invariants and method contracts, are used for reasoning about complex or infinitely many program execution paths. We investigate their sematic properties which are required to generate tests satisfying full feasible branch coverage.

1.2 Contributions

The proposed dissertation extends the state-of-the-art of software fault detection approaches that are based on deductive verification technology. The formal basis of the techniques are a first-order dynamic logic [Harel, 1984] and a sequent calculus that combines symbolic execution and first-order theorem proving. These techniques are implemented in the KeY tool [Beckert et al., 2007]. In this thesis the pronoun "we" refers to the author of this thesis. The following list summarizes our contributions.

- We have developed a deductive software fault detection approach that uses and extends verification technology, and we have developed the theory behind it. We belief that the approach is applicable also to other verification tools that follow similar ideas as the KeY tool.

- We have discovered fundamental problems that occur when trying to detect faults deductively. The problems are caused by quantifiers and program abstractions (loop invariants and method contracts) and differ from the problems that occur with quantifiers and program abstractions in verification. We have invented novel techniques to handle these problems:
  - We have developed a technique for counterexample generation, respectively model generation, for first-order logic formulas with quantifiers. This technique is also important for test data generation when specifications and program annotations with quantifiers are used.
  - We have developed a technique for deducing the existence of software faults from a failed verification attempt when loop invariants and method contracts are used. The technique unifies verification and fault detection by reusing the information that was obtained through a verification attempt.
- We have developed several test generation techniques that extend and complement verification and deductive software fault detection.
  - We have developed a new version of a test generation approach that derives test cases from proofs (VBT) and we have developed a new theory behind it that is based on the theory of the deductive fault detection approach.
  - We have developed test generation approaches that combine VBT with more traditional test generation techniques such as black-box and capture & replay-based testing tools. The VBT technique and the traditional testing techniques benefit from this combination.
- The described techniques do not just exist side-by-side. All the techniques are based on the same verification technology and information is shared and reused between these techniques. We have achieved a combination of verification, deductive fault detection, and test generation based on a common theory, in one framework, and with a combined methodology.
- Prototypes of all technique are implemented in the KeY tool and are evaluated or have been tested.

The techniques and approaches that we have developed are addressed in the following subsections.

10

1.2.1 Counterexample Generation from Invalid Verification Conditions with Quantifiers

Verification conditions are first-order logic (FOL) formulas that are obtained during a verification attempt. It is important to detect if verification conditions have counterexamples in order to stop proof attempts that cannot succeed and in order to analyze the reason for verification failure. This requires the ability to generate models, i.e. interpretations, that satisfy first-order logic (FOL) formulas. Satisfiability modulo theory (SMT) solvers are state-of-the-art techniques for handling this problem. A major bottleneck is, however, the handling of quantified formulas.

We propose a model generation technique that is not explicitly restricted to a specific class of formulas. Consequently, the technique is not a decision procedure, i.e., it may not terminate. However, it can solve more general formulas than SMT solvers can solve in cases where it terminates. For example, assume we want to show the satisfiability of the formula

$$\forall x.(x \geqslant 0 \rightarrow prev(next(x)) = x) \tag{1.1}$$

where *prev* and *next* are uninterpreted function symbols. The formula stems from a verification condition. Some state-of-the-art SMT solvers – concretely we have tested Z3 [de Moura and Bjørner, 2008], CVC3 [Barrett and Tinelli, 2007], Yices [Dutertre and de Moura, 2006a] – are not capable to solve this formula in contrast to our proposed technique. The reason is that this formula is not in the decidable fragment of the SMT solvers because it combines arithmetics, uninterpreted functions, and quantification.

Our contribution is a model generation technique for quantified formulas that is powered by verification technology. The model generation technique can be used either stand-alone for model generation, or as a precomputation step for SMT solvers to eliminate quantifiers. Quantifier elimination in this sense is sound for showing satisfiability but not for refutational or validity proofs.

This technique is described in Chapter 6 and is based on the papers [Gladisch, 2010b] and [Gladisch, 2010a]. In [Gladisch, 2010b] we describe the theory of this technique with a soundness proof and in [Gladisch, 2010a] we describe an implementation of the technique and its evaluation.

11

1.2.2 Deducing the Existence of Software Faults when Using Program Abstractions

The method contract and loop invariant rules (*contract rules*) are an important software verification technique for handling method invocations and loops. However, if a verification condition resulting from using a contract rule turns out to be falsifiable, then the user does not know if (a) they could have chosen a stronger contract (respectively abstraction) to verify the program or (b) if the program is not verifiable due to a fault in the program or its requirement specification. We approach this problem and present a novel technique that unifies verification and software fault detection.

The technique extends existing approaches that try to verify a program and in case of verification failure generate counterexamples for verification conditions. In contrast to existing approaches which only check if verification conditions have counterexamples, this approach allows us to conclude the existence of a software fault from falsifiable verification conditions even if contract rules are used during the verification attempt. Checking the existence of a software fault after the verification attempt does not require explicit program testing, symbolic execution, or weakest precondition computation. Instead information obtained from the verification attempt is *reused* to reason about the existence of a software fault. In this way, the technique unifies verification and fault detection.

———— Java + JML (1.1) ————

```
public int sqrtA(int x){
  int i=0;
  /*@loop_invariant (i-1)*(i-1)<=x
   || i==0; modifies i; @*/
  while(i*i<=x){
   i++;
  }
  return i; //fault
}
```

———— Java + JML (1.2) ————

```
public int sqrtB(int x){
  int i=0;
  /*@loop_invariant (i-1)*(i-1)<=x;
   || x==0; modifies i;@*/
  while(i*i<=x){   //weak invariant
   i++;
  }
  return i-1;
}
```

———————— Java + JML —— ———————— Java + JML ——

Fig. 1.1. Examples used in falsifiability preservation analysis

For example, the methods in Listings 1.1 and 1.2 of Figure 1.1 are supposed to compute an integer approximation of the square-root of the argument. Trying to verify the programs using the given loop invariants fails because falsifiable verification conditions are created. The reason for the failure is, however, different in both cases. The method `sqrtA()` has a fault and cannot be verified with any loop invariant whereas method `sqrtB()` is correct but the loop invariant is inappropriate. Our approach tries to show if a contract rule with a given loop invariant or method contract has the required properties in order to deduce the existence of a fault in the program or its requirement specification. In Listing 1.1 this is the case and indeed the discussed approach detects that the method `sqrtA()` has a fault.

This technique is described in Chapters 4 and 5 and is based on the paper [Gladisch, 2009]. The technique has evolved from a test generation technique described in [Gladisch, 2008a].

1.2.3 Verification-based Test Case Generation

The generation of tests from verification proofs has been proposed in [Engel and Hähnle, 2007] and [Beckert and Gladisch, 2007]. Since this technique involves the runtime execution of the considered program, it can find faults that result from the interaction of the program under test (PUT) and its runtime environment. We have extended the original approaches enabling the generation of test cases of different quality such as specification-based tests, white-box tests, and tests that are guaranteed to reveal faults. The test cases with fault detection guarantee are generated with the techniques described in Sections 1.2.1 and 1.2.2. Such test cases help the user finding the fault(s) in the PUT using a program debugger.

The white-box test case generation technique can make use of loop invariants and method contracts and generate test cases that are likely to be missed by techniques based on bounded symbolic execution. These would require an exhaustive inspection of all execution paths which is infeasible in the presence of complex methods and impossible in the presence of loops because loops represent infinitely many paths. The technique was published in [Gladisch, 2008a].

An example that shows the advantages of the presented approach is given in Listing 1.3 of Figure 1.2. In order to execute `A()` the loop body has to be entered at least 11 times and in order to execute `C()` it has to be executed exactly 20 times. In similar programs these numbers

```
 —— Java (1.3) ——————             —— Java + JML (1.4) ———
void foo1(int n){                void D(int n){
 int i=0;                          while(i<n){ ... }
 while(i < n){                    }
   if(i==10){ A();}
   B(); i++;                      void foo2(int n){
 }                                 D(n);
 if(i==20){ C(); }                 if(i==20){ C(); }
}                                 }
 ———————————————— Java —          ———————————— Java + JML —
```

Fig. 1.2. Challenging examples for test generators based on bounded symbolic execution

could be much larger or be the result of complex expressions requiring an exhaustive inspection of all paths in order to find the case where the branch conditions are satisfied. The situation is similar in Listing 1.4. In this case an exhaustive inspection of D() may be required in order to find a path such that after the execution of D() the branch condition $i \doteq 20$ holds (the "$\doteq$" denotes semantic equality). Existing testing techniques are likely to miss these cases because they have a bound on the amount of inspected execution paths. For loops and recursive methods the typical approach is to symbolically execute the first k loop iterations or recursion steps, called k-bounded unwinding, where k is a limiting constant.

In order to create executable tests also technical problems have to be solved. We describe techniques for initializing the PUT with test data which is obtained by the technique described in Section 1.2.1. Another technique we describe is for evaluating the requirement specification using a test oracle.

These techniques are described in Chapter 7. The chapter combines contributions from [Beckert and Gladisch, 2007; Gladisch, 2008a; Engel et al., 2008] where [Beckert and Gladisch, 2007] is one of the tool-chain approaches described below.

1.2.4 Tool-chain Approaches for Test Generation

Verification-based test case generation is a powerful technique because it ensures high code coverage by the generated tests. Yet, traditional

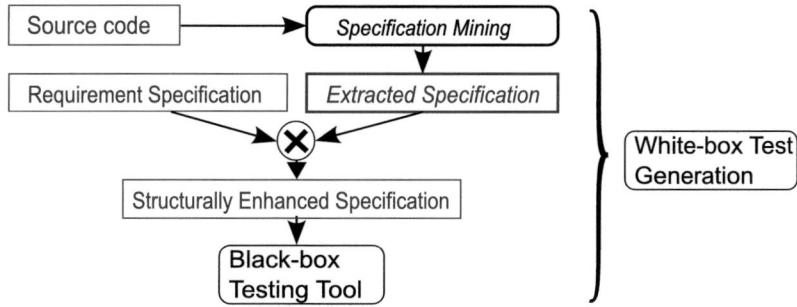

Fig. 1.3. White-box testing by combining specification mining and black-box testing

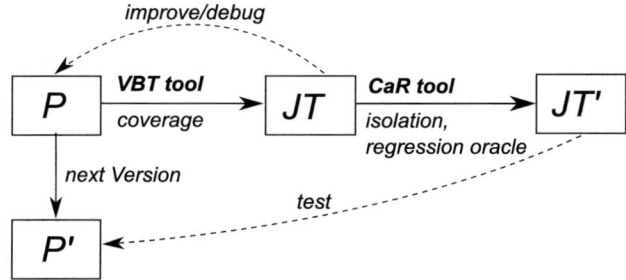

Fig. 1.4. Combining verification-based testing with capture & replay

testing techniques are well established and tests generated using verification technology alone may lack some of the benefits obtained by using more traditional testing techniques. The dissertation investigates two tool-chain approaches that combine and extend verification-based test case generation with traditional approaches such as black-box testing and capture & replay based techniques.

The first approach, illustrated in Figure 1.3, uses a deductive program verification technique to generate specifications for given programs and it then uses these specifications as input for black-box testing tools. Thus, (1) the black-box testing method can make use of information about the program's structure that is contained in the specification, and (2) we separate concerns and get a clear interface between program analysis on the one hand and test-case generation and execution on the other hand.

The second approach, illustrated in Figure 1.4, combines verification-based testing and capture & replay based testing techniques in order to obtain isolated unit regression tests that provide high code coverage. As we have identified, the two groups of techniques have complementary strengths, and are therefore ideal candidates for the proposed tool-chain approach. The first phase produces, for a given system P, unit tests JT with high coverage. However, when using them to test a unit, its environment is tested as well – resulting in a high cost of testing. To solve this problem, the second phase captures the various executions of the test suite JT, which is the output of the first phase. The output of the second phase JT' is a set of unit tests with high code coverage, which use mock objects to test the units in isolation.

The two techniques are described in the Chapters 7 and 8 and are based on the papers [Beckert and Gladisch, 2007] and [Gladisch et al., 2010], respectively.

1.3 Outline

The dissertation is divided into three parts.

Part I. This part describes the verification framework that the presented techniques are based on. Chapter 2 describes the logic, the calculus, and the overall approach of the KeY tool. The sections describing the calculus components explain how verification works in KeY and provide several examples. Chapter 3 introduces the specification language JML which is used in examples of this dissertation.

Part II. This part consists of purely deductive techniques that solve specific problems for detecting software-faults if a verification attempt is not successful. These techniques are also the most significant contributions of this dissertation. Chapter 4 describes our general approach and motivates the need for the techniques described in the following chapters. Chapter 6 describes a technique for counterexample generation from first-order logic formulas with quantifiers. Chapter 5 describes a technique for deducing the existence of software faults from a failed verification attempt when loop invariants and method contracts are used.

Part III. The third part is dedicated to test generation approaches and techniques which *extend* the formal verification and fault detection approach described in the previous parts. Technically, the test generation techniques are also *based* on the techniques of the previous chapters and therefore an integration of verification, deductive fault detection, and testing is achieved in one tool. In Chapter 7 several techniques and approaches are described for test case generation and for the generation of executable tests. The chapter combines contribution from several published papers as well as previously unpublished content. Chapter 8 describes a tool-chain approach for the generation of isolated regression unit tests. Candidates for the first component in the tool-chain are, e.g., the approaches described in Chapter 7.

Related work, proofs, and experiments or evaluations are provided in the respective chapters. Final conclusions of this thesis are given in Chapter 9.

1.4 Publications of the Author

The following list contains publications that have directly contributed to this dissertation.

[Gladisch, 2010a] Christoph Gladisch. Test data generation for programs with quantified first-order logic specifications. In Alexandre Petrenko, Adenilso da Silva Simão, and José Carlos Maldonado, editors, *Proceedings, Testing Software and Systems - 22nd IFIP WG 6.1 International Conference, ICTSS 2010, Natal, Brazil*, volume 6435 of *LNCS*, pages 158–173. Springer, 2010a.

[Gladisch, 2010b] Christoph Gladisch. Satisfiability solving and model generation for quantified first-order logic formulas. In Bernhard Beckert and Claude Marché, editors, *Conf. Post. Proc., Formal Verification of Object-Oriented Software, International Conference, FoVeOOS 2010, Paris, France*, volume 6528 of *LNCS*. Springer, 2010b. (Best student paper and presentation award)

[Gladisch et al., 2010] Christoph Gladisch, Shmuel Tyszberowicz, Bernhard Beckert, and Amiram Yehudai. Generating regression unit tests using a combination of verification and capture & replay. In Gordon Fraser and Angelo Gargantini, editors, *Proceedings, Tests and Proofs, Forth International Conference, TAP 2010, Málaga, Spain*, volume 6143 of *LNCS*, pages 61–76. Springer, 2010.

[Gladisch, 2009] Christoph Gladisch. Could we have chosen a better loop invariant or method contract? In Catherine Dubois, editor, *Proceedings, Tests and Proofs, Third International Conference, TAP 2009, Zurich, Switzerland*, volume 5668 of *LNCS*, pages 74–89. Springer, 2009.

[Gladisch, 2008a] Christoph Gladisch. Verification-based test case generation for full feasible branch coverage. In Antonio Cerone and Stefan Gruner, editors, *Proceedings, Sixth IEEE International Conference on Software Engineering and Formal Methods, SEFM 2008, Cape Town, South Africa*, pages 159–168. IEEE Computer Society, 2008a.

[Engel et al., 2008] Christian Engel, Christoph Gladisch, Vladimir Klebanov, and Philipp Rümmer. Integrating verification and testing of object-oriented software. In Bernhard Beckert and Reiner Hähnle, editors, *Proceedings, Tests and Proofs, Second International Conference, TAP 2008, Prato, Italy*, volume 4966 of *LNCS*, pages 182–191. Springer, 2008.

[Beckert and Gladisch, 2007] Bernhard Beckert and Christoph Gladisch. White-box testing by combining deduction-based specification extraction and black-box testing. In Yuri Gurevich and Bertrand Meyer, editors, *Proceedings, Tests and Proofs, First International Conference, TAP 2007, Zurich, Switzerland*, volume 4454 of *LNCS*, pages 207–216. Springer, 2007.

Additional scientific contributions by the author are provided in the following list.

[Gladisch, 2008c] Christoph Gladisch. Verification-based test case generation with loop invariants and method specifications. In Bernhard Beckert und Reiner Hähnle, editors, Tests and Proofs: Papers Presented at the Second International Conference, TAP 2008, Prato, Italy, Reports of the Faculty of Informatics 5/2008, University of Koblenz-Landau, April 2008c.

[Gladisch, 2008b] Christoph Gladisch. *Extending KeY for the Verification of C Programs*. VDM Verlag Dr. Müller e.K., 2008b.

[Gladisch, 2007] Christoph Gladisch. How C differs from Java for symbolic program execution. In Hendrik Tews, editor, Proceedings, C/C++ Verification Workshop, Oxford, United Kingdom, Technical Report ICIS-R07015, Radboud University Nijmegen, Juli 2007.

Part I

Foundations

2

The Formalism and Techniques of KeY

2.1 Introduction

The KeY tool [Beckert et al., 2007] is a verification and test generation tool for a subset of JAVA and a superset of JAVA CARD [Chen, 2000], the latter is a standardized subset of JAVA for programming of SmartCards. At its core, KeY is an automated and interactive theorem prover for an instance of first-order dynamic logic (DL) [Harel, 1984; Harel et al., 2000]. The logic combines first-order logic (FOL) formulas with programs allowing to express, e.g., correctness properties of programs. The techniques presented in this thesis were developed on top of the KeY tool. Hence, the details of the techniques are specific to the formalism and techniques of the KeY tool.

The history of the KeY tool dates back to the year 1998. It has been developed throughout several research projects by research groups at Universität Koblenz-Landau, Chalmers University, and the Karlsruhe Institute of Technology where the KeY project was initiated. At the 9th International KeY Symposium 2010 – one of the annual meetings of the research groups – statistics about the tool were presented by Richard Bubel. According to these statistics KeY's source code consisted at this point of 174,732 *source lines of code* (SLOC) and 1755 calculus rules. The rule base is so big because the rules encode the semantics of JAVA as well as axioms of certain theories.

KeY's approach to verification is to reduce DL formulas which express properties of programs to FOL formulas and then to prove the FOL formulas. In contrast to the majority of verification tools at this time, a *strict* separation between program analysis and first-order theorem proving is not made in the KeY approach. This is because both tasks are achieved by rule applications within the KeY tool and the application of program reduction rules and first-order theorem proving rules can be interleaved.

The techniques described in this thesis do not require any extension of the logic or the calculus of KeY. The dynamic logic JAVA CARD DL and the calculus described in this chapter are the same as in the *KeY Book* [Beckert et al., 2007]. Most of the definitions and lemmas in this chapter stem from the KeY Book. We present, however, a subset of the definitions and lemmas from the KeY Book which is relevant for understanding this thesis. Since the lemmas stem from the KeY Book, they are not proved here. We refer the reader to the original source for further details about the definitions and lemmas.

Structure of this chapter. Similarly as in the KeY Book the first-order logic subset of JAVA CARD DL is presented first. In contrast to the KeY Book we define a more concrete instance of first-order logic, called JAVA CARD FOL, which uses the same type system and signature as JAVA CARD DL. On the one hand this enables us to refer to more concrete sets of FOL terms and formulas and on the other hand we hope to simplify the presentation of the dynamic logic.

We assume that the reader is familiar with first-order logic and can use Section 2.2 as a reference rather than for learning it. In Section 2.3 we define JAVA CARD DL as an extension of JAVA CARD FOL. Concrete JAVA CARD DL formulas are used as examples in Section 2.4 where a subset of KeY's calculus is defined. Section 2.4 explains how software verification works in KeY and we advise the reader to place their main focus on this section.

2.2 The First-order Logic JAVA CARD FOL

2.2.1 Syntax

In order to reason about JAVA programs, fields and program variables are represented as function symbols in JAVA CARD FOL. Each program is associated with an instance of JAVA CARD FOL whose type system and signature is derived from the program.

The type system distinguishes between *static*, *dynamic*, and *abstract* types. Each JAVA object has a dynamic type, e.g., the type of the object created by **new** C() is C. In contrast, terms and expressions have static types. Static types restrict the possible syntactical compositions of terms or expressions. The connection between static and dynamic types is that an expression or a term with a static type A can have a value whose dynamic type may be more specific than A. In JAVA the dynamic type is also called the runtime type. A static type can also be an abstract class type or interface type but the type of an object is never an abstract class type or interface type.

Definition 2.1. *A type hierarchy for a* JAVA CARD *program P is a quadruple $(\mathcal{T}, \mathcal{T}_d, \mathcal{T}_a, \sqsubseteq)$ of*

- *a finite set of* static types $\mathcal{T}$,
- *a finite set of* dynamic types $\mathcal{T}_d$,
- *a finite set of* abstract types $\mathcal{T}_a$, *and*
- *a* subtype relation $\sqsubseteq$ *on $\mathcal{T}$,*

satisfying the conditions of Figure 2.1.

We say that A is a subtype of B if $A \sqsubseteq B$. The set of non-empty static types is denoted by $\mathcal{T}_q := \mathcal{T} \backslash \{\bot\}$.

Since the details of the type hierarchy are not important to understand this thesis, but are still required in order to define the same logic as in the KeY Book, we have placed these conditions in Figure 2.1. To summarize, KeY's type hierarchy imports all relevant types and type relations from the JAVA program and extends them. Additionally the types $\bot$ and $\top$ are added to the type hierarchy in order to ensure that all types have a common subtype and supertype. The type `integer` is used in order to refer to any of the primitive JAVA types `byte`, `short`, `int`, `long`, or `char`. The values of these types belong to the type `integerDomain` which we will define as $\mathbb{Z}$ in Section 2.2.2.

Definition 2.2. *Let T be a type hierarchy for a program P, then a* JAVA CARD FOL *signature (for T) is a tuple*

$$\Sigma = (\mathrm{VSym}, \mathrm{FSym}_r, \mathrm{FSym}_{nr}, \mathrm{PSym}_r, \mathrm{PSym}_{nr}, \alpha)$$

consisting of:

- *a typing function α such that*[1]
    - $\alpha(v) \in \mathcal{T}_q$ *for all $v \in \mathrm{VSym}$,*
    - $\alpha(f) \in \mathcal{T}_q^* \times \mathcal{T}_q$ *for all $f \in \mathrm{FSym}$, and*

---

[1] We use the standard notation A^* to denote the set of (possibly empty) sequences of elements of A.

- $\mathcal{T} = \mathcal{T}_d \cup \mathcal{T}_a$
- boolean $\in \mathcal{T}_d$ denotes the boolean type
- Null $\in \mathcal{T}_d$ denotes the type of the constant `null`
- $A \in \mathcal{T}_d$ for all non-abstract class types A declared in P or imported into P.
- $A \in \mathcal{T}_a$ for all interface and abstract class types A declared in P or imported into P
- $\sqsubseteq$ is a reflexive partial order on $\mathcal{T}$,
- $\{\texttt{integer}, \texttt{byte}, \texttt{short}, \texttt{int}, \texttt{long}, \texttt{char}\} \subset \mathcal{T}_a$ denotes the integer types
- integerDomain $\in \mathcal{T}_d$
- integerDomain $\sqsubseteq A \sqsubseteq$ integer, for all $A \in \{\texttt{integer}, \texttt{byte}, \texttt{short}, \texttt{int}, \texttt{long}, \texttt{char}\}$
- There is an *empty type* $\bot \in \mathcal{T}_a$ and a *universal type* $\top \in \mathcal{T}_d$.
- $\bot \sqsubseteq A \sqsubseteq \top$ for all $A \in \mathcal{T}$.
- $C \sqsubseteq D$ iff C is implicitly or explicitly declared as a subtype of D (using the keywords `extends` or `implements`), for all (abstract) class or interface types C, D declared in or imported into P
- For all array types A occurring in P, $A \in \mathcal{T}$ and $A[]^i \in \mathcal{T}_d$ for $0 \leqslant i \leqslant n$ for some n where $A[]^i$ denotes $A \underbrace{[\,]\ldots[\,]}_{i \text{ times}}$ for short and $A[]^0 = A$.
- $\mathcal{T}$ is closed under greatest lower bounds w.r.t. $\sqsubseteq$. We write $A \sqcap B$ for the greatest lower bound of A and B and call it the *intersection type* of A and B. The existence of $A \sqcap B$ also guarantees the existence of the least upper bound $A \sqcup B$ of A and B, called the *union type* of A and B.
- Every non-empty abstract type $A \in \mathcal{T}_a \backslash \{\bot\}$ has a non-abstract subtype: $B \in \mathcal{T}_d$ with $B \sqsubseteq A$.

Fig. 2.1. Type hierarchy of JAVA CARD FOL and JAVA CARD DL

- $\alpha(p) \in \mathcal{T}_q^*$ *for all* $p \in \text{PSym}$.

We use the following notations:

- $v : A$ *for* $\alpha(v) = A$,
- $f : A_1, \ldots, A_n \to A$ *for* $\alpha(f) = ((A_1, \ldots, A_n), A)$, *and*
- $p : A_1, \ldots, A_n$ *for* $\alpha(p) = (A_1, \ldots, A_n)$.
- *a set* VSym *of variables,*
- *the set* FSym *of function symbols with:*

$$\text{FSym} = \text{FSym}_r \cup \text{FSym}_{nr}$$

where FSym_r *is the set of* rigid *function symbols and* FSym_{nr} *is the set of* non-rigid *function symbols containing at least the symbols defined in Table 2.1 such that*

$$\text{FSym}_r \cap \text{FSym}_{nr} = \emptyset$$

The set FSym_r includes at least the following symbols:

- $(A) \in \mathrm{FSym}_r$ with $(A) : \top \to A$ for any $A \in \mathcal{T}_q$, called the *cast to type A*,
- $\texttt{null} \in \mathrm{FSym}_r$ with $\texttt{null} : \mathrm{Null}$,
- $\mathrm{A::get} \in \mathrm{FSym}_r$ with $\mathrm{A::get} : \texttt{integer} \to A$ for any $\texttt{A} \in \mathcal{T}_d \backslash \{\mathrm{Null}\}$
- $0, 1, 2, \ldots \in \mathrm{FSym}_r$ of type $\texttt{integer}$,
- $- \in \mathrm{FSym}_r$ $- : \texttt{integer} \to \texttt{integer}$, called *unary minus*
- $\{+, -, *, /\} \subset \mathrm{FSym}_r$ with $\circ : \texttt{integer}, \texttt{integer} \to \texttt{integer}$, for each $\circ \in \{+, -, *, /\}$,

The set FSym_{nr} includes at least the following symbols:

- $[\,] \in \mathrm{FSym}_{nr}$ with $[\,] : \top, \texttt{integer} \to \top$ called *array access*,
- $length \in \mathrm{FSym}_{nr}$ with $length : \top \to \texttt{integer}$ called *length of an array*,
- $A.\texttt{<nextToCreate>} \in \mathrm{FSym}_{nr}$ for any $A \in \mathcal{T}_d$ with $A.\texttt{<nextToCreate>} : \texttt{integer}$,
- $\texttt{<created>} \in \mathrm{FSym}_{nr}$ with $\texttt{<created>} : Object \to \texttt{boolean}$,
- $id : A \in \mathrm{FSym}_{nr}$ For all local variables and static field declarations "$\texttt{A id;}$" in P,
- $id : (C \to A) \in \mathrm{FSym}_{nr}$ For all non-static field declarations "$\texttt{A id;}$" in a class C in P

Table 2.1. Rigid and non-rigid function symbols

- *the set* PSym *of predicate symbols with:*

$$\mathrm{PSym} = \mathrm{PSym}_r \cup \mathrm{PSym}_{nr}$$

where PSym_r *is the set of* rigid *predicate symbols and* PSym_{nr} *is the set of* non-rigid *predicate symbols containing at least the symbols defined in Table 2.2 such that*

$$\mathrm{PSym}_r \cap \mathrm{PSym}_{nr} = \emptyset$$

A constant symbol *is a function symbol* c *with* $\alpha(c) = ((), A)$ *for some type A.*

Function and predicate symbols are divided into *rigid* and *non-rigid* symbols. Rigid symbols are those that have a fixed interpretation

The sets PSym_r and PSym_{nr} include at least the following symbols:

- $\{\doteq, \neq\} \subset \mathrm{PSym}_r$ with $\doteq: \top, \top$ and $\neq: \top, \top$
- $\boxminus A \in \mathrm{PSym}_r$ with $\boxminus A : \top$ for any $A \in \mathcal{T}$, called the *type predicate of type A*,
- $\{<, \leqslant, \geqslant, >\} \subset \mathrm{PSym}_r$ for each $\circ \in \{<, \leqslant, \geqslant, >\}$, $p : (\mathtt{integer}, \mathtt{integer})$
- $inReachableState \in \mathrm{PSym}_{nr}$

Table 2.2. Rigid and non-rigid predicate symbols

throughout the Kripke structure such as the constant '0' or the function '+'. Non-rigid symbols are those, whose value, respectively interpretation, can vary between different program states. For instance, the non-rigid function symbols in Table 2.1 include all fields and program variables of the JAVA program because their values can be changed. Note that a program variable $id \in \mathrm{FSym}_{nr}$ is called a constant in terms of the logic because it is a function symbol with no arguments. In contrast, an object field is a function which takes the object reference as argument and returns the values of the field.

The function symbols `A::get`, `A.<nextToCreate>`, and `<created>`, are used to model JAVA's object creation mechanism. The functions `<created>` and `A.<nextToCreate>`, and are called *implicit* fields because they are a static and a non-static field, respectively, which exist in the logic but not in the JAVA program. When an object is created, then its implicit field `<created>` is set to true and `A::get` returns the reference to the newly created object. In order to create a new reference the static field `A.<nextToCreate>` is incremented and the reference is accessed by the term `A::get(A.<nextToCreate>)`. We will define `A::get` as an injective function to ensure that $\mathtt{A::get}(x) \neq \mathtt{A::get}(y)$ if $x \neq y$.

Next we define the sets of terms and formulas as well as the notion of free variables and ground terms and formulas.

Definition 2.3. *Given a signature Σ, we inductively define the system of sets $\{\mathrm{Trm}_A^{FOL}\}_{A \in \mathcal{T}}$ of first-order logic terms of static type A to be the least system of sets such that*

- $x \in \mathrm{Trm}_A^{FOL}$ *for any variable* $x : A \in \mathrm{VSym}$,
- $f(t_1, \ldots, t_n) \in \mathrm{Trm}_A^{FOL}$ *for any function symbol* $f : A_1, \ldots, A_n \rightarrow A \in \mathrm{FSym}$, *and terms* $t_i \in \mathrm{Trm}_{A_i'}^{FOL}$ *with* $A_i' \sqsubseteq A_i$ *for* $i = 1, \ldots, n$.
- (if ϕ then t_1 else t_2) $\in \mathrm{Trm}_A^{FOL}$ *for all* $\phi \in \mathrm{Fml}^{FOL}$ *(see Def. 2.4) and all terms* $t_1 \in \mathrm{Trm}_{A_1}^{FOL}, t_2 \in \mathrm{Trm}_{A_2}^{FOL}$ *with* $A = A_1 \sqcup A_2$;
- (ifExMin $x.\phi$ then t_1 else t_2) $\in \mathrm{Trm}_A^{FOL}$ *for all* $\phi \in \mathrm{Fml}^{FOL}$ *(see Def. 2.4) and all terms* $t_1 \in \mathrm{Trm}_{A_1}^{FOL}, t_2 \in \mathrm{Trm}_{A_2}^{FOL}$ *with* $A = A_1 \sqcup A_2$;

For type cast terms, we write $(A)t$ *instead of* $(A)(t)$. *We write the static type of* t *as* $\sigma(t) := A$ *for any term* $t \in \mathrm{Trm}_A^{FOL}$.

Definition 2.4. *We inductively define the set of first-order logic formulas* Fml^{FOL} *to be the least set such that*

- $p(t_1, \ldots, t_n) \in \mathrm{Fml}^{FOL}$ *for any predicate symbol* $p : A_1, \ldots, A_n$ *and terms* $t_i \in \mathrm{Trm}_{A_i'}^{FOL}$ *with* $A_i' \sqsubseteq A_i$, *for* $i = 1, \ldots, n$,
- $\mathrm{true}, \mathrm{false} \in \mathrm{Fml}^{FOL}$
- $\neg\phi, (\phi \vee \psi), (\phi \wedge \psi), (\phi \rightarrow \psi) \in \mathrm{Fml}^{FOL}$ *for any* $\phi, \psi \in \mathrm{Fml}^{FOL}$.
- $\forall x.\phi, \exists x.\phi \in \mathrm{Fml}^{FOL}$ *for any* $\phi \in \mathrm{Fml}^{FOL}$ *and any variable* x.

For type predicate formulas, we write $t \sqsubseteq A$ *instead of* $\sqsubseteq A(t)$. *For* $\circ \in \{\doteq, \neq, \leqslant, <, >, \geqslant\}$, *we write* $t_1 \circ t_2$ *instead of* $\circ(t_1, t_2)$. *An atomic formula or atom is a formula of the shape* $p(t_1, \ldots, t_n)$ *(including* $t_1 \doteq t_2$ *and* $t \sqsubseteq A$). *A literal is an atom or a negated atom* $\neg p(t_1, \ldots, t_n)$.

Definition 2.5. *We define* $fv(t)$, *the set of free variables of a term* t, *by*

- $fv(v) = \{v\}$ *for* $v \in \mathrm{VSym}$, *and*
- $fv(f(t_1, \ldots, t_n)) = \bigcup_{i=1,\ldots,n} fv(t_i)$.
- $fv(\mathrm{if}\ \phi\ \mathrm{then}\ t_1\ \mathrm{else}\ t_2) = fv(\phi) \cup fv(t_1) \cup fv(t_2)$

A term t *is called* ground *iff* $fv(t) = \emptyset$.

The set of free variables of a formula is defined by

- $fv(p(t_1, \ldots, t_n)) = \bigcup_{i=1,\ldots,n} fv(t_i)$,
- $fv(\mathrm{true}) = fv(\mathrm{false}) = \emptyset$,

- $fv(\neg\phi) = fv(\phi),$
- $fv(\phi \wedge \psi) = fv(\phi \vee \psi) = fv(\phi \rightarrow \psi) = fv(\phi) \cup fv(\psi),$ *and*
- $fv(\forall x.\phi) = fv(\exists x.\phi) = fv(\phi)\backslash\{x\}.$

A formula ϕ is called closed *or* ground *iff $fv(\phi) = \emptyset$.*

2.2.2 Semantics

The meaning of function and predicate symbols is determined by an interpretation function. A valid a formula must hold for all interpretations except that for some of the symbols such as '0' or '+' we are interested only in their fixed interpretation. Due to this restriction on the interpretation of a subset of the signature the notion of a partial model is introduced.

Definition 2.6. *A partial model is a quintuple $(T, \mathcal{D}, \preceq, \delta, \mathcal{I})$ of*

- *a type hierarchy $T = (\mathcal{T}, \mathcal{T}_d, \mathcal{T}_a, \sqsubseteq),$*
- *a domain (also called universe) $\mathcal{D},$*
- *a binary relation $\preceq$ on $\mathcal{D},$*
- *a dynamic type function $\delta : \mathcal{D} \rightarrow \mathcal{T}_d,$ and*
- *an interpretation $\mathcal{I},$*

such that, if we define

$$\mathcal{D}^A := \{d \in \mathcal{D}|\delta(d) \sqsubseteq A\},$$

to be the set of all domain elements that "fit" the type A, it holds that

- *$\mathcal{D}^A$ is non-empty for all $A \in \mathcal{T}_d,$*
- *$\mathbb{Z} = \mathcal{D}^{\text{integer}}, \{tt, ff\} = \mathbb{B} = \mathcal{D}^{\text{boolean}}, \{\text{null}\} = \mathcal{D}^{Null},$*
- *$\delta(\mathbb{Z}) = \text{integerDomain}, \delta(\mathbb{B}) = \text{boolean}, \delta(\{\text{null}\}) = \text{Null},$*
- *for all dynamic types $A \in \mathcal{T}_d\backslash\{Null\}$ with $A \sqsubseteq \text{Object}$ there is a countably infinite set $\mathcal{D}^A \subset \mathcal{D},$*
- *the binary relation $\preceq$ has the following properties for all $x, y \in \mathcal{D}$*
  - *$x \preceq x$ (reflexivity),*
  - *$x \preceq y$ and $y \preceq x$ implies $x = y$ (antisymmetry)*
  - *$x \preceq y$ and $y \preceq z$ implies $x \preceq z$ (transitivity), and*
  - *any non-empty subset $\mathcal{D}_{sub} \subseteq \mathcal{D}$ has a least element $\min_{\preceq}(\mathcal{D}_{sub}),$ i.e., $\min_{\preceq}(\mathcal{D}_{sub}) \preceq y$ for all $y \in \mathcal{D}_{sub}$ (well-orderedness).*
- *for any $f : A_1, \ldots, A_n \rightarrow A \in \text{FSym}, \mathcal{I}$ yields a function*

$$\mathcal{I}(f) : \mathcal{D}^{A_1} \times \ldots \times \mathcal{D}^{A_n} \rightarrow \mathcal{D}^A,$$

and $\mathcal{I}$ is restricted according to Def. 2.7, and

- *for any $p : A_1, \ldots, A_n \in \text{PSym}$, $\mathcal{I}$ yields a subset*

$$\mathcal{I}(p) \subseteq \mathcal{D}^{A_1} \times \ldots \times \mathcal{D}^{A_n},$$

and $\mathcal{I}$ is restricted according to Def. 2.8.

Furthermore, functions and predicates which have a fixed interpretation are called interpreted *functions, respectively predicates. Otherwise, they are called* uninterpreted *functions, respectively predicates.*

The interpretation function maps constants to elements of a domain, function symbols to functions over the domain, and predicates to relations over the domain. The domain, also known as universe, is divided into sub-domains for the different types of the type hierarchy. The domain is ordered by a well-ordering $\preceq$ which is a total ordering such that every non-empty subset $\mathcal{D}_{sub} \subseteq \mathcal{D}$ has a least element $\min_{\prec}(\mathcal{D}_{sub})$. The well-ordering is required in order to define the semantics of quantified updates in Section 2.3.2.1.

Fixed interpretations of function and predicate symbols are given in the Definitions 2.7 and 2.8, respectively. Note, the logic may contain also other symbols which have a fixed interpretation.

Definition 2.7. *A partial model $(T, \mathcal{D}, \preceq, \delta, \mathcal{I})$ has the following restrictions on the interpretations of functions:*

- *the usual mathematical interpretations of the constants $0, 1, 2, \ldots$, and of the binary arithmetic functions $+, -, *$ denoting addition, subtraction, multiplication, respectively and of the unary function '$-$' denoting negation on the domain $\mathbb{Z}$,*
- $\mathcal{I}(/)(x,y) = z$ *such that* $\begin{cases} 0 \leqslant x - y * z < |y| & \text{if } y \neq 0 \\ \text{arbitrary fixed } d \in \mathcal{D}^{\text{integer}} & \text{otherwise} \end{cases}$
- *for type cast,* $\mathcal{I}((A))(x) = \begin{cases} x & \text{if } \delta(x) \sqsubseteq A \\ \text{arbitrary fixed } d \in \mathcal{D}^A & \text{otherwise} \end{cases}$
- $\mathcal{I}(\text{A::get}) \in \mathcal{D}^A$. *Restricted to the set of non-negative integers, A::get is interpreted as a bijective mapping onto an object repository. For negative integers, A::get is also defined, but its values are unknown. The* index *of an object o is the non-negative integer i such that $\mathcal{I}(\text{A::get})(i) = o$ holds.*
- $\mathcal{I}(\texttt{null})$ *is the* null *constant of* JAVA CARD

Definition 2.8. *A partial model $(T, \mathcal{D}, \preceq, \delta, \mathcal{I})$ has the following restrictions on the interpretations of predicates:*

- $\mathcal{I}(\doteq) = \{(d, d) | d \in \mathcal{D}\}$,
- $\mathcal{I}(\neq) = \{(a, b) | a, b \in \mathcal{D} \text{ and not } a = b\}$,
- the usual mathematical interpretations of the predicate symbols $<, \leqslant, \geqslant, >$ on the domain $\mathbb{Z}$ hold which denote order relations
- $\mathcal{I}(\sqsubseteq A) = \mathcal{D}^A$
- $\mathcal{I}(inReachableState)$ holds in exactly those states that are reachable by a JAVA CARD program. Note that we assume a certain restriction of the interpretation of this predicate at this point and post-pone the explanation of the connection between interpretations and states to Section 2.3.

The meaning of the predicate $\sqsubseteq A$ is similar to the JAVA operator `instanceof` but the predicate allows to reason also about the extended type hierarchy of the logic.

In the following we define how the values of terms and formulas are determined if a variable assignment and a partial model are given. Terms are evaluated by the function valuation function *val* and formulas are evaluated by the validity relation $\models$.

Definition 2.9. *Given a partial model* $(T, \mathcal{D}, \preceq, \delta, \mathcal{I})$, *a variable assignment is a function* $\beta : \text{VSym} \to \mathcal{D}$, *such that*

$$\beta(x) \in \mathcal{D}^A \quad \text{for all} \quad x : A \in \text{VSym}.$$

We also define the modification β_x^d *of a variable assignment* β *for any variable* $x : A$ *and any domain element* $d \in \mathcal{D}^A$ *by:*

$$\beta_x^d(y) := \begin{cases} d & \text{if } y = x \\ \beta(y) & \text{otherwise} \end{cases}$$

Definition 2.10. *Let* $\mathcal{M} = (T, \mathcal{D}, \preceq, \delta, \mathcal{I})$ *be a partial model, and* β *a variable assignment. We inductively define the valuation function* $val_{\mathcal{M},\beta}$ *by*

$$val_{\mathcal{M},\beta}(x) = \beta(x) \text{ for any variable } x.$$

$$val_{\mathcal{M},\beta}(f(t_1, \dots, t_n)) = \mathcal{I}(f)(val_{\mathcal{M},\beta}(t_1), \dots, val_{\mathcal{M},\beta}(t_n)).$$

$$val_{\mathcal{M},\beta}(\text{if } \varphi \text{ then } t_1 \text{ else } t_2) = \begin{cases} val_{\mathcal{M},\beta}(t_1) \text{ if } \mathcal{M}, \beta \models \varphi \\ val_{\mathcal{M},\beta}(t_2) \text{ if } \mathcal{M}, \beta \nvDash \varphi \end{cases}$$

$$val_{\mathcal{M},\beta}(\text{ifExMin } x.\phi \text{ then } t_1 \text{ else } t_2) =$$

$$\begin{cases} val_{\mathcal{M},\beta_x^d}(t_1) & \textit{if there is some } d \in \mathcal{D}^A \textit{ such that } \mathcal{M}, \beta_x^d \vDash \\ & \phi \textit{ and } d \preceq d' \textit{ for any } d' \in \mathcal{D}^A \textit{ with} \\ & \mathcal{M}, \beta_x^{d'} \vDash \phi \textit{ (where } A \textit{ is the type of } x) \\ \\ val_{\mathcal{M},\beta_x^d}(t_2) & \textit{otherwise} \end{cases}$$

For a ground term t, we simply write $val_{\mathcal{M}}(t)$*, since* $val_{\mathcal{M},\beta}(t)$ *is independent of* β*.*

The constructs (if ϕ then t_1 else t_2) and (ifExMin $x.\phi$ then t_1 else t_2) do not extend the expressibility of first-order logic but they reduce the size of formulas and simplify the definition of the calculus. Formulas with occurrences of these constructs can be rewritten to equivalent formulas without these constructs. The KeY Book does not define simplification rules for these terms but rather describes how these terms can be modelled in first-order logic. The term (if ϕ then t_1 else t_2) evaluates to t_1 if ϕ evaluates to true and it evaluates to t_2 if ϕ evaluates to false. The meaning of the term (ifExMin $x.\phi$ then t_1 else t_2) is described in the KeY Book as follows. If there is some d such that ϕ holds, then the whole term evaluates to the value denoted by t_1 under the variable assignment $\beta_x^{d'}$, where d' is the least element[2] satisfying ϕ. Otherwise, if ϕ does not hold for any x, then t_2 is evaluated.

Definition 2.11. *Let* $\mathcal{M} = (T, \mathcal{D}, \preceq, \delta, \mathcal{I})$ *be a partial model, and* β *a variable assignment. We inductively define the validity relation* $\vDash$ *by*

- $\mathcal{M}, \beta \vDash p(t_1, \ldots, t_n)$ *iff* $(val_{\mathcal{M},\beta}(t_1), \ldots, val_{\mathcal{M},\beta}(t_n)) \in \mathcal{I}(p)$.
- $\mathcal{M}, \beta \vDash$ *true.*
- $\mathcal{M}, \beta \nvDash$ *false.*
- $\mathcal{M}, \beta \vDash \neg\phi$ *iff* $\mathcal{M}, \beta \nvDash \phi$.
- $\mathcal{M}, \beta \vDash \phi \wedge \psi$ *iff* $\mathcal{M}, \beta \vDash \phi$ *and* $\mathcal{M}, \beta \vDash \psi$.
- $\mathcal{M}, \beta \vDash \phi \vee \psi$ *iff* $\mathcal{M}, \beta \vDash \phi$ *or* $\mathcal{M}, \beta \vDash \psi$*, or both.*
- $\mathcal{M}, \beta \vDash \phi \rightarrow \psi$ *iff if* $\mathcal{M}, \beta \vDash \phi$*, then also* $\mathcal{M}, \beta \vDash \psi$.
- $\mathcal{M}, \beta \vDash \forall x.\phi$ *(for a variable* $x : A$*) iff* $\mathcal{M}, \beta_x^d \vDash \phi$ *for every* $d \in \mathcal{D}^A$.
- $\mathcal{M}, \beta \vDash \exists x.\phi$ *(for a variable* $x : A$*) iff there is some* $d \in \mathcal{D}^A$ *such that* $\mathcal{M}, \beta_x^d \vDash \phi$.

---

[2] The condition which checks if a least element satisfying ϕ exists is modelled as $\exists x.(\phi \wedge \forall y.([y/x]\phi \rightarrow quanUpdateLeq(x,y)))$, where the predicate *quanUpdateLeq* represents the well-ordering $\preceq$.

Furthermore, if $\mathcal{M}, \beta \vDash \phi$, we say that ϕ is valid in the partial model $\mathcal{M}$ under the variable assignment β. For a closed formula ϕ, we write $\mathcal{M} \vDash \phi$, since β is then irrelevant.

In this thesis we are interested in different properties of formulas. Based on the validity relation of Definition 2.11 we introduce the standard notions of validity, satisfiability, unsatisfiability, falsifiability, and consequence in the following definition and define non-standard notions of validity and consequence in Definition 2.13.

Definition 2.12. *Let a fixed type hierarchy and signature be given.*

- *A formula ϕ is* logically valid, *denoted by $\vDash \phi$, if $\mathcal{M}, \beta \vDash \phi$ for any partial model $\mathcal{M}$ and any variable assignment β.*
- *A formula ϕ is* satisfiable *if $\mathcal{M}, \beta \vDash \phi$ for some partial model $\mathcal{M}$ and some variable assignment β.*
- *A formula is* unsatisfiable *if it is not satisfiable.*
- *A formula ϕ is* falsifiable *or it has as a* counterexample *if $\mathcal{M}, \beta \nvDash \phi$ for some partial model $\mathcal{M}$ and variable assignment β.*
- *A formula ϕ is the (local)* consequence *of a set Φ of formulas, denoted by $\Phi \vDash \phi$, iff for all partial models $\mathcal{M}$ and variable assignments β, $\mathcal{M}, \beta \vDash \bigwedge_{\varphi \in \Phi} \varphi$ implies $\mathcal{M}, \beta \vDash \phi$.*

Definition 2.13. *Let a fixed type hierarchy and signature be given.*

- *If $\mathcal{M}, \beta \vDash_A \phi$, where $A \subseteq (\mathrm{FSym}_{nr} \cup \mathrm{PSym}_{nr})$, we say that ϕ is valid in the partial model $\mathcal{M}$ modulo A under the variable assignment β. The relation $\mathcal{M}, \beta \vDash_A \phi$ holds iff for all partial models $\mathcal{M}' = (T, \mathcal{D}, \preceq, \delta, \mathcal{I}')$, where $\mathcal{M}$ and $\mathcal{M}'$ are identical except for the interpretation of A,[3] it holds that $\mathcal{M}', \beta \vDash \phi$.*
- *A formula ϕ is the (semi-local)* consequence *of a set Φ of formulas modulo A, denoted by $\Phi \vDash_A \phi$, iff for all partial models $\mathcal{M}$ and variable assignments β, $\mathcal{M}, \beta \vDash_A \bigwedge_{\varphi \in \Phi} \varphi$ implies $\mathcal{M}, \beta \vDash \phi$.*

The validity relation $\vDash_A$ is generally stronger than the validity relation $\vDash$. For instance let $val_{\mathcal{M}, \beta}(a) = 1$, then $\mathcal{M}, \beta \vDash a \doteq 1$ holds. In contrast, $\mathcal{M}, \beta \vDash_{\{a\}} a \doteq 1$ does not hold because the relation requires that the formula $a \doteq 1$ is true for all interpretations of a. The stronger relation is needed in order to define the semi-local consequence relation in the last item of the definition.

---

[3] $\mathcal{I}(X) = \mathcal{I}'(X)$ for all symbols $X \in (\mathrm{FSym}_r \cup \mathrm{FSym}_{nr} \cup \mathrm{PSym}_r \cup \mathrm{PSym}_{nr}) \backslash A$.

Generally, the semi-local consequence relation $\models_A$ is weaker than the local consequence relation. It is needed if a formula on the left hand side of the relation contains Skolem functions. A Skolem function is an uninterpreted function (see Def. 2.6) which does not occur in the proof structure yet. A typical situation is, e.g., to replace a quantified variable by a Skolem function. This technique is called Skolemization. For instance, in order to prove the validity of the formula $\forall x.x + 1 \doteq 1 + x$ one can prove the validity of the formula $sk + 1 \doteq 1 + sk$ instead, where sk is the Skolem function.

The difference between the local and semi-local consequence relations is that if φ_{sk} is the formula obtained from φ using Skolemization, then $\{\varphi_{sk}\} \models_{\{sk\}} \varphi$ holds but $\{\varphi_{sk}\} \models \varphi$ does not necessarily hold. Consider, e.g., the case where $\varphi = \forall x.(x > a \rightarrow x > b)$ and $\varphi_{sk} = sk > a \rightarrow sk > b$. If $\mathcal{M} \models a < b$ and $\mathcal{M} \models sk < a$, then $\mathcal{M} \models \varphi_{sk}$ holds but $\mathcal{M} \models \varphi$ does not hold and therefore $\{\varphi_{sk}\} \models \varphi$ does not hold. In contrast the semi-local consequence relation $\{\varphi_{sk}\} \models_{\{sk\}} \varphi$ does hold because the premiss $\mathcal{M} \models_{\{sk\}} \varphi_{sk}$ does not hold.

Finally, we use the following notation to denote the equivalence between terms or formulas.

Definition 2.14. *Given terms t and t' and formulas ϕ and ϕ', we write*

- $t \equiv t'$ *if* $\models t \doteq t'$
- $\phi \equiv \phi'$ *if* $\models \phi \leftrightarrow \phi'$

2.3 The Dynamic Logic Java Card DL

First-order dynamic logic (DL) [Harel, 1984] is a multi-modal logic. It is an extension of first-order logic where a formula ϕ can be *prepended* by the modal operators $\langle p \rangle$ and $[p]$ for every program p. The formula $[p]\phi$ means that if p terminates, then ϕ holds in the state after the execution of p. Using the termini in [Dijkstra, 1976], $[p]\phi$ is semantically equivalent to the weakest precondition $wlp(p, \varphi)$. As we consider only sequential and deterministic Java programs the meaning of $\langle p \rangle \phi$ is that the program terminates and that $[p]\phi$ is true. Thus, $[p]\phi \wedge \langle p \rangle true$ is equivalent to $\langle p \rangle \phi$ which is again equivalent to the weakest precondition $wp(p, \varphi)$ in [Dijkstra, 1976]. Different program states are realized as first-order partial models with different interpretations of the non-rigid function symbols. Hence, if p changes the program state this means that the interpretation of non-rigid functions is changed. In the following the set *Formulae* denotes the set of dynamic logic formulas.

An implication of the form *pre* → [*p*]*post* ∈ *Formulae* with *pre*, *post* ∈ *Formulae* corresponds to the Hoare triple {*pre*}*p*{*post*} in Hoare logic [Hoare, 1969].[4] If the precondition *pre* is true in the state before the execution of the program and the program terminates, then the postcondition *post* holds after the execution of the program; if the precondition does not hold before the execution of the program, then no statement is made about the post-state. The implication *pre* → ⟨*p*⟩*post* states additionally that *p* terminates. In contrast to Hoare logic, dynamic logic is closed under the logical operators, i.e., dynamic logic allows the formulas *pre* and *post* to *contain* programs as modal operators.

JAVA CARD DL is an instance of classical dynamic logic [Harel, 1984] and extends it (syntactically) with updates [Beckert, 2001]. Updates are used to capture the essence of programs, namely the state change computed by a program execution. Intuitively, updates can be seen as modal operators although they are not defined as such in the KeY Book. Updates allow an efficient way of handling the aliasing problem by delaying of proof splits.

2.3.1 Syntax

Definition 2.15. *Given a signature* Σ*, we inductively define the system of sets* $\{Terms_A\}_{A \in \mathcal{T}}$ *of terms of static type A to be the least system of sets such that*

- *all syntactic constructors of* Trm_A^{FOL} *according to Def. 2.3 are also constructors of* $Terms_A$*,*
- $\{u\}t \in Terms_A$ *for all updates* $u \in Updates$ *(see Def. 2.16) and all terms* $t \in Terms_A$*.*

In the style of JAVA CARD syntax we often write $t.f$ *instead of* $f(t)$ *and* $a[i]$ *instead of* $[\,](a, i)$*.*

Definition 2.16. *Given a JAVA CARD DL signature* $(\mathrm{VSym}, \mathrm{FSym}_r,$ $\mathrm{FSym}_{nr}, \mathrm{PSym}_r, \mathrm{PSym}_{nr}, \alpha)$ *for a type hierarchy* $(\mathcal{T}, \mathcal{T}_d, \mathcal{T}_a, \sqsubseteq)$*, the set Updates of* syntactic updates *is inductively defined as the least set such that:*

---

[4] The Hoare triple exists only if *pre*, *post* ⊂ Fml^{FOL}.

- $(f(t_1, \ldots, t_n) := t) \in Updates$ *(called* function update*) for all terms* $f(t_1, \ldots, t_n) \in Terms_A$ *(see Def. 2.15) with* $f \in \mathrm{FSym}_{nr}$ *and* $t \in Terms_{A'}$ *s.t.* $A' \sqsubseteq A;$
- $(u_1 \, ; u_2) \in Updates$ *(called* sequential update*);*
- $(u_1 \, \| \, u_2) \in Updates$ *(called* parallel update*);*
- $(\mathtt{for} \ x; \ \phi; \ u) \in Updates$ *(called* quantified update*) for all* $u \in Updates,$ $x \in \mathrm{VSym},$ *and* $\phi \in Formulae$ *(see Def. 2.17);*
- $(\{u_1\}u_2) \in Updates$ *(called* update application*)*

where $u_1, u_2, u \in Updates.$

In a function update $f(t_1, \ldots, t_n) := t$ *the term* $f(t_1, \ldots, t_n)$ *is called the* location term *and* t *is called the* value term.

The atomic updates are always function updates. Function updates are similar to assignments in JAVA. The main difference is that the left and right hand side of the updates are terms and not JAVA expressions. In contrast to expressions, terms may contain quantified variables and they have no side-effects. A side effect occurs if the evaluation of an expression changes the state, hence, e.g. $a := \mathtt{i++}$ is not an update. Important is that the top-level symbol of a location term is a non-rigid function symbol. For instance, $1 + 2 := 4$ is not an update but $f(1, 2) := 4 \in Updates$ if $f \in \mathrm{FSym}_{nr}.$

Definition 2.17. *Given a signature* Σ, *we inductively define the set* Formulae *to be the least set such that*

- *all syntactic constructors of* Fml^{FOL} *according to Def. 2.4 are also constructors of* Formulae *with the extension that the terms of the sets* $\{Terms_A\}_{A \in \mathcal{T}}$ *(see Def. 2.15) are used in Def. 2.4,*
- $\{u\}\phi \in Formulae$ *for all* $\phi \in Formulae$ *and* $u \in Updates$ *(see Def. 2.16),*
- $\langle p \rangle \phi, [p]\phi \in Formulae$ *for all* $\phi \in Formulae$ *and any legal sequence* p *of* JAVA CARD *DL program statements. The program may also contain method frame blocks (see Section 2.4.5).*

Furthermore, the modal operator $\langle p \rangle$ *is called* diamond *and* $[p]$ *is called* box *for any program* p.

Definition 2.18. *We define the set $fv(u)$ of free variables of an update u by:*

- $fv(f(t_1, \ldots, t_n) := t) = fv(t) \cup \bigcup_{i=1}^{n} fv(t_i)$,
- $fv(u_1 \,;\, u_2) = fv(u_1) \cup fv(u_2)$,
- $fv(u_1 \,\|\, u_2) = fv(u_1) \cup fv(u_2)$,
- $fv(\texttt{for } x;\, \phi;\, u) = (fv(\phi) \cup fv(u)) \backslash \{x\}$.

For terms and formulas we extend Def. 2.5 as follows:

- $fv(\{u\}t) = fv(u) \cup fv(t)$ *for a term t,*
- $fv(\{u\}\phi) = fv(u) \cup fv(\phi)$ *for a formula ϕ,*
- $fv(\langle p \rangle \phi) = fv(\phi)$ *for a formula ϕ,*
- $fv([p]\phi) = fv(\phi)$ *for a formula ϕ.*

A formula ϕ is called closed iff $fv(\phi) = \emptyset$.

2.3.2 Semantics

Partial models according to Definition 2.6 and program states are the same concept in JAVA CARD DL. Hence, from now on we use the term *state* in order to refer to a partial model. When a program changes the values of fields or program variables, this means that the interpretation of these symbols is changed. In contrast to first-order logic several states may have to be considered in order to evaluate a formula in dynamic logic. The connection between states is given by a Kripke structure.

Definition 2.19. *A JAVA CARD DL Kripke structure $\mathcal{K}_{\preceq}$ is a tuple $(\mathcal{S}, \rho)$ consisting of the set of all partial models $\mathcal{S}$ as defined in Def. 2.6, that we call states, and a program relation ρ such that for all states $S_1, S_2 \in \mathcal{S}$ and any legal sequence p of JAVA CARD DL program statements with possible non-standard JAVA constructs[5]:*

$$\rho(S_1, p, S_2)$$

iff

- *Let $(\mathcal{T}_1, \mathcal{D}_1, \preceq_1, \delta_1, \mathcal{I}_1) = S_1$ and $(\mathcal{T}_2, \mathcal{D}_2, \preceq_2, \delta_2, \mathcal{I}_2) = S_2$, then*
  - $\mathcal{T}_1 = \mathcal{T}_2$
  - $\mathcal{D}_1 = \mathcal{D}_2$
  - $\preceq_1 = \preceq_2$

---

[5] A non-standard JAVA construct of KeY used in this thesis is the *method frame block* which is described in Section 2.4.5.

$- \delta_1 = \delta_2$,

- and p started in S_1 in a static context terminates normally (i.e., without throwing an exception) in S_2 according to the JAVA language specification [Gosling et al., 1996] with extensions for non-standard constructs.

In this context we call S_1 the pre-state and S_2 the post-state of p.

2.3.2.1 Semantics of Updates

An update changes the interpretation of non-rigid function symbols. For instance, the formula $(\{a := b\}a \doteq c) \in Formulae$, where $a \in \mathrm{FSym}_{nr}$ and $b, c \in \mathrm{FSym}$ consists of the (function) update $a := b$ and the *application* of the update operator $\{a := b\}$ on the formula $a \doteq c$.

The meaning of this *update application* is the same as that of the weakest precondition $wp(a := b, a \doteq c)$, i.e., it represents all states such that after the assignment $a := b$ the formula $a \doteq c$ is true – which is equivalent to $b \doteq c$. In contrast to programs updates always terminate.

The semantics of an update is defined by its evaluation into a semantic update. A semantic update maps a state to a new state. The Definitions 2.20, 2.21, and 2.22 are needed for the definition of the semantics of updates in Definition 2.23.

Definition 2.20. *Let* $(\mathrm{VSym}, \mathrm{FSym}_r, \mathrm{FSym}_{nr}, \mathrm{PSym}_r, \mathrm{PSym}_{nr}, \alpha)$ *be a signature for a type hierarchy. A* semantic update *is a triple*

$$(f, (d_1, \ldots, d_n), d)$$

such that

- $f : A_1, \ldots, A_n \to A \in \mathrm{FSym}_{nr}$,
- $d_i \in \mathcal{D}^{A_i}$ $(i \leqslant i \leqslant n)$, and
- $d \in \mathcal{D}^A$.

Definition 2.21. *A set CU of semantic updates is called* consistent *if for all* $(f, (d_1, \ldots, d_n), d), (f', (d'_1, \ldots, d'_m), d') \in CU$,

$$d = d' \text{ if } f = f', n = m, \text{ and } d_i = d'_i \ (1 \leqslant i \leqslant n) .$$

Let $\mathcal{CU}$ denote the set of consistent semantic updates.

Definition 2.22. *Let* $(\text{VSym}, \text{FSym}_r, \text{FSym}_{nr}, \text{PSym}_r, \text{PSym}_{nr}, \alpha)$ *be a signature for a given type hierarchy and further let* $S = (T, \mathcal{D}, \preceq, \delta, \mathcal{I})$ *be a* JAVA CARD *DL state, i.e. partial model, for that signature.*

For any set $CU \in \mathcal{CU}$ *of consistent semantic updates, the modification* $CU(S)$ *is defined as the partial model* $S' = (T, \mathcal{D}, \preceq, \delta, \mathcal{I}')$ *with*

$$\mathcal{I}'(f)(d_1, \ldots, d_n) = \begin{cases} d & \text{if } (f, (d_1, \ldots, d_n), d) \in CU \\ \mathcal{I}(f)(d_1, \ldots, d_n) & \text{otherwise} \end{cases}$$

for all $f : A_1, \ldots, A_n \to A \in \text{FSym}$ *and* $d_i \in \mathcal{D}^{A_i}$ $(1 \leqslant i \leqslant n)$ *and* $\mathcal{I}'(p)(d_1, \ldots, d_n) = \mathcal{I}(p)(d_1, \ldots, d_n)$ *for all predicate symbols* $p \in \text{PSym} \backslash \{inReachableState\}$. *The interpretation* $\mathcal{I}'(inReachableState)$ *satisfies Definition 2.8.*[6]

In this context S *is the pre-state and* S' *is the post-state of* CU.

Definition 2.23. *Given a signature for a type hierarchy, let* $\mathcal{K}_{\preceq} = (\mathcal{S}, \rho)$ *be a* JAVA CARD *DL Kripke structure with ordered domain, let* β *be a variable assignment.*

For every state $\mathcal{S} = (T, \mathcal{D}, \preceq, \delta, \mathcal{I}) \in \mathcal{S}$, *the valuation function* $val_S :$ $\text{Updates} \to \mathcal{CU}$ *for updates is inductively defined by*

- $val_{S,\beta}(f(t_1, \ldots, t_n) := s) = \{(f, (d_1, \ldots, d_n), d)\}$ *where*

$$d_i = val_{S,\beta}(t_i) \quad (1 \leqslant i \leqslant n)$$
$$d = val_{S,\beta}(s),$$

- $val_{S,\beta}(u_1 \,;\, u_2) = (U_1 \cup U_2) \backslash C$ *where*

$U_1 = val_{S,\beta}(u_1)$
$U_2 = val_{S',\beta}(u_2) \quad$ *with* $S' = val_{S,\beta}(u_1)(S)$
$C = \{(f, (d_1, \ldots, d_n), d) | (f, (d_1, \ldots, d_n), d) \in U_1 \text{ and}$
$\qquad\qquad\qquad (f, (d_1, \ldots, d_n), d') \in U_2 \text{ for some } d' \neq d\},$

- $val_{S,\beta}(u_1 \,\|\, u_2) = (U_1 \cup U_2) \backslash C$ *where*

$U_1 = val_{S,\beta}(u_1)$
$U_2 = val_{S,\beta}(u_2)$
$C = \{(f, (d_1, \ldots, d_n), d) | (f, (d_1, \ldots, d_n), d) \in U_1 \text{ and}$
$\qquad\qquad\qquad (f, (d_1, \ldots, d_n), d') \in U_2 \text{ for some } d' \neq d\},$

---

[6] The function symbol *inReachableState* is a so-called *location dependent symbol*. For simplicity we only give a special treatment for this symbol.

- $val_{S,\beta}(\texttt{for } x;\ \phi;\ u) = U$ where

$$U = \{(f,(d_1,\ldots,d_n),d)|\ there\ is\ a \in \mathcal{D}^A\ such\ that$$
$$((f,(d_1,\ldots,d_n),d),a) \in dom\ and$$
$$b \not\preceq a\ for\ all\ ((f,(d_1,\ldots,d_n),d'),b) \in dom\}$$

with $dom = \bigcup_{a\in\{d\in\mathcal{D}^A|S,\beta_x^d\models\phi\}}(val_{S,\beta_x^a}(u) \times \{a\})$, and A is the type of x,

- $val_{S,\beta}(\{u_1\}u_2) = val_{S',\beta}(u_2)$ with $S' = val_{S,\beta}(u_1)(S)$.

For an update u without free variables we simply write $val_S(u)$ since $val_{S,\beta}(u)$ is independent of β.

In the following we give examples for the evaluation of syntactic updates to semantic updates. The updates are evaluated in a state $S \in \mathcal{S}$ of a Kripke structure and $\mathcal{I}$ is the interpretation function of S. For a shorter notation we write $g^{\mathcal{I}}$ to denote the interpretation of a function symbol $g \in$ FSym. Furthermore, we assume that $f, a, b \in$ FSym$_{nr}$, and $x \in$ VSym are of compatible types in the respective case.

The function update $f(1) := a$ evaluates to the consistent set of semantic updates $\{((f,(1^{\mathcal{I}})),a^{\mathcal{I}})\}$ and the sequential update $(f(1) := 3\,;f(2) := 4)$ evaluates to the set $\{((f,(1^{\mathcal{I}})),3^{\mathcal{I}}),((f,(2^{\mathcal{I}})),4^{\mathcal{I}})\}$ of consistent semantic updates. More interesting is the case when a *clash* occurs as in the update

$$f(1) := 3\,;f(1) := 4 \tag{2.1}$$

The two function sub-updates assign different values to the location $(f,(1^{\mathcal{I}}))$. In this case the set C of the sequential update according to Definition 2.23 is $\{((f,(1^{\mathcal{I}})),3^{\mathcal{I}})\}$. The set of consistent semantic updates is in this case

$$\underbrace{\{((f,(1^{\mathcal{I}})),3^{\mathcal{I}}),((f,(2^{\mathcal{I}})),4^{\mathcal{I}})\}}_{U_1\cup U_2} \setminus \underbrace{\{((f,(1^{\mathcal{I}})),3^{\mathcal{I}})\}}_{C} = ((f,(2^{\mathcal{I}})),4^{\mathcal{I}})$$

The update (2.1) is equivalent to the update $f(1) := 4$. Hence, in case of a clash the latter update *wins*.

In order to show the difference between sequential and parallel updates consider the following example.

$$a := b\,;b := a \tag{2.2}$$

The update (2.2) evaluates to the set

$$\{(a, ()), b^{\mathcal{I}}), ((b, ()), val_{\{(a,()),b^{\mathcal{I}})\}(S)}, \beta(a))\} \tag{2.3}$$

The state modification $\{(a, ()), b^{\mathcal{I}})\}(S)$ results in a state where a is interpreted as $b^{\mathcal{I}}$. Therefore (2.3) simplifies to

$$\{(a, ()), b^{\mathcal{I}}), (b, ()), b^{\mathcal{I}})\}$$

In contrast the value terms of a parallel update are evaluated in the same state S. The parallel update

$$a := b \, || \, b := a$$

evaluates therefore to

$$\{(a, ()), b^{\mathcal{I}}), (b, ()), a^{\mathcal{I}})\}$$

This set of semantic update modifies a state such that the values of a and b are swapped.

Quantified updates can be informally seen as an infinite composition of parallel updates. A quantified update can be used, e.g., in order to initialize the values of an array arr to 0, which can be written as $(\mathbf{for}\ x;\ \text{true};\ arr[x] := 0)$.

The update

$$\mathbf{for}\ x;\ 0 \leqslant x \wedge x \leqslant 2;\ f(x) := x \tag{2.4}$$

is equivalent to the parallel update

$$f(2) := 2 \, || \, f(1) := 1 \, || \, f(0) := 0$$

and it evaluates to the following set of consistent semantic updates:

$$\{((f, (2^{\mathcal{I}})), 2^{\mathcal{I}}), ((f, (1^{\mathcal{I}})), 1^{\mathcal{I}}), ((f, (0^{\mathcal{I}})), 0^{\mathcal{I}})\}$$

Quantified updates may, however, have clashes as it is the case with the following update.

$$\mathbf{for}\ x;\ \underbrace{x \doteq 0 \vee x \doteq 1}_{\phi};\ a := x \tag{2.5}$$

In this case the set dom and the well-ordering $\preceq$ come into play. The set dom for this update is

$$\{(((a, ()), 0^{\mathcal{I}}), 0^{\mathcal{I}}), (((a, ()), 1^{\mathcal{I}}), 1^{\mathcal{I}})\}$$

because only for the variable assignments $\beta_x^{0^{\mathcal{I}}}$ and $\beta_x^{1^{\mathcal{I}}}$, ϕ evaluates to true. The definition says that in case of a clash the update with the least value of x according to the well-ordering $\preceq$ *wins*. Hence, from the set *dom* we derive the following consistent set

$$\{((a, ()), 0^{\mathcal{I}})\}$$

The update (2.5) is therefore equivalent to the parallel update $(a := 1 \,||\, a := 0)$ but not to the update $(a := 0 \,||\, a := 1)$.

The final example shows an update application.

$$\{a := b\}(a := a) \tag{2.6}$$

An update application does not affect the top-level function symbol of the location term, i.e., the left hand side of $a := a$ is not affected. The semantic update for $a := b$ is $((a, ()), b^{\mathcal{I}})$. The update (2.6) evaluates therefore to

$$\{val_{\{((a,()),b^{\mathcal{I}})\}}(S),\beta}(a := a)\} = \{((a, ()), b^{\mathcal{I}})\}$$

In contrast to the top-level function symbol of the location term, an update application does affect the sub-terms of the location term. For instance the update application

$$\{a := b\}(f(a) := a)$$

evaluates to

$$\{((f, (b^{\mathcal{I}})), b^{\mathcal{I}})\}.$$

2.3.2.2 Semantics of Terms and Formulas

With the notions of a Kripke structure and semantic updates it is easy to define the semantics of JAVA CARD DL terms and formulas. The definition of the semantics of terms and formulas in Section 2.2.2 is extended here. A term or formula which is in the scope of a modal operator is evaluated in the post-state of the modal operator. Similarly, a term or formula which is in the scope of an update is evaluated in the post-state of the update.

Definition 2.24. *Given a signature for a type hierarchy, let $\mathcal{K}_{\preceq} = (\mathcal{S}, \rho)$ be a JAVA CARD DL Kripke structure, and let β be a variable assignment.*

For every state $S = (T, \mathcal{D}, \preceq, \delta, \mathcal{I})$, the valuation function val_S is inductively defined according to Definition 2.10 (note that $S = \mathcal{M}$) with the following extension

$$val_{S,\beta}(\{u\}(t)) = val_{S',\beta}(t) \text{ with } S' = val_{S,\beta}(u)(S).$$

Since $val_{S,\beta}(t)$ does not depend on β if t is ground, we write $val_S(t)$ in that case.

Definition 2.25. *Given a signature for a type hierarchy, let $\mathcal{K}_{\preceq} = (\mathcal{S}, \rho)$ be a JAVA CARD DL Kripke structure, and let p be a JAVA CARD program.*

For every state $S = (T, \mathcal{D}, \preceq, \delta, \mathcal{I})$, the validity relation $\vDash$ for JAVA CARD DL formulas is inductively defined according to Definition 2.11 (note that $S = \mathcal{M}$) and the following extensions

- *$S, \beta \vDash \{u\}\phi$ iff $S', \beta \vDash \phi$ with $S' = val_{S,\beta}(u)(S)$*
- *$S, \beta \vDash [p]\phi$ iff there exists some state $S' \in \mathcal{S}$ such that $(S, p, S') \in \rho$ and $S', \beta \vDash \phi$*
- *$S, \beta \vDash \langle p \rangle \phi$ iff $S', \beta \vDash \phi$ for every state $S' \in \mathcal{S}$ with $(S, p, S') \in \rho$*

We write $S \vDash \phi$ for a closed formula ϕ, since β is then irrelevant.

The formula $[p]\phi$ expresses partial correctness and $\langle p \rangle \phi$ expresses total correctness.

As one can see the valuation function of updates plays the same role for updates as the program relation ρ for programs. In contrast to updates, programs do not always terminate and they may throw exceptions. For this reason there are two modal operators for every program which have different semantics depending on the termination of the program. If a program does not terminate or throws an exception, then according to Definition 2.19 there is no post-state of the program satisfying the program relation ρ. In this case the formula $[p]\phi$ evaluates to true for any $\phi \in Formulae$ and $\langle p \rangle \phi$ evaluates to false which is one of the facts stated in the following lemma.

Lemma 2.26. *For every program p and $\phi \in Formulae$.*

- $\langle p \rangle \phi \equiv \neg [p] \neg \phi$

- $\langle p \rangle \phi \equiv (\langle p \rangle \text{true}) \wedge ([p]\phi)$

If P is a non-terminating program, then for any $\phi \in$ Formulae

- $\langle p \rangle \phi \equiv \text{false}$
- $[p]\phi \equiv \text{true}$

Lemma 2.27. *Let $\varphi \in$ Formulae, if $\vDash \varphi$, then for any update $u \in$ Updates, $\vDash \{u\}\varphi$ holds.*

Lemma 2.27 does not stem from the KeY Book and is therefore proved here.

Proof of Lemma 2.27. Since for any $s \in \mathcal{S}$, $s \vDash \varphi$ holds, it is also the case for $s' = val_s(u)$ that $s' \vDash \varphi$ because $s' \in \mathcal{S}$. ∎

Definition 2.28. *A JAVA CARD DL term t is rigid*

- *if $t = x$ and $x \in$ VSym,*
- *if $t = f(t_1, \ldots, t_n)$, $f \in$ FSym$_r$ and the sub-terms t_i with $(1 \leqslant i \leqslant n)$ are rigid,*
- *if $t = \{u\}(s)$ and s is rigid,*
- *if $t = (\text{if } \phi \text{ then } t_1 \text{ else } t_2)$ and the formula ϕ is rigid and the sub-terms t_1, t_2 are rigid,*
- *if $t = (\text{ifExMin } x.\phi \text{ then } t_1 \text{ else } t_2)$ and the formula ϕ is rigid and the sub-terms t_1, t_2 are rigid.*

A JAVA CARD DL formula ϕ is rigid

- *if $\phi = p(t_1, \ldots, t_n)$, $p \in$ PSym$_r$ and the terms t_i with $(1 \leqslant i \leqslant n)$ are rigid,*
- *if $\phi = \text{true}$ or $\phi = \text{false}$,*
- *if $\phi = \neg\psi$ and ψ is rigid,*
- *$\phi = (\psi_1 \vee \psi_2)$, $\phi = (\psi_1 \wedge \psi_2)$, or $\phi = (\psi_1 \to \psi_2)$, and ψ_1, ψ_2 are rigid,*
- *if $\phi = \forall x.\psi$ or $\phi = \exists x.\psi$, and ψ is rigid,*
- *$\phi = \{u\}\psi$ and ψ is rigid.*

2.4 Calculus

The calculus of KeY is divided into several groups of calculus rules such as first-order rules, update simplification rules, program reduction rules, and contract rules. Since programs and formulas are combined in dynamic logic the calculus consists of rules for reasoning about first-order logic formulas as well as of rule for program analysis by symbolic execution. KeY's rule base consists of about 1755 rules where most of the rules model the semantics of JAVA programs. The correctness of the program rules has been validated using different techniques as described in [Trentelman, 2005] and [Ahrendt et al., 2005]. A more general discussion about the correctness of verification systems is found in [Beckert and Klebanov, 2006].

In the following sections we show only a subset of rules which is relevant for understanding this thesis. Furthermore, we have simplified the rules in Sections 2.4.5 and 2.4.6 which model the semantics of programs. This is because most of the technical details are not necessary for understanding the techniques described in this thesis. However, the implementation of the described techniques works with the original rules. Many rules of KeY's calculus also encode theories such as Presburger arithmetic which are not described in this thesis. The calculus rules for Presburger and non-linear arithmetic are formalized in [Rümmer, 2007, 2008] and we assume that the reader can follow our arithmetic transformations without seeing the concrete rules. For further details about KeY's calculus we refer the reader to the KeY Book.

2.4.1 Sequents, Rules, and Proofs

For proving the validity of formulas (Def. 2.12) KeY uses a sequent calculus. The sequent calculus rules create a tree structure that we call a proof tree. The root of the proof tree is the formula whose validity is to be proven. The goal of the calculus is to replace the formula by new formulas, that are in a way simpler, until axioms are derived. If all leaves of the proof tree are axioms, then soundness of the calculus ensures that the formula at the root of the proof tree is a consequence of the axioms, i.e., it is valid.

The syntactic structure of sequents, rules, rule schemas, and proofs is defined in the Definitions 2.29, 2.30, 2.32, and 2.31. Examples are shown in Section 2.4.3 and the following sections. Definition 2.34 describes a generalization of rule schemas which applies to almost all sequent rules of the calculus. Finally, Propositions 2.35 and 2.36 state soundness and relative completeness of KeY's calculus.

Definition 2.29. *A* sequent *is of the form* $\Gamma \implies \Delta$*, where* Γ, Δ *are finite sets of closed (see Def. 2.5 and 2.18) JAVA CARD DL formulas.*

The left-hand side Γ is called antecedent *and the right-hand side Δ is called* succedent *of the sequent.*

The semantics of a sequent

$$\phi_1, \ldots, \phi_m \Longrightarrow \psi_1, \ldots, \psi_n$$

is the same as that of the formula

$$(\phi_1 \wedge \ldots \wedge \phi_m) \rightarrow (\psi_1 \vee \ldots \vee \psi_n).$$

We write $\bigwedge\Gamma$ to abbreviate $\bigwedge_{\phi \in \Gamma} \phi$ and we write $\bigvee\Delta$ to abbreviate $\bigvee_{\psi \in \Delta} \psi$.

Definition 2.30. *A* rule *R is a binary relation between (a) the set of all tuples of sequents and (b) the set of all sequents.*

If $R(\langle P_1, \ldots, P_k \rangle, C)$ $(k \geqslant 0)$, then the conclusion *C is* derivable *from the* premisses *$P_1, \ldots, P_k$ using rule R.*

Definition 2.31. *A* proof tree *is a finite tree (shown with the root at the bottom), such that*

- *each node of the tree is annotated with a sequent,*
- *each inner node of the tree is annotated with one rule that has at least one premiss. The sequent of the node is the rule conclusion. The direct descendants of the nodes are the premisses of the rule.*
- *If a leaf node is annotated with a rule, then the rule has no premisses and is called a* closing rule.

Furthermore

- *A* proof tree *for a formula ϕ is a proof tree where the root sequent is annotated with $\Longrightarrow \phi$.*
- *A* branch *of a proof tree is a path from the root to one of the leaves. A branch is* closed *if the leaf is annotated with one of the closing rules. A proof tree is* closed *if all its branches are closed, i.e., every leaf is annotated with a closing rule.*
- *A closed proof tree (for a formula resp. a sequent ϕ) is also called a* proof *(for ϕ) and ϕ is in this case* derivable *in the calculus.*

Definition 2.32. *A rule schema is of the form*

$$\frac{P_1 \quad P_2 \quad \ldots \quad P_k}{C} \qquad (k \geqslant 0)$$

where $P_1, \ldots, P_k$ and C are schematic sequents, i.e., sequents containing schema variables.

Remark 2.33. Despite the distinction between a rule (Def. 2.30) and a rule schema (Def. 2.32) we will conveniently use the term rule to refer to a rule schema in the following sections and chapters.

Definition 2.34. *Let $A, A^1, \ldots, A^k, B, B^1, \ldots, B^k \subset Formulae$. If*

$$\frac{A^1 \Longrightarrow B^1 \quad \ldots \quad A^k \Longrightarrow B^k}{A \Longrightarrow B}$$

is an instance of a rule schema, then

$$\frac{\Gamma, \mathcal{U} A^1 \Longrightarrow \mathcal{U} B^1, \Delta \quad \ldots \quad \Gamma, \mathcal{U} A^k \Longrightarrow \mathcal{U} B^k, \Delta}{\Gamma, \mathcal{U} A \Longrightarrow \mathcal{U} B, \Delta}$$

is an inference rule of our DL calculus, where $\mathcal{U}$ is an arbitrary syntactic update, and Γ, Δ are finite sets of context formulas.

The notation $\mathcal{U} \Phi$ with $\{\phi_1, \ldots, \phi_n\} = \Phi \subset Formulae$ is an abbreviation for $\{\mathcal{U}\phi_1, \ldots, \mathcal{U}\phi_n\}$.

If, however, the symbol $(*)$ is added to the rule schema, the context $\Gamma, \Delta, \mathcal{U}$ must be empty, i.e., only instances of the schema itself are inference rules.

Proposition 2.35. *If a sequent $\Gamma \Longrightarrow \Delta$ is derivable (see Def. 2.31) in the JAVA CARD DL calculus, then it is valid, i.e., the formula $\bigwedge \Gamma \rightarrow \bigvee \Delta$ is logically valid (Def. 2.12).*

Proposition 2.36. *If a sequent $\Gamma \Longrightarrow \Delta$ is valid, i.e., the formula $\bigwedge \Gamma \rightarrow \bigvee \Delta$ is logically valid (Def. 2.12), then there is a finite set Γ_{FOL} of logically valid first-order formulae such that the sequent*

$$\Gamma_{FOL}, \Gamma \Longrightarrow \Delta$$

is derivable in the JAVA CARD DL calculus.

Propositions 2.35 and 2.36 state the soundness and relative completeness properties of the calculus and were established for a simplified version of KeY's dynamic logic and calculus in [Platzer, 2004; Beckert and Platzer, 2006]. As mentioned in the beginning of this section, additional arguments support Proposition 2.35 [Trentelman, 2005; Ahrendt et al., 2005; Beckert and Klebanov, 2006].

2.4.2 How Verification Works in KeY

The principal verification approach can be divided into three phases:

1. Program reduction rules are applied leading to a proof tree where branches in the proof tree correspond to case distinction in the program control flow. The proof construction in this phase can be seen as *symbolic execution* [King, 1976] of the program. After this phase the program parts are replaced by updates.
2. The state change performed by the program on each execution trace is captured by an update on each branch. In this phase the updates simplification calculus is applied in order to obtain first-order logic formulas. Effectively, this step performs weakest precondition computation.
3. At this stage all information from the original program has been transformed into first-order logic formulas. It remains to use the first-order logic rules in order to prove the remaining proof obligations.

Similar phases exist in other verification systems where a different tool for each of such phases is used in a tool-chain. In contrast to other systems, the KeY tool integrates the three phases in one calculus and allows using SMT solvers in addition to that. As calculus rules can be applied in any order if applicable, i.e., the separation between the phases is not strict in KeY. For instance, the three phases can be performed for the first statement of the program before proceeding to the next statement.

2.4.3 Calculus Component: First-order Logic Rules

The following example illustrates how the propositional rules of Table 2.3 are used. In this example the formula $((A \wedge B) \rightarrow C) \rightarrow (\neg(A \wedge B) \vee C)$ is proven where $A, B, C \in Formulae$. The formula has no particular meaning, rather it has been constructed to show several different rule applications while keeping the example small.

Propositional Rules

$$\text{notRight} \quad \frac{\phi \Longrightarrow}{\Longrightarrow \neg\phi} \qquad \text{andRight} \quad \frac{\Longrightarrow \phi \quad \Longrightarrow \psi}{\Longrightarrow \phi \wedge \psi} \qquad \text{orRight} \quad \frac{\Longrightarrow \phi, \psi}{\Longrightarrow \phi \vee \psi}$$

$$\text{notLeft} \quad \frac{\Longrightarrow \phi}{\neg\phi \Longrightarrow} \qquad \text{andLeft} \quad \frac{\phi, \psi \Longrightarrow}{\phi \wedge \psi \Longrightarrow} \qquad \text{orLeft} \quad \frac{\phi \Longrightarrow \quad \psi \Longrightarrow}{\phi \vee \psi \Longrightarrow}$$

$$\text{impLeft} \quad \frac{\psi \Longrightarrow \quad \Longrightarrow \phi}{\phi \to \psi \Longrightarrow} \qquad \text{impRight} \quad \frac{\phi \Longrightarrow \psi}{\Longrightarrow \phi \to \psi} \qquad \text{cut} \quad \frac{\phi \Longrightarrow \quad \neg\phi \Longrightarrow}{\Longrightarrow}$$

$$\text{close} \quad \frac{}{\phi \Longrightarrow \phi} \qquad \text{closeFalse} \quad \frac{}{\text{false} \Longrightarrow} \qquad \text{closeTrue} \quad \frac{}{\Longrightarrow \text{true}}$$

$$\text{unitProp} \quad \frac{\psi, \phi \Longrightarrow}{\phi \to \psi, \phi \Longrightarrow}$$

Quantifier Skolemization Rules

$$\text{allRight} \quad \frac{\Longrightarrow [x\backslash sk](\phi)}{\Longrightarrow \forall x.\phi} \qquad \text{exLeft} \quad \frac{[x\backslash sk](\phi) \Longrightarrow}{\exists x.\phi \Longrightarrow}$$

where sk is a new constant of type $\alpha(sk) = \alpha(x)$

Quantifier Instantiation Rules

$$\text{allLeft} \quad \frac{\forall x.\phi, [x\backslash t](\phi) \Longrightarrow}{\forall x.\phi \Longrightarrow} \qquad \text{exRight} \quad \frac{\Longrightarrow \exists x.\phi, [x\backslash t](\phi)}{\Longrightarrow \exists \ x.\phi}$$

where $t \in \text{Trm}_A^{FOL}$ with $A \sqsubseteq \alpha(x)$, and either
a) $\phi \in \text{Fml}^{FOL}$ (classical first-order), or
b) t is a rigid ground term (see Def. 2.28) (DL extension).

Table 2.3. Classical first-order rules

A proof tree is constructed bottom-up, i.e., the leaf of a proof branch is matched with a rule conclusion and the rule premises become the new leaves. In this example the proof tree starts with the root sequent

$$\Longrightarrow ((A \wedge B) \to C) \to (\neg(A \wedge B) \vee C) \tag{2.7}$$

and is constructed by *application* of the rules impRight, orRight, notRight, impLeft, close, andLeft, andRight, close, close in the given order. Closed branches are marked with '*'.

$$\cfrac{\cfrac{*}{C, A \wedge B \Rightarrow C} \text{ close} \qquad \cfrac{B_1}{A \wedge B \Rightarrow A \wedge B, C} \text{ (see below)}}{\cfrac{(A \wedge B) \rightarrow C, A \wedge B \Rightarrow C}{\cfrac{(A \wedge B) \rightarrow C \Rightarrow \neg(A \wedge B), C}{\cfrac{(A \wedge B) \rightarrow C \Rightarrow \neg(A \wedge B) \vee C}{\Rightarrow ((A \wedge B) \rightarrow C) \rightarrow (\neg(A \wedge B) \vee C)} \text{ impRight}} \text{ orRight}} \text{ notRight}} \text{ impLeft}}$$

The branch B_1 is continued as follows.

$$\cfrac{\cfrac{\cfrac{*}{A, B \Rightarrow A, C} \text{ close} \qquad \cfrac{*}{A, B \Rightarrow B, C} \text{ close}}{A, B \Rightarrow A \wedge B, C} \text{ andRight}}{A \wedge B \Rightarrow A \wedge B, C} \text{ andLeft}$$

Since all branches are closed, the proof tree is closed, and the Formula (2.7) is proven.

Note that in order to reduce computational complexity a good strategy is to delay the application of the *branching rules* andRight, orLeft, and impLeft as much as possible. This example further illustrates the symmetry between the rules andRight, orLeft on the one hand and orRight, andLeft on the other hand.

The next example shows how quantifier Skolemization and instantiation rules of Table 2.3 are used. The formula to be proven is

$$(\exists x. \forall y. p(x, y)) \rightarrow (\forall v. \exists u. p(u, v))$$

where $p \in \text{PSym}_r$ and $x, y, v, u \in \text{VSym}$ are of the same type. The formula is proved by the following proof tree where $sk_1, sk_2 \in \text{FSym}_r$ are fresh symbols, i.e., they do not occur in the proof tree before their first usage.

$$\cfrac{\cfrac{\cfrac{\cfrac{\cfrac{\cfrac{*}{\forall y. p(sk_1, y), p(sk_1, sk_2) \Rightarrow p(sk_1, sk_2), \exists u. p(u, sk_2)} \text{ close}}{\forall y. p(sk_1, y), p(sk_1, sk_2) \Rightarrow \exists u. p(u, sk_2)} \text{ exRight}}{\forall y. p(sk_1, y) \Rightarrow \exists u. p(u, sk_2)} \text{ allLeft}}{\forall y. p(sk_1, y) \Rightarrow \forall v. \exists u. p(u, v)} \text{ allRight}}{\exists x. \forall y. p(x, y) \Rightarrow \forall v. \exists u. p(u, v)} \text{ exLeft}}{\Rightarrow (\exists x. \forall y. p(x, y)) \rightarrow (\forall v. \exists u. p(u, v))} \text{ impRight}$$

This example shows that the existential quantifier in the antecedent and the universal quantifier in the succedent can be easily eliminated

eqLeft	$\dfrac{t_1 \doteq t_2, \phi, \phi[t_1 \backslash t_2] \Longrightarrow}{t_1 \doteq t_2, \phi \Longrightarrow}$	eqRight	$\dfrac{t_1 \doteq t_2 \Longrightarrow \phi, \phi[t_1 \backslash t_2]}{t_1 \doteq t_2 \Longrightarrow \phi}$
	if $\sigma(t_2) \sqsubseteq \sigma(t_1)$ and (a)		if $\sigma(t_2) \sqsubseteq \sigma(t_1)$ and (a)

eqLeft'	$\dfrac{t_1 \doteq t_2, \phi, \phi[t_1 \backslash (A)t_2] \Longrightarrow}{t_1 \doteq t_2, \phi \Longrightarrow}$	eqRight'	$\dfrac{t_1 \doteq t_2 \Longrightarrow \phi, \phi[t_1 \backslash (A)t_2]}{t_1 \doteq t_2 \Longrightarrow \phi}$
	with $A := \sigma(t_1)$ and (a)		with $A := \sigma(t_1)$ and (a)

eqSymmLeft	$\dfrac{t_2 \doteq t_1 \Longrightarrow}{t_1 \doteq t_2 \Longrightarrow}$	eqClose	$\dfrac{}{\Longrightarrow t \doteq t}$

(a) It is required that $\phi \in \mathrm{Fml}^{FOL}$ and ϕ has an occurrence of t_1. The notation $\sigma(t)$ is defined in Definition 2.3.

Table 2.4. Equality rules

by *Skolemization*, i.e., the quantified variable is replaced by a new constant without losing information. In contrast, existentially quantified formulas in the succedent and universally quantified formulas in the antecedent cannot be eliminated without loosing information. Quantified formulas that require instantiation cause challenging problems in many situations, some of them will be investigated in the next part of the thesis.

Finally, the next proof tree shows an example that makes use of rules from Tables 2.3 and 2.4. We assume that $\sigma(x) = \sigma(a) = \sigma(b)$.

$$
\dfrac{
\dfrac{
\dfrac{
\dfrac{
\dfrac{
\dfrac{
\dfrac{*}{\forall x.x = f(x), f(a) = a, a = b \Longrightarrow a = a} \text{ eqClose}
}{\forall x.x = f(x), f(a) = a, a = b \Longrightarrow f(a) = a} \text{ eqLeft}
}{\forall x.x = f(x), f(a) = a, a = b \Longrightarrow f(a) = b} \text{ eqRight}
}{\forall x.x = f(x), a = f(a), a = b \Longrightarrow f(a) = b} \text{ eqSymmLeft}
}{\forall x.x = f(x), a = b \Longrightarrow f(a) = b} \text{ allLeft}
}{((\forall x.x = f(x)) \wedge a = b) \Longrightarrow f(a) = b} \text{ andLeft}
}{\Longrightarrow ((\forall x.x = f(x)) \wedge a = b) \rightarrow f(a) = b} \text{ impRight}
$$

2.4.4 Calculus Component: Update Simplification Rules

Updates are the connecting link between programs and first-order logic formulas and are therefore presented before showing the program reduction rules in Section 2.4.5. Updates express the state-change that is performed by a program. The update simplification calculus is capable to accumulate updates and then to evaluate first-order formulas in the state expressed by those updates. We first give some general simplification laws for updates in Section 2.4.4.1 and then show how to *apply* updates on updates, terms, and formulas in Section 2.4.4.2. Application of an update means the evaluation of an updates, term, or formula in the post-state of an update. When using the update simplification calculus typically an update is created *in front* of the program modality as will be described in Section 2.4.5. This update is *typically* converted into update normal form during verification as defined below.

Definition 2.37. *An update u is in* update normal form *if it has the form*

$$\mathtt{for}\ \bar{x}_1;\ \phi_1;\ u_1\ ||\ \ldots\ ||\ \mathtt{for}\ \bar{x}_n;\ \phi_n;\ u_n$$

where the u_i are function updates (see Def 2.16) and $\bar{x}_1, \ldots, \bar{x}_n$ denote vectors of variables, i.e., more than one variable can be quantified.

We often write u_i instead of for *$\bar{x}_i$; ϕ_i; u_i if $x \notin fv(u_i)$ and $\phi = $ true.*

2.4.4.1 General Simplification Laws

The update simplification calculus is defined in form of equivalence relations rather than sequent rules. The equivalence or rewriting rules are applied from left to right, i.e., the left-hand side of the relation is substituted by the right-hand side. In the KeY tool the application of these rules is not made explicit in the proof tree. Instead the result of using multiple update simplification steps is shown in the proof tree as one update simplification rule.

Definition 2.38. *Let $u_1, u_2 \in$ Updates. The relation*

$$\equiv \subseteq Updates \times Updates$$

is defined by

$$u_1 \equiv u_2 \quad iff \quad val_{S,\beta}(u_1) = val_{S,\beta}(u_2)$$

for all variable assignments β and JAVA CARD DL states S.

Lemma 2.39. *For all $u_1, u_2, u_3 \in$ Updates the following holds:*

- $u_1 \parallel (u_2 \parallel u_3) \equiv (u_1 \parallel u_2) \parallel u_3$
- $u_1 \,;\, (u_2 \,;\, u_3) \equiv (u_1 \,;\, u_2) \,;\, u_3$

Lemma 2.40. *Let $x \in$ VSym, $\phi \in$ Formulae, and $u \in$ Updates. If ϕ is logically valid and $x \notin fv(\phi) \cup fv(u)$ then*

$$(\texttt{for } x;\ \phi;\ u) \equiv u.$$

Lemma 2.41. *For all $u_1, u_2 \in$ Updates:*

$$u_1 \,;\, u_2 \equiv u_1 \parallel \{u_1\}u_2$$

2.4.4.2 Update Application

The following lemmas represent substitution rules for applying an update to an update (Lemma 2.42), to a term (Lemma 2.43), and to a formula (Lemma 2.45).

Lemma 2.42. *Let an arbitrary update $u \in$ Updates and function updates $u_1, \ldots, u_n \in$ Updates be given. Then,*

- $\{u\}(f(t_1, \ldots, t_n) := s) \equiv f(\{u\}t_1, \ldots, \{u\}t_n) := \{u\}s$
- *if none of the variables in the variable lists $\bar{x}_i$ occur in u*

$$
\begin{aligned}
&\{u\}(\texttt{for } \bar{x}_1;\ \phi_1;\ u_1 \parallel \ldots \parallel \texttt{for } \bar{x}_n;\ \phi_n;\ u_n) \equiv \\
&\quad \texttt{for } \bar{x}_1;\ \{u\}\phi_1;\ \{u\}u_1 \parallel \ldots \parallel \texttt{for } \bar{x}_n;\ \{u\}\phi_n;\ \{u\}u_n)
\end{aligned}
$$

For instance, the update application $\{a := b\}a := a$ simplifies to $a := \{a := b\}a$. The example shows that the update is not applied to the top-level function symbol of the location term. It is applied, however, to the sub-terms of the top-level function symbol. For instance, the update application $\{a := b\}f(a) := a$ simplifies to $f(\{a := b\}a) := \{a := b\}a$.

Lemma 2.43. *Let*

$$u = \texttt{for } \bar{x}_1;\ \phi_1;\ u_1 \parallel \ldots \parallel \texttt{for } \bar{x}_n;\ \phi_n;\ u_n$$

be an update in normal form. Then,

- *for all rigid terms $t \in$ Terms (see Def. 2.28),*

$$\{u\}t = t,$$

- *for all terms $f(a_1, \ldots, a_n) \in$ Terms,*

$$\{u\}f(a_1, \ldots, a_n) \equiv \text{if } C_m \text{ then } T_m \text{ else } ($$

$$\vdots$$

$$\text{if } C_1 \text{ then } T_1 \text{ else } f(\{u\}a_1, \ldots, \{u\}a_n)$$

$$\vdots$$

$$)$$

where $C_1, \ldots, C_m$ are guard formulas expressing that the i-th sub-update of u affects the term $f(a_1, \ldots, a_n)$, and $T_1, \ldots, T_m$ are terms that describe the value of the expression in these cases.
C_i and T_i are defined as follows. Suppose that the i-th part of u is of the form

$$\texttt{for } (z_1, \ldots, z_l); \ \phi_i; \ g(b_1, \ldots, b_k) := s_i.$$

Then, the formula C_i is defined by

$$C_i = \begin{cases} \exists z_1. \cdots \exists z_l. C_i' & \text{if } f = g \text{ and } n = k \\ \text{false} & \text{otherwise} \end{cases}$$

$$C_i' = \phi_i \wedge (\{u\}a_1) \doteq b_1 \wedge \cdots \wedge (\{u\}a_k) \doteq b_k$$

and the terms T_i are constructed from the s_i by applying substitutions that instantiate the occurring variables with the smallest of clashing values (corresponding to the clash semantics of quantified updates):

$$[z_1/(\text{ifExMin } z_1'.\exists z_2. \cdots \exists z_l.C_i'' \text{ then } z_1' \text{ else } z_1^{sk})]$$
$$[z_2/(\text{ifExMin } z_2'.\exists z_3. \cdots \exists z_l.C_i'' \text{ then } z_2' \text{ else } z_2^{sk})]$$

$$\vdots$$

$$[z_l/(\text{ifExMin } z_l'.C_i'' \text{ then } z_l' \text{ else } z_l^{sk})]s_i$$

where $C_i'' = [z_1/z_1', \ldots, z_l/z_l']C_i'$ and $z_1^{sk}, \ldots, z_l^{sk} \in$ FSym are fresh functions.

- *for all $u_1 \in$ Updates and $t \in$ Terms,*

$$\{u\}(\{u_1\}t) \equiv \{u \, ; u_1\}t \quad .$$

Remark 2.44. Lemma 2.43 fixes a *typing mistake* in the definition of the terms T_i that was made in the respective lemma in the KeY Book. A formal definition of the update simplification calculus with a soundness and completeness proof is presented in [Rümmer, 2008].

In the following paragraphs we show examples of using the second equivalence (rule) of Lemma 2.43.

First we consider the application of a single function update on a term such as

$$\{g(b_1, \ldots, b_k) := s\} f(a_1, \ldots, a_n)$$

where $g \neq f$ or $k \neq n$. Note, that the update can also be written as a quantified update of the form $(\texttt{for } y; \text{ true}; g(b_1, \ldots, b_k) := s)$ where y does not occur in the function update. In this example C is false and the if-cascade which has the form

$$\text{if } C \text{ then } T \text{ else } f(\{g(b_1, \ldots, b_k) := s\}a_1, \ldots, \{g(b_1, \ldots, b_k) := s\}a_n)$$

simplifies to

$$f(\{g(b_1, \ldots, b_k) := s\}a_1, \ldots, \{g(b_1, \ldots, b_k) := s\}a_n)$$

The update is propagated to the sub-terms of $f(a_1, \ldots, a_n)$ but f remains the top-level function symbol. Hence, the update is not effective on f.

Now we look at more concrete examples where the conditions $g = f$ and $k = n$ are satisfied such as in the following update application.

$$\{f(b) := s\} f(a) \tag{2.8}$$

A function update has no quantified variables and the formula ϕ is not present. In this case C is the same as C' and there are no substitutions for variables in T, i.e., T is simply s_i. The (ifExMin .... then ... else ...) term has in this case the same semantics as the (if ... then ... else ...) term (see Def. 2.10). According to Lemma 2.43 the update application (2.8) is equivalent to

$$\text{if } \underbrace{(\{f(b) := s\}a) \doteq b}_{C} \text{ then } \underbrace{s}_{T} \text{ else } f(\{f(b) := s\}a)$$

The condition C checks if $f(b)$ and $f(a)$ are aliased, i.e., if they refer to the same location. If this is the case, then the update is effective on $f(a)$ and the resulting term is s. Otherwise, the update is not effective on $f(a)$ but possibly on a which results in $f(\{f(b) := s\}a)$.

Next, we consider the application of a parallel update to a term.

$$\underbrace{\{a := 1 \,||\, f(1) := 2 \,||\, f(3) := 4\}}_{u} f(a)$$

This update application rewrites by equivalence transformations to the if-cascade

$$\text{if } (\{u\}a) \doteq 3 \text{ then } 4 \text{ else } (\text{if } (\{u\}a) \doteq 1 \text{ then } 2 \text{ else } f(\{u\}a)) \quad (2.9)$$

The condition $(\{u\}a) \doteq 3$ can be simplified to false and the condition $(\{u\}a) \doteq 1$ can be simplified to true. Hence, the Term (2.9) simplifies to 2.

Finally, we consider the application of a quantified update to a term (see also Section 2.3.2.1):

$$\underbrace{\{\texttt{for } x; \overbrace{0 \leqslant z \wedge z \leqslant 2}^{\phi}; f(z) := z\}}_{u} f(1) \quad (2.10)$$

This update application is equivalent to

$$\text{if } C \text{ then } T \text{ else } f(\{u\}1)$$

where C is defined as

$$\exists z. \overbrace{0 \leqslant z \wedge z \leqslant 2}^{\phi} \wedge (\{u\}1) \doteq z)$$

and can be simplified to true, and T is defined as

$$[z/(\text{ifExMin } z'.[z/z']\overbrace{0 \leqslant z \wedge z \leqslant 2}^{\phi} \wedge (\{u\}1) \doteq z \text{ then } z' \text{ else } z^{sk})]z$$

which can be simplified to

$$\begin{aligned}
&\text{ifExMin } z'.[z/z']0 \leqslant z \wedge z \leqslant 2 \wedge (\{u\}1) \doteq z' \text{ then } z' \text{ else } z^{sk} \\
\equiv~ &\text{ifExMin } z'.0 \leqslant z' \wedge z' \leqslant 2 \wedge 1 \doteq z' \text{ then } z' \text{ else } z^{sk} \\
\equiv~ &\text{ifExMin } z'.1 \doteq z' \text{ then } z' \text{ else } z^{sk} \quad\quad (2.11) \\
\equiv~ &1
\end{aligned}$$

We have simplified the Term (2.11) by following its semantics according to Definition 2.10. KeY is capable to do such simplifications automatically with rewriting rules presented in [Rümmer, 2008].

The following lemma shows equivalence relations for handling update applications on formulas. Reading the equivalence relations as rewriting equations, the applied update is in most cases propagated to sub-formulas and terms.

Lemma 2.45. *Let $u \in Updates$ be an update, then:*

- $\{u\}p(t_1,\dots,t_n) \equiv p(\{u\}t_1,\dots,\{u\}t_n)$,
- $\{u\}\,\text{true} \equiv \text{true}$ *and* $\{u\}\,\text{false} \equiv \text{false}$,
- $\{u\}(\neg\phi) \equiv \neg\{u\}\phi$,
- $\{u\}(\phi \circ \psi) \equiv \{u\}\phi \circ \{u\}\psi$ *for* $\circ \in \{\vee, \wedge, \rightarrow\}$,
- $\{u\}\forall x.\phi \equiv \forall x.\{u\}\phi$ *and* $\{u\}\exists x.\phi \equiv \exists x.\{u\}\phi$ *provided that* $x \notin fv(u)$,
- $\{u\}(\{u_1\}\phi) \equiv \{u\,;u_1\}$.

2.4.5 Calculus Component: Program Reduction Rules

When a program is executed on a processor the state of the program is determined by the values of program memory locations, the program pointer, and the method call stack. In a sense, these concepts have counterparts in a dynamic logic formula with a modal operator.

A verification condition with an occurrence of the program to be verified has *typically* the form

$$\Gamma \implies \mathcal{U}\langle\pi\,stmt\,;\omega\rangle\phi, \Delta \qquad (2.12)$$

The formulas $\Gamma \cup \Delta$ and the update $\mathcal{U}$ determine the values of memory locations, i.e., the state in which $\langle\pi\,stmt\,;\omega\rangle\phi$ is evaluated. The prefix π is a stack with information required to determine where program execution shall continue if a jump statement such as **return**, **throw**, **break**, or **continue** is encountered. The prefix may contain labeled opening braces **label:{**, opening try blocks **try{**, and opening method frames **MF(v,C,se):{**, where **v**, **C**, and **se** contain context information of the method call. The method frame can be seen as a special labelled block that is the jump-target of the return statement. The statement *stmt* is the current or first *active statement* that is to be executed. Program reduction rules given in Table 2.5 operate always on the first active statement. The rest of the program that is executed after *stmt* is abbreviated by ω. With this intuition in mind program reduction rules perform execution of the program with symbolic values which is called *symbolic execution* [King, 1976]. Broadly speaking, the sequent (2.12) can be read as the Hoare triple

$$\{\bigwedge\Gamma \wedge \neg\bigvee\Delta\}\mathcal{U}\pi\ stmt;\ \omega\ \{\phi\}$$

$$\text{assignment } \frac{\Rightarrow \{loc := se^*\}\langle\pi\ \omega\rangle\phi}{\Rightarrow \langle\pi\ loc\ \texttt{=}\ se\texttt{;}\ \omega\rangle\phi}$$

$$\text{ifElseSplit } \frac{se^* \Rightarrow \langle\pi\ p\ \omega\rangle\phi \quad \neg se^* \Rightarrow \langle\pi\ q\ \omega\rangle\phi}{\Rightarrow \langle\pi\ \texttt{if(}se\texttt{)}\ p\ \texttt{else}\ q\ \omega\rangle\phi}$$

$$\text{loopUnwind } \frac{\Rightarrow \langle\pi\ \texttt{if(}e\texttt{)\{}\ p\ \texttt{while(}e\texttt{)}p\texttt{\}}\ \omega\rangle\phi}{\Rightarrow \langle\pi\ \texttt{while(}e\texttt{)}p\ \omega\rangle\phi}$$

$$\text{methodExpand } \frac{\Rightarrow \langle\pi\ \texttt{MF(}lhs, C, se\texttt{):\{}body\texttt{\}}\ \omega\rangle\phi}{\Rightarrow \langle\pi\ lhs\ \texttt{=}\ se.mname(v_1,\dots,v_n)\texttt{@}C\texttt{;}\ \omega\rangle\phi}$$

$$\text{methodReturn } \frac{\Rightarrow \langle\pi\ v\ \texttt{=}\ se\texttt{;}\ \omega\rangle\phi}{\Rightarrow \langle\pi\ \texttt{MF(}v,\dots\texttt{):\{return}\ se\texttt{;}p\texttt{\}}\ \omega\rangle\phi}$$

$$\text{methodEmpty } \frac{\Rightarrow \langle\pi\ \omega\rangle\phi}{\Rightarrow \langle\pi\ \texttt{MF(}v,\dots\texttt{):\{\}}\ \omega\rangle\phi}$$

$$\text{methodThrow } \frac{\Rightarrow \langle\pi\ \texttt{throw}\ se\texttt{;}\ \omega\rangle\phi}{\Rightarrow \langle\pi\ \texttt{MF(}v,\dots\texttt{):\{throw}\ se\texttt{;}p\texttt{\}}\ \omega\rangle\phi}$$

$$\text{tryCatchThrow } \cfrac{\Longrightarrow \langle\pi\ \texttt{if(}se\ \texttt{== null)\{}}{\qquad\texttt{try\{throw new NullPointerException();\}}}$$

tryCatchThrow

$$\Longrightarrow \langle\pi\ \texttt{if(}se\ \texttt{== null)\{}$$
$$\quad\texttt{try\{throw new NullPointerException();\}}$$
$$\qquad\texttt{catch(}T\ v\texttt{)\{}\ q\ \texttt{\} finally \{}\ r\ \texttt{\}}$$
$$\quad\texttt{\} else if (}se\ \texttt{instanceof}\ T\texttt{) \{}$$
$$\qquad T\ v\ \texttt{;}\ v\ \texttt{=}\ se\ \texttt{;}\ q\ \texttt{;}\ r$$
$$\quad\texttt{\} else \{}$$
$$\qquad T\ v\ \texttt{=}\ se\texttt{;}\ r\ \texttt{;}\ \texttt{throw}\ v\texttt{;\}}\ \omega\rangle\phi$$

$$\overline{\Longrightarrow \langle\pi\ \texttt{try\{throw}\ se\texttt{;}\ p\ \texttt{\}}}$$
$$\qquad\texttt{catch(}T\ v\texttt{)\{}\ q\ \texttt{\}}\ \texttt{finally\{}\ r\ \texttt{\}}\ \omega\rangle\phi$$

$$\text{createObject } \cfrac{\begin{array}{l}\Rightarrow \{loc := \text{C::get}(C.\texttt{<nextToCreate>})\}\{loc.\texttt{<created>} := \texttt{true}\}\\ \{C.\texttt{<nextToCreate>} := C.\texttt{<nextToCreate>} + 1\}\\ \langle\pi\ \omega\rangle\phi\end{array}}{\Rightarrow \langle\pi\ loc\ \texttt{=}\ \texttt{new}C\texttt{();}\ \omega\rangle\phi}$$

$$\text{throwDia } \frac{\Longrightarrow \text{false}}{\Longrightarrow \langle\texttt{throw}\ se\texttt{;}\ \omega\rangle\phi} \qquad \text{throwBox } \frac{\Longrightarrow \text{true}}{\Longrightarrow [\texttt{throw}\ se\texttt{;}\ \omega]\phi}$$

The notation se^* represents the translation of the simple expression se into a term or formula depending on the context (see Remark 2.47). The notation $mname(v_1,\dots,v_n)@C$ identifies the method $mname$ that is defined in the class C.

Table 2.5. Simplified program reduction rules

$$\text{emptyDiamond} \quad \dfrac{\Rightarrow \phi}{\Rightarrow \langle\rangle\phi} \qquad\qquad \text{emptyBox} \quad \dfrac{\Rightarrow \phi}{\Rightarrow [\,]\phi}$$

$$\text{diamondLeft} \quad \dfrac{\Rightarrow [p]\neg\phi}{\langle p\rangle\phi \Rightarrow} \qquad\qquad \text{boxLeft} \quad \dfrac{\Rightarrow \langle p\rangle\neg\phi}{[p]\phi \Rightarrow}$$

$$\text{diamondToBox} \quad \dfrac{\Rightarrow [p]\phi \qquad \Rightarrow \langle p\rangle\text{true}}{\Rightarrow \langle p\rangle\phi}$$

Table 2.6. Non-program rules for modalities

After symbolic execution of the first active statement the formulas $\Gamma \cup \Delta$ and the update $\mathcal{U}$ may be updated reflecting the new program state. The prefix π is updated if the program enters or leaves a program method or a program block that may be the target of a jump statement.

Remark 2.46. The rules in Table 2.5 are simplified rules of KeY's calculus which capture only the essential idea of the original rules. The actual rules of the KeY tool are equipped with additional case distinctions in order to check if exceptions should be thrown such as `NullPointerException`-, `ArrayIndexOutOfBounds`-exceptions, as well as other exceptions.

2.4.5.1 Example 1

In the following we show a simple example that illustrates the three phases of verification as described in Section 2.4.2. Note, however, that calculus rules can be applied in any order if applicable.

Consider the program

```
if(a<b) d=b-a; else d=a-b;
```

where a, b, and d are program variables of type `int`. The goal is to prove that after the execution of this program d stores the absolute difference between a and b. This requirement can be formalized by the verification condition

$$\langle \texttt{if(a<b) d=b-a; else d=a-b;} \rangle \underbrace{((d \doteq b - a \lor d \doteq a - b) \land d \geqslant 0)}_{post}$$

where the formula *post* is the postcondition. The prefix π and the postfix ω as used in Table 2.5 are empty and therefore do not occur in the modal operator. The logical constants a, b, and d represent the program variables a, b, and d respectively.

In the following proof tree, according to phase 1, mainly program reduction and modality rules from Tables 2.5 and 2.6 are applied.

$$\cfrac{\cfrac{\cfrac{\cfrac{\boldsymbol{B_2}}{a < b \Longrightarrow \{d := b - a\}post}}{a < b \Longrightarrow \{d := b - a\}\langle\rangle post}\text{ emptyDiamond}}{a < b \Longrightarrow \langle\texttt{d=b-a;}\rangle post}\text{ assignment} \qquad \boldsymbol{B_1}}{\Longrightarrow \langle\texttt{if(a<b) d=b-a; else d=a-b;}\rangle post}\text{ ifElseSplit}$$

On branch B_2 the case is considered where $a < b$ holds after the application of the ifElseSplit rule while on branch B_1, that we show below, the case is considered where $\neg(a < b)$ holds.

$$\cfrac{\cfrac{\cfrac{\boldsymbol{B_3}}{\neg a < b \Longrightarrow \{d := a - b\}post}}{\neg a < b \Longrightarrow \{d := a - b\}\langle\rangle post}\text{ emptyDiamond}}{\neg a < b \Longrightarrow \langle\texttt{d=a-b;}\rangle post}\text{ assignment}$$

Notice that the program has been replaced by two updates on the branches B_2 and B_3. The effective computation performed by the program is now captured by the updates. In phase 2 the update simplification calculus is applied in order to obtain first-order logic formulas. As both branches are very similar we show only the continuation of branch B_2. The following derivation is obtained using Lemmas 2.45 and 2.43.

$$\cfrac{\cfrac{\boldsymbol{B_4}}{a < b \Longrightarrow ((b - a \doteq b - a \vee b - a \doteq a - b) \wedge b - a \geqslant 0)}}{a < b \Longrightarrow \{d := b - a\}\underbrace{((d \doteq b - a \vee d \doteq a - b) \wedge d \geqslant 0)}_{post}}$$

The application of update simplification rules is not made explicit in the proof tree when using the KeY tool. At this point the leaf of the branch consists only of first-order logic formulas. Finally, in phase 3 first-order logic rules and arithmetic rules are used to extend branch B_4.

$$\cfrac{\cfrac{\cfrac{\cfrac{*}{a < b \Longrightarrow \text{true}, b - a \doteq a - b}}{a < b \Longrightarrow b - a \doteq b - a, b - a \doteq a - b}}{a < b \Longrightarrow b - a \doteq b - a \vee b - a \doteq a - b} \quad \cfrac{\cfrac{\cfrac{*}{\vdots}}{a < b \Longrightarrow b \geqslant a}}{a < b \Longrightarrow b - a \geqslant 0}}{a < b \Longrightarrow ((b - a \doteq b - a \vee b - a \doteq a - b) \wedge b - a \geqslant 0)}$$

Note, that the arithmetic rules are not provided in this thesis. The calculus for arithmetics is described in [Rümmer, 2007, 2008].

Remark 2.47. We use the notation se^* to denote the translation of a simple expression, i.e. an expression without side-effects, into a term or formula in the respective case. The KeY tool features the choice between different semantics for the JAVA operators +, -, *, and /. In this thesis we use infinite integer semantics for the sake of simplicity.

2.4.5.2 Example 2

The next example shows the application of some of the other rules shown in Tables 2.5 and 2.6. Another purpose of the example is to demonstrate bounded symbolic execution with *finite loop unwinding* as this is a common technique used by software fault detection methods. The method `sqrt` of Listing 2.1 will serve as our running example and in latter chapters we will refer to this example.

—— JAVA (2.1) ————————————————————————

```java
1   public int sqrt(int x){
2     int i=0;
3     while(i*i<=x){
4       i=i+1;
5     }
6     return i-1; }
```

————————————————————————————— JAVA ——

The method `sqrt` computes the square root of its argument by incrementing `i` up to the value of the square root of the argument. In this example finite unwinding of loops is considered. We verify the program only for the input value $x \doteq 0$. Verification of the method for more general input values requires to use the loop invariant rule which will be discussed in Section 2.4.6.

The verification condition for the method `sqrt` with restriction to the input value $x \doteq 0$ reads as follows (let $X^2 = X * X$).

$$\underbrace{x \doteq 0, o \neq \texttt{null}}_{\Gamma} \Longrightarrow \langle \texttt{r=o.sqrt(x);} \rangle \underbrace{(r^2 \leqslant x \land (r+1)^2 > x)}_{\varphi} \quad (2.13)$$

Note that like in the previous example the constants x, o, r represent the program variables `x,o,r` respectively. The first statement to be executed is the invocation of the method `sqrt`. Generally when a method is invoked, *dynamic dispatch* has to be performed which chooses different implementations of the invoked method depending on the dynamic type of o. KeY implements dynamic dispatch by creating an if-cascade that checks the dynamic type of the target object o. Dynamic dispatch is realized by the following rule.

$$\textsf{methodCall} \ \frac{\Longrightarrow \langle \pi\, T_{lhs}\, v_0\, ;\, paramDecl\, ;\, ifCascade\, ;\, lhs{=}v_0\, ;\ \ \omega \rangle \phi}{\Longrightarrow \langle \pi\, lhs{=}se.mname\,(se_1,\ldots,\,se_n)\, ;\, \omega \rangle \phi}$$

where *paramDecl* abbreviates

$$T_{se_1}p_1{=}se_1\, ;\, \ldots\, ;\, T_{se_n}p_n{=}se_n\, ;$$

and *ifCascade* abbreviates

```
if (se instanceof C₁)
    v₀  = se.mname (p₁,...,pₙ)@C₁ ;
else if (se instanceof C₂)
    v₀  = se.mname (p₁,...,pₙ)@C₂ ;
⋮
else if (se instanceof Cₖ₋₁)
    v₀  = se.mname (p₁,...,pₙ)@Cₖ₋₁ ;
else v₀  = se.mname (p₁,...,pₙ)@Cₖ ;
```

The symbols $C_1,\ldots,C_k$ represent classes which contain a definition of the method *mname*, where C_i is more specific than C_{i+1} for $0 < i < k$. The notation $mname(v_1,\ldots,v_n)@C$ identifies the method *mname* that is defined in the class C.

We consider dynamic dispatch as a technical detail and omit it in the following. In the following chapters we assume that the dynamic type of the target object, here represented by o, is known and allow to use the rule methodExpand directly, i.e., without prior usage of the rule methodCall. The actual rules of KeY additionally check if $se \doteq null$ (see Remark 2.46).

Following the example the application of the rule methodExpand yields the sequent

$$\Gamma \Longrightarrow \langle \underbrace{\texttt{MF(r,C,o)}}_{\pi}:\{\texttt{int i=0; while(i*i<=x)\{...\}}\rangle\varphi \qquad (2.14)$$

The method frame MF(r,C,o) stores information about the context of the method invocation. In this example only the argument r is important as it represents the expression that will be assigned the return value of the method.

Declarations have no effect on the semantics of DL formulas, i.e., for all states $s \in \mathcal{S}$ of a Kripke structure $(\mathcal{S}, \rho)$ we have $(s, decl, s) \in \rho$, where *decl* is a declaration. We therefore treat the statement `int i=0;` like an ordinary assignment. Using the rule **assignment** we obtain the sequent

$$\Gamma \Longrightarrow \{i := 0\}\langle\pi \text{ while(i*i<=x)\{i=i+1;\}}\ldots\rangle\varphi \qquad (2.15)$$

In the next step the loop is unwound once using the rule **loopUnwind**.

$$\Gamma \Longrightarrow \{i := 0\}\langle\pi \text{ if(i*i<=x)\{i=i+1;while(i*i<=x)\{i=i+1;\}\}}\ldots\rangle\varphi \qquad (2.16)$$

The rule **ifElseSplit** makes a case distinction on the if-condition. Here we use a variant of the **ifElseSplit** rule for an if-statement without an else-branch and obtain the following two sequents

$$\underbrace{x \doteq 0, o \neq \texttt{null}}_{\Gamma}, \{i := 0\}i * i \leqslant x \Longrightarrow \{i := 0\} \langle\pi \text{ i=i+1;}$$
$$\text{while(i*i<=x)}\ldots\rangle\varphi$$
$$(2.17)$$

and

$$\underbrace{x \doteq 0, o \neq \texttt{null}}_{\Gamma}, \{i := 0\}\neg(i*i \leqslant x) \Longrightarrow \{i := 0\}\langle\pi \text{ return i-1;}\ldots\rangle\varphi$$
$$(2.18)$$

Note that the update in front of the formula $i * i \leqslant x$, respectively the formula $\neg(i * i \leqslant x)$, results from the generalisation of rules according to Definition 2.34.

The antecedent of sequent 2.18 evaluates to false as can be seen when simplifying $\{i := 0\}\neg i * i \leqslant x$ to $0 > x$ and considering the condition $x \doteq 0$. The rule **closeFalse** of Table 2.3 closes this branch. The formulas in the antecedent of the sequent 2.18 constitute the path-condition, i.e., the condition to be satisfied in order to execute the program on the current execution path. If the path-condition is false, then the path cannot be executed. In this case the execution path of this branch is *infeasible*.

Since the branch with the sequent 2.18 is closed, the proof construction continues with the branch that ended with Sequent 2.17. Figure 2.2 shows the structure of the proof up to this point as well as the continuation of the branch where the loop is unwinded again. Only the path where the loop body is executed exactly once represents a feasible path. The last sequent of the open branch B_1 is:

$$
\begin{array}{cc}
\begin{array}{c}
* \\ \hline
\ldots, \text{false} \Longrightarrow \ldots \\ \hline
x \doteq 0, \ldots, \mathbf{1} \leqslant \mathbf{0} \Longrightarrow \Delta \\ \hline
\boldsymbol{x} \doteq \mathbf{0}, \ldots, 1 \leqslant x \Longrightarrow \Delta \\ \hline
\Gamma', \mathbf{1} * \mathbf{1} \leqslant x \Longrightarrow \Delta \\ \hline
\Gamma', \{\boldsymbol{i} := \mathbf{1}\}\boldsymbol{i} * \boldsymbol{i} \leqslant \boldsymbol{x} \Longrightarrow \Delta
\end{array}
&
\begin{array}{c}
\boldsymbol{B_1} \\ \hline
\Gamma', 1 > x \Longrightarrow \Delta' \\ \hline
\Gamma', \neg\mathbf{1} \leqslant \boldsymbol{x} \Longrightarrow \Delta' \\ \hline
\Gamma', \neg\mathbf{1} * \mathbf{1} \leqslant x \Longrightarrow \Delta' \\ \hline
\Gamma', \neg\{\boldsymbol{i} := \mathbf{1}\}\boldsymbol{i} * \boldsymbol{i} \leqslant \boldsymbol{x} \Longrightarrow \Delta'
\end{array}
\end{array}
$$

$$
\begin{array}{c}
\hline
\Gamma' \Longrightarrow \{i := 1\}\langle\pi\ \texttt{if(i*i<=x)\{i=i+1;while(ii<= x)\{...}\rangle\varphi \\ \hline
\Gamma' \Longrightarrow \{i := 1\}\langle\pi\ \texttt{while(i*i<=x)\{i=i+1;\} ...}\rangle\varphi \\ \hline
\Gamma' \Longrightarrow \{\boldsymbol{i} := \mathbf{0}\}\{\boldsymbol{i} := \boldsymbol{i} + \mathbf{1}\}\langle\pi\texttt{while...}\rangle\varphi \\ \hline
\underbrace{x \doteq 0, o \neq \texttt{null}, 0 \leqslant x}_{\Gamma'} \Longrightarrow \{i := 0\}\langle\pi\texttt{i=i+1;while...}\rangle\varphi \\ \hline
x \doteq 0, o \neq \texttt{null}, \mathbf{0} * \mathbf{0} \leqslant \boldsymbol{x} \Longrightarrow \{i := 0\}\langle\pi\texttt{i=i+1;while...}\rangle\varphi
\end{array}
\qquad
\begin{array}{c}
* \\ \hline
\vdots
\end{array}
$$

$$
\begin{array}{c}
\hline
x \doteq 0, o \neq \texttt{null}, \{\boldsymbol{i} := \mathbf{0}\}\boldsymbol{i} * \boldsymbol{i} \leqslant \boldsymbol{x} \Longrightarrow \{i := 0\}\langle\pi\texttt{i=i+1;while ...}\rangle\varphi \quad (2.18) \\ \hline
(2.16) \\ \hline
(2.15) \\ \hline
(2.14) \\ \hline
(2.13)
\end{array}
$$

Fig. 2.2. Structure of the proof and continuation of the branch with the Sequent (2.17)

$$
\underbrace{x \doteq 0, o \neq \texttt{null}, 0 \leqslant x}_{\Gamma'}, 1 > x \Longrightarrow \{i := 1\}\langle\overbrace{\texttt{MF(r,C,o):\{}}^{\pi}\ \texttt{return i-1;\}}\rangle\varphi \tag{2.19}
$$

The method frame MF(r,C,o):{, that we abbreviated previously with π, stores information that is required for handling the return statement by rule methodReturn. Application of the rule methodReturn yields:

$$
x \doteq 0, o \neq \texttt{null}, 0 \leqslant x, 1 > x \Longrightarrow \{i := 0\}\langle\texttt{r=i-1;}\rangle\varphi \tag{2.20}
$$

The construction of the single open branch B_1 continues as shown in Figure 2.3.

2.4.6 Calculus Component: Contract Rules

2.4.6.1 Basic Variants of Contract Rules

The contract rules are the method contract rule and the loop invariant rule. These rules abstract a method or a loop with a contract. In this way verification of programs can be modularized. The correctness of

$$
\cfrac{
\cfrac{
\cfrac{
\cfrac{
\cfrac{*}{\vdots \;\; using \; arithmetic \; rules}
}{x \doteq 0, \ldots \Longrightarrow (0^2 \leqslant x \land (0+1)^2 > x)}
}{x \doteq 0, \ldots \Longrightarrow \{i := 1 \,||\, r := 0\}(r^2 \leqslant x \land (r+1)^2 > x)}
}{x \doteq 0, \ldots \Longrightarrow \{i := 1 \,||\, r := 1 - 1\}(r^2 \leqslant x \land (r+1)^2 > x)}
}{x \doteq 0, o \neq \texttt{null}, 0 \leqslant x, 1 > x \Longrightarrow \{i := 1\}\langle \texttt{r=i-1;}\rangle \underbrace{(r^2 \leqslant x \land (r+1)^2 > x)}_{\varphi}}
$$

$$(2.20)$$

$$(2.19)$$

Fig. 2.3. Continuation of the branch B_1 from Figure 2.2

the abstraction is shown once and then the abstraction is used as a surrogate whenever the method or loop is encountered during verification. Due to the dependency of showing and assuming the correctness of the abstraction we refer to the abstractions as contracts. Technically, there is no distinction between a specification and a contract. However, the term specification emphasizes the requirements of a program while the term contract emphasizes a dependency between entities.

Definition 2.48. *A specification or contract is a quadruple*

$$(pre, post, mod, term)$$

specifying the behavior of a method, constructor, or loop.

- *pre ∈ Formulae is the precondition,*
- *post ∈ Formulae is the postcondition,*
- *mod is a modifier set for the method, constructor, or loop (see Section 2.4.6.2),*
- *The termination marker term is an element from the set {partial, total}; the marker is set to total if and only if the contract requires the method, constructor, or loop to terminate, otherwise term is set to partial.*

A specification typically describes the behavior of a method but it can specify the behavior of any statement or sequence of statements. For instance a loop invariant $I \in Formulae$ is the pre- and postcondition of a loop's body and the loop itself. A stronger postcondition of the loop is $I \land \neg c$ where $c \in Formulae$ is the loop condition, i.e., the loop iterates

Method Contract Rule*	Loop Invariant Rule*

Method Contract Rule*

1: $\quad \Gamma \Rightarrow \{U\}pre_m, \Delta$

2*: $\quad \Rightarrow pre_m \rightarrow \langle\!\langle m \rangle\!\rangle post_m$

3: $\quad \Rightarrow post_m \rightarrow \langle\!\langle \pi\omega \rangle\!\rangle post$

$\overline{\quad\quad \Gamma \Rightarrow \{U\}\langle\!\langle \pi m; \omega \rangle\!\rangle post, \Delta \quad\quad}$

Loop Invariant Rule*

1: $\quad \Gamma \Rightarrow \{U\}I, \Delta$

2: $\quad \Rightarrow I \wedge c \rightarrow [\text{b}]I$

3: $\quad \Rightarrow (I \wedge \neg c) \rightarrow [\pi\omega]post$

$\overline{\quad \Gamma \Rightarrow \{U\}[\pi \texttt{ while(c)\{b;\}}\omega]post, \Delta \quad}$

Fig. 2.4. Contract Rules

while c is true. The specification of a loop is therefore a quadruple of the form $(I, I \wedge \neg c, mod, term)$.

Besides the modularization, the loop invariant rule realizes also induction on the iteration of loops. This enables the verification of programs with loops which have arbitrary or runtime-dependent numbers of loop iterations. The method contract rule can be used in combination with an induction rule in order to handle recursive method calls.

Different variants of the contract rules exists. Firstly, they differ depending on how many technical details of the programming language are handled, e.g. if jump-statements such as break, continue, throw, and return are handled. Secondly, they differ depending on whether modifier sets are supported or not.

In this section we describe the contract rules in their simplest form (see Figure 2.4) without handling of jump statements and modifier sets. The formulas $pre_m, post_m \in Formulae$ constitute the contract of the method invocation m and $I \in Formulae$ is called the loop invariant of the loop while(c){b;}. The following description applies to both rules of Figure 2.4.

In Premiss 1 the goal is to show that the precondition pre_m resp. the loop invariant I holds in the state before the execution of the method resp. the loop.

In Premiss 2 of the method contract rule the goal is to show that pre_m and $post_m$ constitute a correct contract of m. We have annotated this premiss with '*' because in the KeY tool this branch of the method contract rule is omitted. Instead, the correctness of the contract is just assumed and *should* be ensured by a separate verification proof. The motivation behind this is modularity of proofs. The correctness of the method contract is proven once and is assumed in other proofs.

Premiss 2 of the loop invariant rule ensures that the formula I is actually an invariant of the loop body. Since I has to be an invariant for all iterations of the loop the context Γ, Δ, and $\{U\}$ is omitted, otherwise only the pre-state of the first iteration would be regarded. If the loop invariant I is preserved by each loop iteration, then it is also an invariant of the whole loop.

While the goal of the Premisses 1 and 2 is to show that the abstraction is correct and applicable, in Premiss 3 the abstraction is used as surrogate for the method invocation, respectively the loop execution. The formulas $post_m$ and $I \wedge \neg c$ describe the state after the execution of the method or loop, respectively.

Note that in case of recursive method calls, the application of the method contract rule with a proof of the Premiss 2 does not terminate unless it is combined with induction.

2.4.6.2 Modifier Sets and Anonymising Updates

The rules in Figure 2.4 are annotated with * which means that the rule generalizations of Definition 2.34 do not apply. The reason is that the context information in $\Gamma, \Delta,$ and $\{U\}$ may not be satisfied in the post-state of the method invocation or loop execution. Thus, the context information must be omitted in Premiss 2 of the loop invariant rule and in Premiss 3 of both rules. However, the context information is often required for a successful proof. One option is to encode this information in pre_m and $post_m$, respectively in I. This approach is, however, problematic because it adds complexity to the proof and the contract and, even worse, the context information is generally not known beforehand. A better approach is to assume by default that the context information holds in the post-state and to allow specifying where it does not hold. The latter technique is realized by modifier sets as defined next.

Definition 2.49. *(Syntax of Modifier Sets). Let* $(\text{VSym}, \text{FSym}_r, \text{FSym}_{nr}, \text{PSym}_r, \text{PSym}_{nr}, \alpha)$ *be a signature for a type hierarchy.*

A modifier set Mod is a set of pairs $\langle \phi, f(t_1, \dots, t_n) \rangle$ *with* $\phi \in$ *Formulae and* $f(t_1, \dots, t_n) \in$ *Terms with* $f \in \text{FSym}_{nr}$.

Definition 2.50. *(Semantics of Modifier Sets). Given a signature for a type hierarchy* T, *let* $\mathcal{K}_{\preceq} = (\mathcal{S}, \rho)$ *be a* JAVA CARD *DL Kripke structure, and let* β *be a variable assignment.*

A pair $(S_1, S_2) = ((T, \mathcal{D}, \preceq, \delta, \mathcal{I}_1) \times (T, \mathcal{D}, \preceq, \delta, \mathcal{I}_2)) \in \mathcal{S} \times \mathcal{S}$ *of states satisfies a modifier set Mod, denoted by*

$$(S_1, S_2) \models Mod,$$

iff, for

a) all $f : A_1, \ldots, A_n \to A \in \mathrm{FSym}_{nr}$,
b) all $(d_1, \ldots, d_n) \in \mathcal{D}^{A_1} \times \ldots \times \mathcal{D}^{A_n}$

the following holds:

$$\mathcal{I}_1(f)(d_1, \ldots, d_n) \neq \mathcal{I}_2(f)(d_1, \ldots, d_n)$$

<u>*implies*</u> *that there is a pair $\langle \phi, f(t_1, \ldots, t_n) \rangle \in Mod$ and a variable assignment β such that*

$$d_i = val_{S_1, \beta}(t_i) \quad (1 \leqslant i \leqslant n)$$

and

$$S_1, \beta \vDash \phi.$$

Furthermore, a modifier set is minimal *if the underlined implication in this definition is replaced by "if and only if". We write $Mod(p)$ to denote an arbitrary but fixed minimal modifier set for a program p.*

The modifier set Mod is correct *for a program p, if*

$$(S_1, S_2) \vDash Mod$$

for all state pairs $(S_1, p, S_2) \in \rho$.

A modifier set for a program is a set of terms with side conditions. The purpose of using a modifier set as part of a contract or specification is to specify which of these terms – modelling program variables, fields, and arrays – are modified by the program. All other program variables, fields, and arrays, are assumed to be not modifiable by the program. For example, a correct modifier set for the assignment `o.b=1` is $\{\langle \text{true}, b(x) \rangle\}$, where $x \in \mathrm{VSym}$. Note that the field `b` is modelled as a function $b \in \mathrm{FSym}_{nr}$. A minimal modifier set for `o.b=1` is, e.g., $\{\langle \text{true}, b(o) \rangle\}$. The minimal modifier set is not unique because the sets $\{\langle o \doteq o, b(o) \rangle\}$ and $\{\langle \text{true}, b(o) \rangle, \langle \text{false}, c(o) \rangle\}$ are minimal for `o.b=1` as well.

Remark 2.51. Techniques for proving the correctness of modifier sets are not discussed in this thesis. As it is the case with method contracts the correctness of modifier sets has to be shown in separate proofs. We assume that the modifier sets in the examples of this thesis are correct if not stated otherwise.

Modifier sets are utilized in KeY proofs through *anonymising updates*. An anonymising update assigns unspecified values to memory locations which are mentioned in the modifier set. Hence, anonymising update correspond to the `havoc` command in Boogie [Barnett et al., 2006] language. For the construction of anonymising updates an extension of the update language is not necessary.

Definition 2.52. *(Anonymising Update w.r.t. a Modifier Set). Let a signature* $(\mathrm{VSym}, \mathrm{FSym}_r, \mathrm{FSym}_{nr}, \mathrm{PSym}_r, \mathrm{PSym}_{nr}, \alpha)$ *for a type hierarchy, a modifier set* M, *and a sequent* $\Gamma \Longrightarrow \Delta$ *be given. For every* $\langle \phi_i, f_i(t_1^i, \ldots, t_{n_i}^i) \rangle \in M$ *with* $f_i : A_1, \ldots, A_{n_i} \to A$, *let* $f_i^{sk} \in \mathrm{FSym}$ *be a fresh (w.r.t.* $\Gamma \cup \Delta$) *function symbol with the same type as* f_i, *i.e.,* f_i^{sk} *does not occur in* $\Gamma \cup \Delta$.
If

$$M = \{ \langle \phi_1, f_1(t_1^1, \ldots, t_{n_1}^1) \rangle, \ldots, \langle \phi_k, f_k(t_1^k, \ldots, t_{n_k}^k) \rangle \}$$

then the update $\mathcal{V}_M$ *is defined as*

$$\mathcal{V}_M = u_1 \, \| \, \ldots \, \| \, u_k$$

with

$$u_i = \mathtt{for} \; x_1^i; \; \mathtt{true}; \; \ldots \mathtt{for} \; x_{l_i}; \; \phi_i; \; f_i(t_1^i, \ldots, t_{n_i}^i) := f_i^{sk}(t_1^i, \ldots, t_{n_i}^i)$$

where

$$\{ x_1^i, \ldots, x_{l_i}^i \} = fv(\phi_i) \cup fv(t_1^i) \cup \ldots \cup fv(t_{n_i}^i)$$

is called an anonymising update *with respect to* M.

An anonymising update assigns unspecified values to function symbols which occur in the corresponding modifier set. This happens by assigning to those function symbols the values of Skolem functions, i.e., fresh functions which do not occur in the proof. For instance, given the modifier set $M = \{ \langle \mathrm{true}, f(a) \rangle, \langle \varphi, g(x) \rangle \}$ the corresponding anonymising update is

$$f(a) := f^{sk}(a) \, \| \, \mathtt{for} \; x; \; \varphi; \; g(x) := g^{sk}(x)$$

where f^{sk} and g^{sk} are fresh function symbols.

Method Contract Rule (mContract)

1: $\Rightarrow pre_m$

2*: $\Rightarrow pre_m \rightarrow \langle\!\langle m \rangle\!\rangle post_m$ $(*)$

3: $\Rightarrow \mathcal{V}_M(post_m \rightarrow \langle\!\langle \pi\omega \rangle\!\rangle post)$

$\Rightarrow \langle\!\langle \pi m;\omega \rangle\!\rangle post$

Loop Invariant Rule (loopInv)

1: $\Rightarrow I$

2: $\Rightarrow \mathcal{V}_M(I \wedge c \rightarrow [\mathtt{b}]I)$

3: $\Rightarrow \mathcal{V}_M((I \wedge \neg c) \rightarrow [\pi\omega]post)$

$\Rightarrow [\pi \ \mathtt{while(c)\{b;\}}\omega]post$

where $\mathcal{V}_M$ is an anonymising update w.r.t. the modifier set M and M is a correct modifier set for m, respectively $\mathtt{b}$ and $\mathtt{c}$.

Fig. 2.5. Contract Rules

2.4.6.3 Contract Rules with Anonymising Updates

Figure 2.5 shows variants of the contract rules which, in contrast to the contract rules of Figure 2.4, can be generalized according to Definition 2.34. This means that contextual information that is stored in Γ, Δ, and in updates is available on all three branches of both rules. An exception is, however, the Premiss 2 of the method contract rule where the contextual information is omitted. As described in Section 2.4.6.1, in order to support modularity the Premiss 2 is proven in a separate proof and the contract is assume to be correct in other proofs. In order to allow this assumption in all contexts the specific contextual information Γ, Δ, and $\mathcal{U}$ is omitted.

The context information refers to the pre-state of the method, respectively the loop. Due to the anonymising updates $\mathcal{V}_M$ this information can be used in the post-state of the method, respectively the loop. Functions whose interpretation is modified by the program, and which may be in conflict with the context information, are assigned unspecified values through the anonymising update.

In the following example we show how the loop invariant rule in Figure 2.5 is used in order to verify the Program 2.1 for arbitrary numbers of loop iterations. The specification (see Def. 2.48) of the method $\mathtt{sqrt}$ is the quadruple (let $X^2 = X * X$).

$$(\underbrace{x \geqslant 0 \wedge \neg o \doteq \mathtt{null}}_{\text{precondition}}, \underbrace{r^2 \leqslant x \wedge (r+1)^2 > x}_{\text{postcondition}}, \underbrace{\{\langle\text{true}, i\rangle\}}_{\text{mod.}}, \underbrace{partial}_{\text{term.}}) \quad (2.21)$$

The modifier set specifies that the program variable $\mathtt{i}$ may be modified. In JAVA program variables are local and are not accessible outside the method in which they are defined. Therefore, in JML specifications (see Chapter 3) modifier sets do not contain program variables or method parameters but rather object fields and static fields. As mentioned in Remark 2.51 we do not check the correctness of modifier sets.

Since the variants of the loop invariant rule in Figures 2.4 and 2.5 do not support total correctness proofs, i.e., these variants of the rule do not ensure the termination of loop, the specification requires only partial correctness of the method `sqrt`. From the specification (2.21) we construct the following proof obligation

$$\underbrace{x \geqslant 0, \neg o \doteq \texttt{null}}_{\Gamma} \Longrightarrow [\texttt{r=o.sqrt(x);}] \underbrace{(r^2 \leqslant x \wedge (r+1)^2 > x)}_{\varphi} \quad (2.22)$$

and obtain the following partial proof tree by applying of the rules methodCall, assignment, and loopInv.

$$\cfrac{\cfrac{B_1 \qquad\qquad B_2 \qquad\qquad B_3}{\Gamma \Longrightarrow \{i := 0\}[\pi \ \texttt{while(i*i<=x)\{i=i+1;\} return i;}]\varphi} \ \text{loopInv}}{\cfrac{\Gamma \Longrightarrow [\pi \ \texttt{int i=0; while(i*i<=x)\{i=i+1;\} return i;}]\varphi}{\Gamma \Longrightarrow [\texttt{r=o.sqrt(x);}]\varphi}}$$

For the application of the loop invariant rule in the last step the loop invariant I and the modifier set M we use are

$$(i-1)^2 \leqslant x \vee i \doteq 0 \qquad \text{and} \qquad \{\langle \text{true}, i \rangle\}$$

respectively. The modifier set yields the anonymising update $\mathcal{V}_M = \{i := i'\}$, where i' is a fresh function symbol. Application of the loop invariant rule on the last sequent of the proof tree results in the following three sequents.

$$\mathbf{B_1} : \quad \Gamma \Longrightarrow \{i := 0\} \overbrace{((i-1)^2 \leqslant x \vee i \doteq 0)}^{I}$$

$$\mathbf{B_2} : \quad \Gamma \Longrightarrow \{i := 0\}\{i := i'\}(I \wedge i^2 \leqslant x \to [\texttt{i=i+1}]I)$$

$$\mathbf{B_3} : \quad \Gamma \Longrightarrow \{i := 0\}\{i := i'\}((I \wedge \neg(i^2 \leqslant x)) \to [\pi \ \underbrace{\texttt{return i-1;}}_{\omega}]\varphi)$$

The anonymising update $\{i := i'\}$, where i' is the fresh constant, overrides the update $\{i := 0\}$. Thus, $\{i := 0\}\{i := i'\}I$ simplifies to $\{i := i'\}I$. In this way the value of i in the pre-state is not in conflict with its value in other states.

Finally, Figures 2.6, 2.7, and 2.8 show how the three branches B_1, B_2, and B_3 close, respectively. The proof trees shown in the figures make use of the rules introduced throughout this chapter as well as of arithmetic rules.

$$* $$
$$\Gamma \Rightarrow ((0-1)^2 \leqslant x, \mathbf{true}$$
$$\Gamma \Rightarrow ((0-1)^2 \leqslant x, \mathbf{0 \doteq 0}$$
$$\Gamma \Rightarrow ((0-1)^2 \leqslant x \vee 0 \doteq 0$$
$$\Gamma \Rightarrow \{i := 0\}((i-1)^2 \leqslant x \vee i \doteq 0)$$

Fig. 2.6. Branch B_1 of the example

$$* $$
$$\Gamma, \dots, i'^2 \leqslant x \Rightarrow i'^2 \leqslant x, i' + 1 \doteq 0$$
$$\Gamma' \Rightarrow (i'+1-1)^2 \leqslant x, i' + 1 \doteq 0$$
$$\Gamma' \Rightarrow (i'+1-1)^2 \leqslant x \vee i' + 1 \doteq 0$$
$$\Gamma' \Rightarrow \{i := i'+1\}((i-1)^2 \leqslant x \vee i \doteq 0)$$
$$\Gamma' \Rightarrow \{i := i'\}\{i := i+1\}I$$
$$\Gamma' \Rightarrow \{i := i'\}\{i := i+1\}[]I$$

$$\overbrace{\qquad\qquad\qquad}^{\Gamma'}$$
$$\Gamma, (((i'-1)^2 \leqslant x \vee i' \doteq 0) \wedge i'^2 \leqslant x) \Rightarrow \{i := i'\}[\mathsf{i=i+1}]I$$
$$\Gamma \Rightarrow (((i'-1)^2 \leqslant x \vee i' \doteq 0) \wedge i'^2 \leqslant x) \rightarrow \{i := i'\}[\mathsf{i=i+1}]I$$
$$\Gamma \Rightarrow \{i := i'\}((((i-1)^2 \leqslant x \vee i \doteq 0) \wedge i^2 \leqslant x) \rightarrow [\mathsf{i=i+1}]I)$$
$$\Gamma \Rightarrow \{i := 0\}\{i := i'\}((\underbrace{((i-1)^2 \leqslant x \vee i \doteq 0)}_{I} \wedge i^2 \leqslant x) \rightarrow [\mathsf{i=i+1}]I)$$

Fig. 2.7. Branch B_2 of the example

Branch $B_{3.1}$

$$
\cfrac{
\cfrac{
\cfrac{
\cfrac{
\cfrac{
\cfrac{*}{\ldots, \textbf{false} \Rightarrow \ldots}
}{\ldots, x \geqslant 0, 0 > x \Rightarrow \ldots}
}{\ldots, x \geqslant 0, i' \doteq 0, 0^2 > x \Rightarrow \ldots}
}{\ldots, x \geqslant 0, i' \doteq 0, i'^2 > x \Rightarrow \ldots} \qquad \cfrac{*}{\ldots, ((i'-1)^2 \leqslant x \Rightarrow (i'-1)^2 \leqslant x}
}{\underbrace{x \geqslant 0, \neg o \doteq \texttt{null}, (i'-1)^2 \leqslant x \vee i' \doteq 0, i'^2 > x}_{\Gamma} \Rightarrow (i'-1)^2 \leqslant x}
}
$$

Branch B_3

$$
\cfrac{
\cfrac{
\cfrac{
\cfrac{
\cfrac{
\cfrac{
\cfrac{
\cfrac{
\cfrac{
\cfrac{
\cfrac{
\cfrac{
\cfrac{
\boldsymbol{B_{3.1}} \qquad \cfrac{*}{\Gamma, \ldots, i'^2 > x \Rightarrow i'^2 > x}
}{\Gamma, \ldots, i'^2 > x \Rightarrow (i'-1)^2 \leqslant x \wedge i'^2 > x}
}{\Gamma, \ldots, \neg i'^2 \leqslant x \Rightarrow (i'-1)^2 \leqslant x \wedge i'^2 > x}
}{\Gamma' \Rightarrow (i'-1)^2 \leqslant x \wedge (i'-1+1)^2 > x}
}{\Gamma' \Rightarrow \{i := i' \,||\, r := i'-1\}(r^2 \leqslant x \wedge (r+1)^2 > x)}
}{\Gamma' \Rightarrow \{i := i' \,||\, r := i'-1\}[](r^2 \leqslant x \wedge (r+1)^2 > x)}
}{\Gamma' \Rightarrow \{i := i'\}\{r := i-1\}[]\varphi}
}{\Gamma' \Rightarrow \{i := i'\}[\texttt{r=i-1}]\varphi}
}{\underbrace{\Gamma' \Rightarrow \{i := i'\}\overbrace{[\texttt{MF(r,C,o):}}^{\pi}\overbrace{\{\texttt{return i-1;}\}}^{\omega}]\varphi}_{\Gamma'}}
}{\Gamma, (((i'-1)^2 \leqslant x \vee i' \doteq 0) \wedge \neg i'^2 \leqslant x) \Rightarrow \{i := i'\}[\pi\omega]\varphi}
}{\Gamma \Rightarrow (((i'-1)^2 \leqslant x \vee i' \doteq 0) \wedge \neg i'^2 \leqslant x) \rightarrow \{i := i'\}[\pi\omega]\varphi}
}{\Gamma \Rightarrow \{i := i'\}((((i-1)^2 \leqslant x \vee i \doteq 0) \wedge \neg i^2 \leqslant x) \rightarrow [\pi\omega]\varphi)}
}{\Gamma \Rightarrow \{i := 0\}\{i := i'\}((I \wedge \neg(i^2 \leqslant x)) \rightarrow [\pi\omega]\varphi)}
$$

Fig. 2.8. Branch B_3 of the example

3

Java Modeling Language (JML)

3.1 Overview

The Java Modeling Language (JML) is a formal behavioral interface specification language for JAVA [Leavens and Cheon, 2006; Chalin et al., 2005; Leavens et al., 2009]. It has been inspired significantly by the specification language Larch [Guttag et al., 1985; Ellis and Stroustrup, 1990] for C++ and by the specification and programming language Eiffel [Meyer, 1991]. JML is also similar to the specification language Spec# [Barnett, 2004] for C# and the specification language of VCC [Cohen et al., 2009] which have been influenced by JML and its predecessors. In contrast to Z [Abrial et al., 1980; Spivey, 1992] these languages do less abstraction from the program and are syntactically and semantically very close to the target programming language.

JML extends JAVA with special annotations in JAVA-comments for specifying the behavior of methods and the properties of fields. Pre- and postconditions as well as class and loop invariants are specified using side-effect free JAVA expressions with some extensions. In this way, JML enables specifying the syntax and semantics of classes and interfaces in JAVA.

The language supports the essential notations that are used for design-by-contract (DBC) [Leavens and Cheon, 2006; Meyer, 1997]. These are method pre- and postconditions and class invariants. In order to satisfy a contract a method must ensure that, if the method is executed in a state that satisfies the precondition, then in the method's post-state the postcondition is satisfied (see also Section 2.4.6, page 63). Hence, if the client code which is calling a specified method fulfills the precondition of the method, then it can relay on the specified postcon-

—— JAVA + JML (3.1) —————————————————————————————

```
1   /*@ public normal_behavior
2       requires x>=0;
3       ensures \result * \result <= x &&
4               (\result+1) * (\result+1)>x;
5       diverges true;
6   @*/
7   public int sqrt(int x){
8     int i=0;
9     /*@ loop_invariant (i-1)*(i-1)<=x || i==0;
10        modifies i; @*/
11    while(i*i<=x){
12    i=i+1;
13    }
14    return i-1;
15  }
```

——————————————————————————————————— JAVA + JML ——

Fig. 3.1. JML specification of the method `sqrt`

dition after the method call. A class invariant is, in principle, a pre-
and postcondition of all methods. This means that if the class invariant
holds before the execution of a method, then it must hold also after
the execution of the method. More advanced policies exist for class invariants such as visible state semantics [Müller, 2002] but we use this
simplified concept of class invariants.

Besides the specification of interfaces JML also supports loop invariants. A loop invariant (see Section 2.4.6) must hold before and after
every loop iteration. We regard loop invariants, however, not as part
of the requirement specification but rather as auxiliary formulas which
are *in practice* needed for proof construction.

For example, Figure 3.1 shows the specification of the method `sqrt`
which computes an integer approximation of the square root of the
number passed as argument (see also Sections 2.4.5 and 2.4.6). JML
annotations are written in JAVA comments of the form `/*@ ... @*/` or
`//@... .`

In Line 1 of Listing 3.1 the keyword `public` specifies the visibility of the specification. In a public specification only fields with public visibility are allowed. In this way JML allows information hid-
ing. The keyword `normal_behavior` specifies that the method must
not throw an exception. Pre- and postconditions are marked with the

keywords `requires` and `ensures`, respectively. The return value of a method is represented by the keyword `\result`. In Section 2.4.6 we have verified that the method `sqrt` is partially correct, i.e., its termination is not ensured. Partial correctness is expressed by the annotation `diverges true`. Lines 9-10 show the loop invariant and modifier set of the loop respectively.

Throughout this thesis we will use additional JML keywords and constructs which are not shown in Figure 3.1. The construct `\old(`e`)` occurs in postconditions of methods and represents the value that the expression e had in the pre-state of the respective method. Implications in JML are represented by the symbol '`==>`'. An expressions of the form (`\forall` T x; *guard*; *phi*), where T is a JAVA type and *guard* and *phi* are boolean JML expressions, represents the universally quantified formula $\forall x.((\varphi_T(x) \wedge guard) \rightarrow phi)$ with $\varphi_T(x) \in Formulae$.[1] The formula $\varphi_T(x)$ restricts the values of x to the value set of T. For instance, the range of integers is restricted to a finite domain and the range of objects is restricted to not include `null`. Similarly, an expression of the form (`\exists` T x; *guard*; *phi*) represents an existentially quantified formula of the form $\exists x.(\varphi_T(x) \wedge guard \wedge phi)$. Table 3.1 shows a subset of the JML keywords relevant in this thesis. For more details about JML we refer the reader to the cited references.

3.2 Translation of JML Specifications to Dynamic Logic

The KeY tool translates JML annotated JAVA code into dynamic logic proof obligations. Throughout the evolution of the KeY tool different translations of JML to dynamic logic have been realized. This is mainly due to the development of JML itself and modifications of KeY such as the extension of the logic. Hence, there exist several different translations from JML to dynamic logic. For instance, Figure 3.2 shows the translation of the method specification of Figure 3.1 into a dynamic logic formula as it is realized in version 1.6 of the KeY tool.

The predicate inReachableState $\in$ PSym$_r$ in Figure 3.2 is satisfied only in reachable JAVA states. This means for instance that integer values of fields and program variables are within the finite integer bounds of JAVA. The program variable `self` holds the reference to the target object of the method `sqrt` and the implicit field `<created>` states

---

[1] In the formula $\forall x.((\varphi_T(x) \wedge guard) \rightarrow phi)$ we assume the respective representations of the JML expressions *guard* and *phi* as formulas.

Keyword	Description
public	visibility specifier
requires	introduces a precondition
ensures	introduces a postcondition
diverges	introduces a non-termination condition
loop_invariant	introduces a loop invariant
invariant	introduces a class invariant
modifies	introduces a modifier set
modifies \nothing	empty modifier set
nullable	null value is allowed; applicable to fields and return values of methods
\exists	existential quantifier
\forall	universal quantifier
\old	evaluation of an expression in the pre-state of a method
\result	return value of a method

Table 3.1. A subset of JML keywords relevant in this thesis

$$(\text{ inReachableState}$$
$$\land \; self. < created > \doteq \text{TRUE} \land \neg self \doteq null$$
$$\land \; \text{inInt}(x)$$
$$\land \; x \geqslant 0 \;)$$
$$\rightarrow$$
$$\{ \_x := x \}$$

```
[ exc=null; try{
    result=self.sqrt(_x)@C;
} catch(Throwable e){
    exc=e;
}
```

$$](result * result \leqslant x$$
$$\land (result + 1) * (result + 1) > x$$
$$\land exc \doteq \text{null})$$

Fig. 3.2. Translation of the JML specification of the method `sqrt` into dynamic logic

whether the object is created. The predicate inInt $\in$ PSym$_r$ states that its the argument is within JAVA's finite integer bounds.

According to JML semantics, method parameters that occur in the ensures clause are evaluated in the pre-state of the method. In this example the only parameter is x. Following the JML semantics KeY replaces the parameter with a new symbol (here, $\_x$). In this way the value of the parameter is not changed by symbolic execution and it can be used in the postcondition.

The JML expression `diverges true` states that the program does not need to terminate which is why the box modal operator is used (see Def. 2.25, page 42). The method call is surrounded by a try-catch-block because the keyword `normal_behavior` requires that no exception is thrown, but $[\texttt{throw e;}]\phi \equiv \text{true}$ (see Lemma 2.26). Whether an exception was thrown is determined by the program variable `exc` whose value is defined in the modality which is check in the postcondition.

The implementation of the techniques described in this thesis handles such technical details. In the examples of this thesis we assume, however, simplified JAVA semantics that use unbounded integer domain. The examples are constructed such that most of the technical details of the JML translation can be ignored. For instance, if we know that a formal parameter is not changed by a method, then we omit the update $\{\_x := x\}$ and if we know that no exception is thrown, then the try-catch-block showing in Figure 3.2 is omitted. A simplified translation of the JML specification in Figure 3.1 is, for instance, the formula

$$x \geqslant 0, \neg o \doteq \texttt{null} \implies [\texttt{r = o.sqrt(x);}](r^2 \leqslant x \wedge (r+1)^2 > x)$$

which we have used earlier in Section 2.4.6.3 on page 69.

Part II

Deductive Techniques for
Software-fault Detection

4

The Deductive Software-fault Detection Approach

4.1 Introduction

Software verification is an expensive task to a large extent because programs and specifications often have faults and because annotations such as (loop) invariants are often too weak to show desired program properties. During software verification, much time is spent fixing and adjusting the programs, requirement specifications, and program annotations. It is therefore invaluable to detect faults in these software artifacts. Once a program is correct and annotations are strong enough, a state-of-the-art verification tool usually can prove the correctness of the program automatically afterwards.

Although programs and specifications can have different kinds of faults we restrict our view on faults that can be formalized in Hoare-style logics as follows.

Definition 4.1. *A* software fault *exists in the program, in the specification, or in both, iff the program does not satisfy its specification for all states, formalized as a verification condition. Otherwise, the program satisfies its specification for all states and we say that the program is* correct. *The exact formalization depends on how the specification of a program is transformed into a verification condition of the target logic (see Chapter 3). The translation is assumed to be correct.*

The general approach we follow is to start with a verification attempt and if the verification attempt does not succeed, then faults are searched based on the unproved verification conditions. This approach is not new and it has been proposed already in 1980 [Suzuki and Jefferson, 1980]. This thesis goes, however, beyond that basic idea. We extend a verification tool for a *real world* programming language, propose new techniques for challenging issues, and extend this approach for test generation.

Loop statements and quantified formulas are two of the challenging issues in verification and in our approach. The problems are, however, not exactly the same for verification on the one hand and deductive software-fault detection on the other hand. The difference results from the different nature of verification and software-fault detection. In verification the goal is to show a universally quantified property, namely that a program is correct for *all* inputs. In contrast, in software-fault detection the problem is existentially quantified, i.e., the goal is to show the existence of *at least one* input that violates a desired program property. In order to extend the verification process with the ability to detect software faults we concluded that new techniques have to be developed in order to handle loops and quantified formulas.

We introduce two novel techniques in this part of this thesis. Chapter 5 describes a technique for handling the problem with loops and in Chapter 6 a technique is described which handles the problem with quantified formulas. Our general approach of extending verification with software fault detection capability is described in this chapter.

4.2 Properties and Basic Ideas of the Deductive Fault-Detection Approach

Part II of this thesis is dedicated to deductive techniques for software fault detection. With the term *deductive* we want to emphasize that these techniques do not require the execution of the target program in a Java Virtual Machine (JVM). Instead, the program is symbolically executed during a verification attempt. Techniques which execute a program in its runtime environment are described in Part III of this thesis.

Given a program with a specification as input, our approach yields one of the following three answers: the program is correct, the program has a fault, or it is unknown if the program is correct or not. Note that correctness in this sense is solely defined by the logical satisfaction of the specification by the program for all program states.

The fault detection technique is based on information that is obtained by a verification attempt. The technique is therefore not disconnected from the verification process. Instead, both processes overlap and information between verification and fault detection is reused. In this way, the resources required to extend the verification process with the software fault detection capability are minimized.

The approach is not a decision procedure, i.e., termination is not guaranteed. This is because showing the correctness or incorrectness of a program requires to prove the validity of first-order logic formulas which is an undecidable problem. However, since our approach features the possibility of detecting faults, it may terminate in cases where a verification alone would not terminate.

A verification technique is the underlying component of our software fault detection approach. The details of our approach are specific to KeY's verification approach. However, we believe that our extension to verification is also applicable to other verification tools that follow similar paradigms as the KeY tool. Those tools can usually only prove the correctness of a program. With verification-based software fault detection we aim at extending techniques which follow a similar paradigm as the KeY tool with the ability to detect faults in programs – with *programs* we mean a program method or sequence of statements. The program as a whole is not abstracted into, e.g., an (abstract) state machine before the verification. Instead the source code of the program is symbolically executed.

Program abstractions play in fact an important role in our approach. However, these abstractions differ from approaches that transform the whole program into a state machine. The difference is that in the here considered verification approach the abstractions consist of possibly complex first-order logic formulas that can be provided by a user. Furthermore, these abstractions are applied only to selected program parts such as method calls and loops.

We abbreviate the underlying verification technique with VT.

Definition 4.2. *The set Branches denotes all branches of proof trees (see Def. 2.31, page 45).*

- *Let $B \in$ Branches, with $B^{Fml} \in$ Formulae we denote the formula at the leaf of the branch B (see Def. 2.29 for the translation of sequents to formulas). If B is closed we define $B^{Fml} =$ true.*
- *Let $Bs \subset$ Branch, then the set Bs^{Fml} denotes $\bigcup_{B \in Bs} \{B^{Fml}\}$.*
- *Branches$_\varphi$ denotes all branches with the root φ.*

Definition 4.3. *The underlying verification technique for verification-based fault detection is a function $VT :$ Formulae $\rightarrow$ Branches that* *maps a formula to a set of open branches with proof obligations such that*

- $VT(\varphi) \subset Branches_{\varphi}$,
- $true \notin VT(\varphi)^{Fml}$, *i.e., closed branches are not in the set, (this condition is omitted for white-box test case generation described in Section 7.4.2)*
- $VT(\varphi)^{Fml} \vDash_A \varphi$, *where A is the set of new symbols introduced by VT (see Def. 2.13).*

Example. Let $\varphi = (\implies \forall x.(a < x \to \{y := x\}(a < y \wedge y < b)))$. A proof tree for φ is for instance:

$$
\cfrac{
  \cfrac{
    \cfrac{B_1}{a < sk \implies a < sk} \qquad \cfrac{B_2}{a < sk \implies sk < b}
  }{a < sk \implies a < sk \wedge sk < b} \text{andRight}
  \\ \vdots \\
  \implies a < sk \to \{y := sk\}(a < y \wedge y < b)
}{\implies \forall x.(a < x \to \{y := x\}(a < y \wedge y < b))} \text{allRight}
$$

In this case we have

$$
\begin{aligned}
B_1^{Fml} &= (a < sk \to a < sk) \\
B_2^{Fml} &= (a < sk \to sk < b) \\
Branches_{\varphi} &= \{B_1, B_2\} \\
VT(\varphi) &= \{B_1, B_2\} \\
VT(\varphi)^{Fml} &= \{(a < sk \to a < sk), (a < sk \to sk < b)\} \\
A &= \{sk\}
\end{aligned}
$$

The conditions of Definition 4.3 are satisfied. Note that $VT(\varphi)^{Fml} \vDash \varphi$ does not hold which becomes clear when considering, e.g., the interpretation, $\mathcal{I}(a) = 0, \mathcal{I}(sk) = 1, \mathcal{I}(b) = 2$.

$\square$

The function VT represents the input and output relation of KeY's software verification component. It allows for some freedom regarding the logic and formalization of the input formula φ. The verification condition ψ can be expressed, for instance, in Hoare Logic. The definition also allows for freedom regarding the actual transformations performed on φ. With some creativity the concept of a proof tree and a branch can be generalized and adapted to the particular verification technique. For instance, we can imagine using a weakest precondition calculus in order to obtain a set of first-order proof obligations and then discharging each proof obligation by a theorem prover. Such an adaption requires, however, a detailed look at the transformations performed by the verification tool.

The proof tree that is obtained by the verification attempt as well as the calculus for construction of the proof tree play a central role in this thesis. The proof tree contains rich information about the program and its specification. The idea of our approach is to utilize this information in order to detect faults. If a proof attempt does not lead to a closed proof tree, then we consider the proof attempt as failed. However, a failed proof attempt does not imply the existence of a fault in the program or the specification. It is only for practical reasons if a proof attempt is considered as failed. For instance, the KeY tool stops a proof attempt if a timeout is reached, if a maximum amount of rules has been applied, or if analytic rules have been applied exhaustively. A proof attempt can always be continued as long as the proof does not close. The reason is that there is an infinite number of possible applications of non-analytic rules. Those rules introduce new formulas into a proof tree such as the cut-rule and induction-rule in the first-order logic part and the contract rules in the dynamic logic part of the calculus.

A failed proof attempt results in an open proof tree which contains at least one open proof branch and other closed branches potentially. The branches of a proof tree are closely corresponding to an execution tree, i.e., proof branches correspond to execution paths of the program. Closed proof branches correspond to program executions that satisfy the specification of the program. We regard these program executions as correct. When searching for software faults it is therefore reasonable to look at proof branches that were not closed during the proof attempt. This is because if the program has a fault on an execution trace, then the proof tree must have an open proof branch corresponding to this execution trace. The underlying verification step can be seen as a filtering mechanism. In this sense the execution traces on which the program behaves correctly are filtered out by the verification attempt and the remaining open proof branches represent those program executions on which an error may potentially occur.

4.3 The Algorithm

4.3.1 Description of the Algorithm

The deductive fault detection technique is an extension that builds on top of a verification technique and is given as Algorithm 1. The algorithm is a framework that connects other algorithms or techniques which will be described in the following chapters.

Algorithm 1 tryToVerifyOrToFindABug(φ)

1:   $Bs = VT(\varphi)$
2: **if** $Bs = \emptyset$ **then**
3:     **return** "Verified"
4: **else**
5:     **for all** $B \in Bs$ **do**
6:        a) Try to show that B^{Fml} has a counterexample and store it in Ex
7:        b) Try to show that B is validity preserving
8:        **if** showing a) and b) was successful **then**
9:           $res = res \ \cup (B, Ex)$
10:        **end if**
11:     **end for**
12:     **if** $res = \emptyset$ **then**
13:        **return** "Unknown"
14:     **else**
15:        **return** "The program or its specification has faults on trace(es) res"
16:     **end if**
17: **end if**

The input to the Algorithm 1 is a formula φ that expresses the correctness of a program. In Section 2.4.5 and Chapter 3 we have described the form of such formulas in the KeY approach. In Line 1 of the algorithm the verification tool is invoked and the result of the verification attempt is checked in Line 2. According to Definition 4.3, if the verification attempt was successful, then the set of open proof obligations returned by VT is empty and the result "Verified" is returned to the user.

In case the verification attempt was not successful, VT returns a set of open proof branches. The loop in Line 5 iterates over the open proof branches and tries to determine whether the information contained in a branch implies the existence of a counterexample of the input formula

φ. If this is so, then we interpret this as a fault in the program or its specification. Two conditions have to be checked for this purpose.

The condition (a) in Line 6 requires that the open proof obligation of branch B, i.e. B^{Fml}, has a counterexample. When using an interactive prover such as KeY, one option is to let the user decide if B^{Fml} has a counterexample. Automation can be achieved by using, e.g., a satisfiability modulo theories (SMT) solver. Such tools can decide in many cases whether a first-order logic formula is satisfiable or not. This means, however, that B^{Fml} must be a first-order logic formula. An important task of the underlying verification technique is therefore to reduce the original verification condition into a set of first-order logic formulas. Branches whose leaf nodes are not first-order logic formulas cannot be processed by SMT solvers.

We have found through experiments that SMT solvers often cannot decide if the proof obligations generated by KeY have a counterexample or not – even if they are first-order logic formulas. The problem is the limited power of SMT solvers for handling quantified formulas. We describe this problem in Section 4.4.2 and in Chapter 6 we describe a new technique for addressing this problem.

Notation 1 *We denote a branch by a sequence $S_0, \ldots, S_n$ of sequents.*

In this notation the sequent S_0 represents the input formula φ and S_n is the last sequent on the branch which is equivalent to B^{Fml}.

Definition 4.4. *Definition of validity preservation (VP) conditions:*

- *Given a rule R, where P is a rule premiss and C is the conclusion of R. The validity preservation condition VP_P of the rule premiss P is the formula*

$$C \to P$$

  The rule premiss P is validity preserving iff $\vDash VP_P$.
- *A rule R is validity preserving iff for all premisses P of R, $\vDash VP_P$ holds.*
- *The validity preservation condition of a sub-sequence $S_i, \ldots, S_j$ of sequents of a branch $S_0, \ldots, S_n$, with $0 \leqslant i \leqslant j \leqslant n$, is the formula*

$$S_i \to S_j$$

  which is denoted by $VP_{S_i}^{S_j}$. The sequence $S_i, \ldots, S_j$ is validity preserving iff $\vDash VP_{S_i}^{S_j}$.

– A proof branch $S_0, \ldots, S_n$ is validity preserving iff $\models VP_{S_0}^{S_n}$. We abbreviate $VP_{S_0}^{S_n}$ with VP^{S_n}.

Translation from sequents to formulas is assumed according to Definition 2.29.

Remark 4.5. VP_S^S is trivially true.

The condition (b) in Line 7 of the algorithm requires the branch B to be validity preserving. Validity preservation means that the validity of the input formula φ implies the validity of B^{Fml} and also that every model of φ is a model of B^{Fml}. Why validity preservation is important for the algorithm becomes obvious by the following simple theorem.

Theorem 4.6. *Let $S_i, \ldots, S_j$ be a sub-sequence of sequents of a branch $S_0, \ldots, S_n$, with $0 \leqslant i \leqslant j \leqslant n$. If $\models VP_{S_i}^{S_j}$, then any counterexample (Def. 2.12) of S_j is a counterexample of S_i.*

Proof. Assume that $\models VP_{S_i}^{S_j}$ holds, i.e., that $S_i \to S_j$ is valid. The implication is equivalent to the implication $\neg S_j \to \neg S_i$. Let $\mathcal{S}$ be a partial model (see Definitions 2.6 and 2.19) such that $\mathcal{S} \models \neg S_j$. According to Definition 2.12, $\mathcal{S}$ is a counterexample of S_j. The assumptions imply that $\mathcal{S} \models \neg S_i$ holds, i.e., the partial model $\mathcal{S}$ is a counterexample of S_i. ∎

Corollary 4.7. *Given a rule R, let P be a rule premiss and let C be the conclusion of R. If P is validity preserving, then any counterexample of P is also a counterexample of C.*

Proof. VP_P is equivalent to $VP_{S_i}^{S_j}$ where $S_i = C$ and $S_j = P$. ∎

Theorem 4.6 formalizes the essential idea of Algorithm 1. The validity preservation condition of the branch B is equivalent to the formula

$$(\neg B^{Fml}) \to (\neg \varphi) \tag{4.1}$$

If B^{Fml} has a counterexample, then Formula (4.1) implies that φ has a counterexample as well. For example, let $\varphi = \langle \text{x=1} \rangle x \doteq a$ and let $B^{Fml} = 1 \doteq a$, then Formula (4.1) is valid and the state $\mathcal{S}$ with $\mathcal{I}(a) = 2$ is a counterexample of B^{Fml} and of φ.

A counterexample of the initial verification condition implies that the target program does not satisfy its specification for all states (Def. 4.1). Hence, if the conditions (a) and (b) are satisfied in Line 8 of the algorithm, then it is known that the target program or its specification is faulty. Furthermore, since a model for $\neg B^{Fml}$ is also a model for $\neg\varphi$, the model represents the initial state for running the program in order to reveal the fault.

The branch B can be mapped to a program execution trace by following the symbolic execution rules that were applied on the branch. In this way, the described approach does not only detect software faults but it also returns the trace on which the fault occurs together with the counterexample that triggers the execution of the trace. Those traces are collected in the set res in Line 9 and are returned by the algorithm in Line 15. This information is helpful to the user for finding the fault. If the set res is empty, however, then it is unknown if the target program has a fault or not. The latter is the case if either no counterexample for B^{Fml} was found, i.e., showing condition (a) was no successful, or if from a counterexample of B^{Fml} it is not sound to conclude that φ has a counterexample, i.e., showing condition (b) was successful. Showing a condition is not successful if the condition is falsifiable or if after a proof attempt it remains unknown whether it holds or not.

Branches are not always validity preserving. Proving the validity preservation condition as an implication $\varphi \rightarrow B^{Fml}$ is as hard as the verification attempt because the implication contains the original input formula φ of the verification tool. In Chapter 5 we describe a new technique that can very efficiently prove the validity preservation of branches when using contract rules. In Section 4.4.1 we describe which rules of KeY's calculus are validity preserving and which are not.

4.3.2 Example

In this section we use an example to demonstrate how the Algorithm 1 works. The code shown in Figure 4.1 is a modified version of our running example from Chapters 2 and 3. The method `sqrt` is supposed to compute an integer approximation of the square root of the input value. For the purpose of the example we have injected a fault into the method `sqrt`. The fault is at the end of the computation where i is returned instead of $i - 1$.

Algorithm 1 expects a formula as input which expresses the correctness of a program. We use the following translation of the JML specification in Figure 4.1 into a sequent (let $X^2 = X * X$).

$$x \geqslant 0, o \neq \texttt{null} \Longrightarrow \langle \texttt{r=o.sqrt(x);} \rangle (r^2 \leqslant x \wedge (r+1)^2 > x) \qquad (4.2)$$

4. The Deductive Software-fault Detection Approach

——— JAVA + JML (4.1) ———————————————————————————

```
1   /*@ public behavior
2       requires x>=0;
3       ensures \result * \result <= x &&
4               (\result+1) * (\result+1) > x;
5   @*/
6   public int sqrt(int x){
7     int i=0;
8     while(i*i<=x){
9       i=i+1;
10    }
11    return i; //FAULT, it should be i-1
12  }
```

———————————————————————————————— JAVA + JML ———

Fig. 4.1. Variant of the method `sqrt` with a fault.

This sequent is similar to the representation of the verification condition used in Section 2.4.5.2 where we verified the correct version of the method `sqrt` for the case $x \doteq 0$. The actual verification condition generated by the KeY tool is more involved (see Chapter 3), however, the differences can be ignored in this example.

In Line 1 of Algorithm 1 the verification tool is invoked which is in our case the KeY tool. It generates the partial proof tree shown in Figure 4.2 by using finite loop unwinding with at least one loop unwinding. For details about the construction of the proof tree we refer the reader to Section 2.4.5.2 on page 60. The proof tree in Figure 4.2 coincides largely with the proof tree in Figure 2.2, except that the branch B_2 is not closed here. This is because in the verification condition (4.2) the program variable x has no upper bound in the initial state.

Using finite loop unwinding, the correctness of a program can be shown only for a bounded number of loop iterations. Generally there is at least one branch, here B_2, on which the loop remains to be symbolically executed. The strengths of finite loop unwinding are that the rule loopUnwind satisfies the validity preservation property required by Algorithm 1 and that no loop invariant has to be provided.

The closed branch B_0 corresponds to the execution of the method where the loop iterates zero times, i.e., the loop condition is false before the first iteration of the loop. This is possible only if $x < 0$ which contradicts the precondition $x \geqslant 0$. Program traces whose path conditions

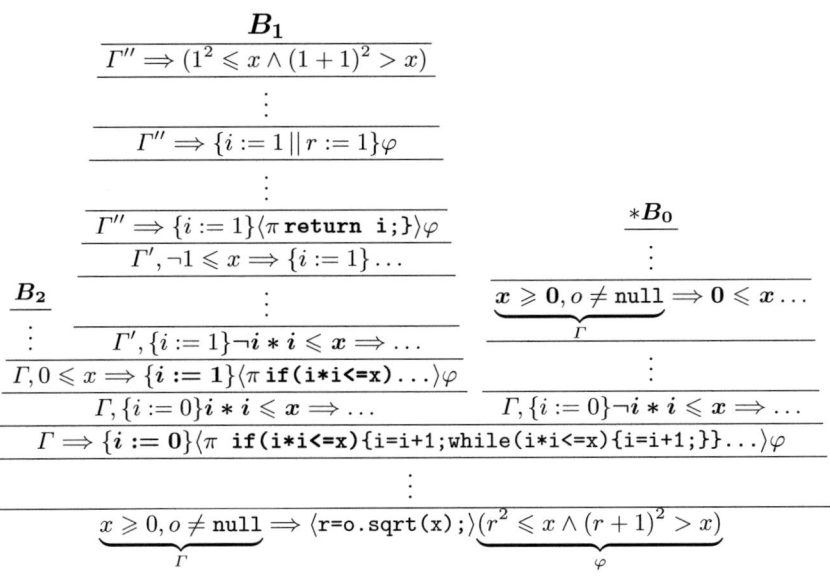

Fig. 4.2. Open proof tree from a verification attempt of the method `sqrt`

cannot be satisfied are closed during the verification attempt. Since Algorithm 1 analyzes only open branches the verification technique works as a filtering mechanism.

Branch B_1 represents the case where the loop execution terminates after one iteration. Further rule applications on B_1 result in the open branch $B_{1,1}$.

$$
\dfrac{
\dfrac{
\dfrac{\quad}{o \neq \texttt{null}, x \doteq 0 \Longrightarrow 1 \leqslant x} \quad B_{1,1} \qquad
\dfrac{\vdots}{o \neq \texttt{null}, x \doteq 0 \Longrightarrow 4 > x} {}^{*}
}{o \neq \texttt{null}, x \doteq 0 \Longrightarrow 1 \leqslant x \wedge 4 > x}
}{
\vdots \\[2pt]
\underbrace{x \geqslant 0, o \neq \texttt{null}, 0 \leqslant x, \neg 1 \leqslant x}_{\Gamma''} \Longrightarrow (1^2 \leqslant x \wedge (1+1)^2 > x)
}
$$

The leaf $B_{1,1}^{Fml}$ is a first-order logic formula. Hence, in order to check if the leaf has a counterexample (Line 6 of the algorithm) an SMT solver can be used. However, when using KeY as the underlying verification tool, it is in some cases not necessary to rely on external tools in order to generate counterexamples. For example, the formula $B_{1,1}^{Fml}$ has a counterexample because it is in a decidable fragment of KeY and cannot be proven. Counterexample generation for integer arithmetic formulas in KeY is described in [Rümmer, 2007].

In Line 7 of the algorithm, validity preservation of $B_{1,1}$ is checked. For the proof tree construction only validity preserving rules were used. Section 4.4.1 explains which rules are validity preserving and which are not. As both conditions (a) and (b) are satisfied for $B_{1,1}$ (Line 8) we can conclude that Formula (4.2) has a counterexample. The counterexample is syntactically given by $o \neq$ null, $x \doteq 0$, and $1 > x$. The branch and its counterexample are finally returned with the statement that the program or its specification has a fault.

4.4 Validity Preservation and Counterexample Generation

4.4.1 Validity Preservation

In this section we show that most of KeY's calculus rules are validity preserving but that special treatment is required for the contract rules. Validity preservation of rules is important because it allows us to conclude the validity preservation of proof branches as stated by the following lemma.

Lemma 4.8. *According to Definition 2.31 the sequents of a proof tree branch are rule premises, except for the sequent at the root. If the sequents of a proof tree branch B are validity preserving rule premises of the rules that were applied on B, then B is validity preserving.*

Proof. Induction Hypothesis: If a branch $S_0, \ldots, S_{k-1}$, with $k \geqslant 0$, is validity preserving, and S_k is a validity preserving rule premiss of a rule which is applied on S_{k-1}, then the branch $S_0, \ldots, S_k$ is validity preserving.

Induction Base ($k = 0$): In this case no rule is applied and the branch consists only of the root sequent S_0. $VP_{S_0}^{S_0}$ is trivially valid.

Induction Step ($k \geqslant 0$): Assume the branch $S_0, \ldots, S_{k-1}$ is validity preserving, i.e. $\vDash S_0 \to S_{k-1}$. Also assume that S_k is a validity preserving rule premiss of a rule that is applied on S_{k-1}, i.e. $\vDash S_{k-1} \to S_k$. We conclude that $\vDash S_0 \to S_k$ which means that the branch $S_0, \ldots, S_k$ is validity preserving. ∎

In the following we select exemplary rules from different rule sets of KeY's calculus and prove their validity preservation property. Most rules of the calculus are equivalence rules.

Definition 4.9. *A rule is an equivalence rule if the conjunction of the rule premises is semantically equivalent to the conclusion of the rule.*

Validity preservation of equivalence rules follows immediately from Definitions 4.4 and 4.9.

Remark 4.10. In a proof of validity preservation of a rule it is sound to use the same rule for proof construction. This is because the proof relies only on the soundness property of the rule and not on its validity preservation property.

Propositional Rules.

The propositional rules in Table 2.3 are equivalence rules. For instance, the validity preservation conditions of the rule premises of the rule

$$\text{andRight} \ \frac{\Longrightarrow \phi \quad \Longrightarrow \psi}{\Longrightarrow \phi \wedge \psi}$$

are $(\phi \wedge \psi) \rightarrow \phi$ for the first premiss and $(\phi \wedge \psi) \rightarrow \psi$ for the second premiss. Both are valid formulas.

In [Harel, 1984] and in [Platzer, 2004; Beckert and Platzer, 2006] where completeness proofs for dynamic logic calculi are given the following additional rules are included in the set of propositional rules.

$$\text{removeLeft} \ \frac{\Longrightarrow}{\phi \Longrightarrow} \quad \text{and} \quad \text{removeRight} \ \frac{\Longrightarrow}{\Longrightarrow \phi}$$

It is sound to remove an arbitrary formula from a sequent. When a formula is removed from a sequent, the sequent is potentially strengthened. The premiss of the rules removeLeft and removeRight implies the conclusion of the rules, respectively, but the conclusion does not necessarily imply the premiss. The latter means that not all instances of this rule schema are validity preserving. The validity preservation condition for the rule schema removeLeft is $\neg \phi \rightarrow$ false. The condition does not hold if, e.g., $\phi =$ false. Similarly, the validity preservation of the rule schema removeRight does not hold if $\phi =$ true.

Remark. The KeY tool implements these rules but with different semantics. The corresponding rules in KeY allow to *hide* an arbitrary formula from a sequent and are called hideLeft and hideRight respectively. The semantic difference to the rules above is that in KeY the hidden formulas can be reintroduced on the same branch which is not allowed in [Harel, 1984; Platzer, 2004; Beckert and Platzer, 2006]. If a hidden formula is not reintroduced on a branch, then the validity preservation on the branch may be violated.

Quantifier Rules.

The quantifier rules consist of Skolemization rules and instantiation rules for universal and existential quantifiers. We regard here only the universal quantifiers, the existential quantifiers behave analogously.

The quantifier Skolemization rules are not equivalence rules but they are validity preserving. The validity preservation condition of the rule

$$\text{allRight} \quad \frac{\implies [x \backslash sk](\phi)}{\implies \forall x.\phi} \qquad (sk \text{ is new})$$

is the formula $\forall x.\phi \to [x \backslash sk](\phi)$ which can be proved as follows.

$$\cfrac{\cfrac{\cfrac{*}{\forall x.\phi, [x \backslash sk](\phi) \implies [x \backslash sk](\phi)} \text{ close}}{\forall x.\phi \implies [x \backslash sk](\phi)} \text{ allRight}}{\implies \forall x.\phi \to [x \backslash sk](\phi)} \text{ impRight}$$

Note that using the rule allRight in this proof is sound as explained in Remark 4.10.

The quantifier instantiation rules are equivalence rules. The validity preservation condition of the rule

$$\text{allLeft} \quad \frac{\forall x.\phi, [x \backslash t](\phi) \implies}{\forall x.\phi \implies}$$

is the formula $(\neg \forall x.\phi) \to \neg (\forall x.\phi \wedge [x \backslash t](\phi))$ and can be proved as follows.

$$\cfrac{\cfrac{\cfrac{\cfrac{\cfrac{*}{\forall x.\phi, [x \backslash t](\phi) \implies \forall x.\phi} \text{ close}}{\forall x.\phi \wedge [x \backslash t](\phi) \implies \forall x.\phi} \text{ andLeft}}{\neg \forall x.\phi, \forall x.\phi \wedge [x \backslash t](\phi) \implies} \text{ notLeft}}{\neg \forall x.\phi \implies \neg (\forall x.\phi \wedge [x \backslash t](\phi))} \text{ notRight}}{\implies (\neg \forall x.\phi) \to \neg (\forall x.\phi \wedge [x \backslash t](\phi))} \text{ impRight}$$

General Validity Preserving Rules.

The instantiation rules add a formula to the sequent and do not remove any formulas from the sequent. This is also the case for the rules eqLeft, eqLeft', eqRight, and eqRight' in Table 2.4. All such rules are validity preserving. This patterns leads us to the following lemma.

Lemma 4.11. *Let $\Gamma, \Delta \subset$ Formulae and $\phi \in$ Formulae. The rules of the form*

$$\frac{\Gamma \Rightarrow \phi, \Delta}{\Gamma \Rightarrow \Delta} \quad and \quad \frac{\Gamma, \phi \Rightarrow \Delta}{\Gamma \Rightarrow \Delta}$$

are validity preserving.

Proof. Since $\Gamma, \phi \Rightarrow \Delta$ is equivalent to $\Gamma \Rightarrow \phi', \Delta$ with $\phi' = \neg\phi$ we prove validity preservation only of the premiss of the left rule. The validity preservation condition of the premiss is $(\bigwedge\Gamma \to \bigvee\Delta) \to (\bigwedge\Gamma \to (\phi \vee \bigvee\Delta))$ which can be proved as follows.

$$\frac{\frac{\overline{\bigvee\Delta, \bigwedge\Gamma \Rightarrow \phi, \bigvee\Delta} \quad \overline{\bigwedge\Gamma \Rightarrow \bigwedge\Gamma, \phi, \bigvee\Delta}}{\frac{\bigwedge\Gamma \to \bigvee\Delta, \bigwedge\Gamma \Rightarrow \phi, \bigvee\Delta}{\frac{\bigwedge\Gamma \to \bigvee\Delta, \bigwedge\Gamma \Rightarrow (\phi \vee \bigvee\Delta)}{\frac{\bigwedge\Gamma \to \bigvee\Delta \Rightarrow \bigwedge\Gamma \to (\phi \vee \bigvee\Delta)}{\Rightarrow (\bigwedge\Gamma \to \bigvee\Delta) \to (\bigwedge\Gamma \to (\phi \vee \bigvee\Delta))} \text{ impRight}} \text{ impRight}} \text{ orRight}} \text{ impLeft}} \text{close}}$$

∎

Lemma 4.11 is not only useful to quickly decide if a rule (premiss) is validity preserving but it can also be used to *fix* the validity preservation of rule premisses. The following lemma states under what condition and how a rule (premiss) can be modified such that it becomes validity preserving.

Lemma 4.12. *Let $\Gamma, \Delta \subset$ Formulae and let $\phi, \phi' \in$ Formulae. Let*

$$\frac{\Rightarrow \phi'}{\Rightarrow \phi} \tag{4.3}$$

be a sound rule. Hence, $\{\phi'\} \models_A \phi$ holds, where A is the set of newly introduced symbols in ϕ' (A may be empty). The following rule is (a) validity preserving and (b) sound.

$$\frac{\Rightarrow \phi', \phi}{\Rightarrow \phi} \tag{4.4}$$

Proof. (a) Rule 4.4 is validity preserving according to Lemma 4.11.
(b) The soundness proof of Rule (4.4) requires us to prove that

$$\{\phi'\} \vDash_A \phi \quad \text{implies} \quad \{\phi' \vee \phi\} \vDash_A \phi. \tag{4.5}$$

We try to prove the opposite and derive a contradiction. Assume the statement (4.5) is false which is possible only if $\{\phi'\} \vDash_A \phi$ is true and $\{\phi' \vee \phi\} \vDash_A \phi$ is false. According to the last item of Definition 2.13 (on page 32) the latter means that there is a partial model $\mathcal{M}^1$ and a variable assignment β^1 such that $\mathcal{M}^1, \beta^1 \vDash_A \phi' \vee \phi$ is true but $\mathcal{M}^1, \beta^1 \vDash \phi$ is false. The condition $\{\phi'\} \vDash_A \phi$ means that for all partial models $\mathcal{M}$ and variable assignments β; $\mathcal{M}, \beta \vDash_A \phi'$ implies $\mathcal{M}, \beta \vDash \phi$. Hence, $\mathcal{M}, \beta \vDash \phi$ can be false only if $\mathcal{M}, \beta \vDash_A \phi'$ is false, under our assumption. From $\mathcal{M}^1, \beta^1 \vDash \phi$ being false follows that $\mathcal{M}^1, \beta^1 \vDash_A \phi'$ is false which contradicts that $\mathcal{M}^1, \beta^1 \vDash_A \phi' \vee \phi$ is true. Hence, the statement (4.5) is true.

∎

Equality, Arithmetic, and Update Simplification Rules.

It is easy to see that the equality rules of Table 2.4, are equivalence rules. The update simplification rules in Section 2.4.4 (page 50) are all defined as equivalence transformations. Also arithmetic rules of KeY [Rümmer, 2007] were designed as equivalence transformations rules and are therefore validity preserving.

Program Reduction Rules.

The program reduction rules (see Section 2.4.5, page 56) were designed as equivalence transformation rules, and hence as validity preserving rules, that mimic the execution of a JAVA program according to the JAVA language specification. Validity preservation of these rules can be shown as in the following example where we prove the validity preservation condition of the first premiss of the rule

$$\text{ifElseSplit} \quad \frac{se^* \Rightarrow \langle \pi \, p \, \omega \rangle \phi \qquad \neg se^* \Rightarrow \langle \pi \, q \, \omega \rangle \phi}{\Rightarrow \langle \pi \, \texttt{if}\,(se)\, p \, \texttt{else} \, q \, \omega \rangle \phi}$$

from Table 2.5. The root of the following proof tree is the validity preservation condition of the first premiss of the rule.

$$\cfrac{\cfrac{\cfrac{\cfrac{*}{se^*, \langle \pi p \omega \rangle \phi \Longrightarrow \langle \pi p \omega \rangle \phi}}{se^*, \neg[\pi p \omega]\neg\phi \Longrightarrow \langle \pi p \omega \rangle \phi} \text{R2}}{se^* \Longrightarrow \langle \pi p \omega \rangle \phi, [\pi p \omega]\neg\phi} \text{R1} \quad \cfrac{\cfrac{*}{se^* \Longrightarrow se^*, \dots}}{se^*, \neg se^* \Longrightarrow \langle \pi p \omega \rangle \phi, [\pi p \omega]\neg\phi}}{\cfrac{\cfrac{se^* \Longrightarrow \langle \pi p \omega \rangle \phi, [\pi \, \texttt{if} \, (se) \, p \, \texttt{else} \, q \, \omega]\neg\phi}{\langle \pi \, \texttt{if} \, (se) \, p \, \texttt{else} \, q \, \omega \rangle \phi, se^* \Longrightarrow \langle \pi p \omega \rangle \phi}}{\langle \pi \, \texttt{if} \, (se) \, p \, \texttt{else} \, q \, \omega \rangle \phi \Longrightarrow (se^* \rightarrow \langle \pi p \omega \rangle \phi)}}$$

For the proof construction we used the following additional sound rules that were not presented in Chapter 2.

$$\text{R1} \; \cfrac{\neg\phi \Longrightarrow}{\Longrightarrow \phi} \qquad\qquad \text{R2} \; \cfrac{\langle \text{p} \rangle \phi \Longrightarrow}{\neg[\text{p}]\neg\phi \Longrightarrow}$$

Soundness of the rule R1 is trivial and soundness of the rule R2 follows from Lemma 2.26.

Contract Rules.

The loop invariant and method contract rules (see Section 2.4.6, page 63) are generally not validity preserving. The validity preservation property depends on the strength of the loop invariant or method contract that is used. For instance, the formula "true" is an invariant of any loop but no properties of the loop can be concluded from it. Hence, a proof obligation is obtained that is not valid, i.e., it has a counterexample, but the original formula expressing the property of the loop may be valid.

In order to fix validity preservation of the contract rules it may be tempting to use Lemma 4.12. The following is a validity preserving variant of the loop invariant rule obtained by using that lemma.

$$\text{loopInvVP} \; \cfrac{\begin{array}{l} \textbf{1:} \;\; \Longrightarrow I, [\pi \, \texttt{while(c)\{b;\}} \, \omega] \textit{\textbf{post}} \\ \textbf{2:} \;\; \Longrightarrow \mathcal{V}_M(I \wedge c \rightarrow [\texttt{b}]I), [\pi \, \texttt{while(c)\{b;\}} \, \omega] \textit{\textbf{post}} \\ \textbf{3:} \;\; \Longrightarrow \mathcal{V}_M((I \wedge \neg c) \rightarrow [\pi\omega]\textit{post}), [\pi \, \texttt{while(c)\{b;\}} \, \omega] \textit{\textbf{post}} \end{array}}{\Longrightarrow [\pi \, \texttt{while(c)\{b;\}} \, \omega] \textit{post}}$$

This rule is, however, problematic for counterexample generation because it prevents the reduction of verification conditions to first-order logic formulas (see Section 4.3.1). When using the rule loopInvVP instead of the rule loopInv the DL-formula cannot be removed from the sequents. Therefore our approach requires to use the rules presented in Section 2.4.6 and we present special techniques for checking the validity preservation of contract rules in Chapter 5.

———— JAVA + JML ————

```
public class C{
  private String[] s;
  /*@ invariant
      s.length>=10;*/
  ...
}
```

$$\left(\begin{array}{l} \forall o : \texttt{C}.o \neq \texttt{null} \rightarrow (\texttt{s}(o) \neq \texttt{null} \wedge \\ \quad (\forall i : \texttt{int}.0 \leqslant i \leqslant \texttt{length}(\texttt{s}(o)) \rightarrow \\ \quad\quad \texttt{acc}_{[]}(\texttt{s}(o), i) \neq \texttt{null})) \end{array} \right) \tag{4.6}$$

———————— JAVA + JML ——

$$\forall o : \texttt{C}.o \neq \texttt{null} \rightarrow \texttt{length}(\texttt{s}(o)) \geqslant 10 \tag{4.7}$$

Fig. 4.3. (left) A field declaration and a class invariant; (right) Quantified formulas occurring in test data constraints generated by KeY from the listing on the left side

4.4.2 Counterexample Generation

In this section we shortly motivate why we propose a special technique for counterexample generation in Chapter 6. SMT solvers are considered as state-of-the-art techniques for generating models, respectively counterexamples, for first-order logic formulas. A major bottleneck is, however, the handling of quantifiers (see, e.g., [Moskal et al., 2008; Nieuwenhuis et al., 2007]). SMT solvers can often create models for quantified formulas if *one* theory is involved. Quantifiers and multiple theories often lead to problems that are not in the decidable fragments of the solvers. In such cases an SMT solver cannot generate a model for the formula.

For example, Figure 4.3 shows a JAVA class with a field declaration and a JML specification of a class invariant. From the field declaration and the class invariant the KeY tool generates the Formulas (4.6) and (4.7), respectively. These formulas are part of verification conditions. Formula (4.6) follows JML's semantics and expresses that the array field s and the elements of the array are not **null**. Formula (4.7) expresses the class invariant, that for all objects of class C the array s has 10 or more elements.

The problem is that state-of-the-art SMT solvers, concretely we have tested Z3 [de Moura and Bjørner, 2008], CVC3 [Barrett and Tinelli, 2007], Yices [Dutertre and de Moura, 2006a], are not capable of generating models or counterexamples for the Formulas (4.6) or (4.7). Although SMT solvers can solve quantified formulas in certain cases, the Formulas (4.6) and (4.7) are not in the decidable logic fragment of the solvers. Note, that a different translation of the code in Figure 4.3 could create formulas that are solvable by SMT solvers, but the general problem of solving quantified formulas remains. We have developed a technique for handling quantified formulas in this context and describe it in Chapter 6.

4.5 Conclusion

Our general approach is an extension for deductive verification techniques. Information obtained from a failed verification attempt is used to determine if the verification condition at the beginning of a proof has a counterexample. If this is so, then the program or its specification has a fault.

The algorithm presented in this chapter is easy to understand and easy to implement. The algorithm is, however, only a framework which delegates more complicated problems to sub-components. The delegated problems to be solved are to check if a formula has a counterexample and to check if a proof branch is validity preserving. Hence, one goal of this chapter was to explain how these techniques are related to our approach and to motivate the need for techniques which address these problems in the following chapters. The algorithm is implemented in the KeY tool. Evaluations are provided for the more interesting sub-algorithms presented in the following chapters.

Counterexamples can be generated directly with KeY in certain cases or with an external tool like an SMT solver. In order to utilize these tools the verification conditions generated by the verification tool must be first-order logic formulas. Therefore certain calculus rule such as the rule loopInvVP (see Section 4.4.1) cannot be used. The actual challenge is, however, to generate counterexamples for quantified formulas. These occur frequently in verification conditions. In Chapter 6 we describe a novel technique for handling the problem of counterexample generation from quantified formulas.

If the leaf node of a branch has a counterexample, our approach is to deduce the existence of a software fault by showing the validity preservation of this branch. When using finite loop unwinding and finite unfolding of method calls, which is also known as bounded symbolic execution, then the branches of the proof tree are validity preserving. However, verification tools typically use contract rules which allow reasoning about arbitrary numbers of loop iterations or method calls. The problem with contract rules is that their validity preservation property depends on the contract that is used. Techniques for handling this problem are addressed in the following chapter.

5

Deducing the Existence of Software Faults when Using Contract Rules

5.1 Introduction

The technique described in this chapter is a sub-component of our general deductive software-fault detection approach described in Chapter 4. It checks conditions for deducing the existence of software faults based on a failed verification attempt. A software correctness proof usually does not succeed on the first proof attempt because often either a) the target program is not correct, i.e., the program does not satisfy the specification, or b) the program is correct but inappropriate *auxiliary* formulas, i.e., loop invariants or method contracts, are used. The user then does not know if they should search for a fault in the program or requirement specification, or search for a different loop invariant or auxiliary method contract.

The technique described in Chapter 4 tries to show the correctness of a program and in case of verification failure it tries to show program incorrectness. The problem of existing techniques following this approach is that counterexamples for verification conditions do not necessarily imply a program incorrectness. The reason for verification failure may be the usage of inappropriate auxiliary formulas resulting in rules which are not validity preserving. Counterexamples of verification conditions only guide the user to find the problem. In contrast, the technique described in this chapter tries to exclude case (b) as the source for verification failure by showing case (a), i.e., it checks if a falsifiable verification condition implies a software fault. The technique does not always give an answer because the problem is undecidable.

The bottlenecks that prevent from concluding the existence of software faults directly from a falsifiable verification condition are the con-

—— JAVA + JML (5.1) ————————————————————

```
1   /*@ public normal_behavior
2     requires x>=0;
3     ensures \result * \result <= x && (\result+1)*(\result+1)>x;
4     diverges true;
5   @*/
6   public int sqrtA(int x){
7     int i=0;
8     /*@ loop_invariant (i-1)*(i-1)<=x || i==0;
9         modifies i; @*/
10    while(i*i<=x){
11      i++;
12    }
13    return i;//FAULT, it should be i-1
14  }
```
———————————————————————————————— JAVA + JML ——

—— JAVA + JML (5.2) ————————————————————

```
1   /*@ public normal_behavior
2     requires x>=0;
3     ensures \result * \result <= x && (\result+1)*(\result+1)>x;
4     diverges true;
5   @*/
6   public int sqrtB(int x){
7     int i=0;
8     /*@ loop_invariant (i-1)*(i-1)<=x || x==0; //weak invariant
9         modifies i; @*/
10    while(i*i<=x){
11      i++;
12    }
13    return i-1;
14  }
```
———————————————————————————————— JAVA + JML ——

Fig. 5.1. Motivating examples

tract rules (loop invariant rule, method contract rule) of the verification calculus (see Section 2.4.6, page 63). These rules are important to reason about programs with loops and method invocation. However, in contrast to first-order logic rules and most other rules that transform the program to a first-order formula, the contract rules are *not always* validity preserving because their validity preservation depends on the instantiation of their rule schema (see Section 4.4.1). Validity preservation (Def. 4.4, page 87) is the property of the rules that enables us concluding that the verification condition at the beginning of the proof attempt is falsifiable. The core of our method described in this chapter is to check if contract rules that occur in a sequence of rule applications are validity preserving for the particular contracts. In this way, if the check succeeds, it enables us to conclude the existence of software faults from falsifiable verification conditions. We describe three variants of this method in this chapter. The final technique, that we call *special validity preservation* checking, truly unifies verification and software fault detection because all information computed during the verification attempt is reused for fault detection.

For example, trying to verify the programs in Listings 5.1 and 5.2 (see Figure 5.1) using the given loop invariants fails because the loop invariant rule, as will be shown in this chapter, creates a falsifiable verification condition. The reason for the failure is, however, different in both cases. The method `sqrtA` has a fault and cannot be verified with any loop invariant whereas method `sqrtB` is correct but the loop invariant is inappropriate. The method described in this chapter tries to show if a contract rule with a given loop invariant or method contract is validity preserving. In Listing 5.1 this is the case and indeed our approach detects that the method `sqrtA` has a fault.

Whether a contract rule is validity preserving or not depends on the *strength* of the auxiliary formulas which instantiate the loop invariant or method contract rule in the respective case, i.e., the loop invariant or method pre- and postconditions. The stronger an auxiliary formula is, the more detailed information it contains about the loop or method invocation it describes. Consequently the described method is capable to detect faults only if contracts are sufficiently strong. The method does not check if a stronger contract exists that would complete the proof or make a contract rule validity preserving. Checking if an appropriate contract exists in order to close a proof is regarded here as the task of the verification engineer during the verification process or in the ideal case the task of a complete and automatic verification tool. Instead the proposed technique is applied after a verification attempt for which contracts were already used. Based on the information obtained from the verification attempt it tries to detect software faults. In this chapter we assume that the input to our technique is provided from Algorithm 1 (page 86). The input consists of proof branches of un-

Method Contract Rule (mContract)	**Loop Invariant Rule** (loopInv)

Method Contract Rule (mContract)

  1: $\Gamma \Rightarrow \mathcal{U} pre_m, \Delta$

  2*: $\quad \Rightarrow pre_m \rightarrow \langle\!\langle m \rangle\!\rangle post_m \qquad (*)$

  3: $\Gamma \Rightarrow \mathcal{U}\mathcal{V}_M(post_m \rightarrow \langle\!\langle \pi\omega \rangle\!\rangle post), \Delta$

$$\overline{\Gamma \Rightarrow \mathcal{U}\langle\!\langle \pi m; \omega \rangle\!\rangle post, \Delta}$$

Loop Invariant Rule (loopInv)

  1: $\Gamma \Rightarrow \mathcal{U}I, \Delta$

  2: $\Gamma \Rightarrow \mathcal{U}\mathcal{V}_M(I \wedge c^* \rightarrow [\text{b}]I), \Delta$

  3: $\Gamma \Rightarrow \mathcal{U}\mathcal{V}_M((I \wedge \neg c^*) \rightarrow [\pi\omega]post), \Delta$

$$\overline{\Gamma \Rightarrow \mathcal{U}[\pi \ \text{while(c)\{b;\}}\omega]post, \Delta}$$

where $\mathcal{V}_M$ is an anonymising update w.r.t. the modifier set M and M is a correct modifier set for m and b respectively.

Fig. 5.2. Contract Rules

proved verification conditions and we assume the existence of a method that determines if a first-order logic formula has a counterexample. A technique for solving the latter problem is described in Chapter 6.

This chapter is an extension of the paper [Gladisch, 2009]. The described techniques have resulted from the refinement of a test case generation technique described in [Gladisch, 2008a].

5.2 What Counterexamples of Contract Rule Premisses Mean

The method contract and loop invariant rules (*contract rules*) (see Section 2.4.6) are a software verification technique for generating verification conditions for programs with method calls and loops. If a verification condition resulting from using a contract rule turns out to be falsifiable, then one cannot always conclude if the target program has a fault or not. This section explains how to interpret falsifiable proof branches, i.e. rule premisses, that these rules generate upon rule application.

For convenience the contract rules from Figure 2.5 are shown in Figure 5.2 with the generalization applied that is described in Definition 2.34 (page 46). The generalization adds the contextual information Γ, Δ and the update $\mathcal{U}$ to the sequents. A contract is a quadruple (see Def. 2.48). The contract used in the method contract rules is the quadruple

$$(pre_m, post_m, M, term)$$

where the modality $\langle\rangle$ is used in the method contract rule if *term=partial* and the modality $[]$ is used if *term=total*. The contract of a loop that is used in the loop invariant rule is the quadruple[1]

$$(I, I \wedge c^*, M, \textit{partial}\ )$$

Note that in Premiss 2 of the loop invariant rule the correctness of the contract of the loop is proven by showing that I is an invariant of the loop body.

Contracts can play different roles in different verification approaches. We distinguish the role of a requirement specification and the role as an auxiliary formula that is required for proof construction. If a program does not satisfy a contract, then depending on the role of the contract one can argue that either the program or the contract has a fault. Depending on the perspective, the falsifiability of a verification condition can be interpreted in different ways. In the following we give different interpretations for the falsifiability of the premisses of contract rules. Table 5.1 on the following page gives an overview of the different cases and interpretations. Below the table a list with abbreviations is shown that we are going to use in the following because both contract rules are considered in parallel. Using the notation of Table 5.1 the verification condition at the root of the proof tree is

$$pre \rightarrow \langle\!\langle ABC \rangle\!\rangle post \tag{5.1}$$

Rule Premiss 1

This premiss ensures that the precondition pre_B, i.e. pre_m or I, is satisfied in the pre-state of the method or loop, respectively. The pre-state is given by the formulas in Γ and Δ and the update $\mathcal{U}$ (see Section 2.4.5, page 56). The formulas Γ and Δ consist of the preconditions of the target program, i.e., the program to be verified, and the path-conditions that led to the current execution point. The update $\mathcal{U}$ describes how the program state has been changed up to this point of execution. Following the abbreviations of Table 5.1 this rule premiss expresses the property

$$pre \rightarrow \langle\!\langle A \rangle\!\rangle pre_B \tag{5.2}$$

Falsifiability of this premiss can be interpreted in two ways.

Firstly, if the precondition pre_B must be satisfied in the verification approach, then falsifiability of this rule premiss implies the existence of a fault in A or pre. For instance, consider the method useSqrt.

---

[1] c^* is the translation of the loop condition into a formula.

Falsifiable Rule Premiss	Type of the contract $pre_B \rightarrow (\!(B)\!) post_B$	Implication for the correctness of the software
1	required	fault exists in pre, A, or pre_B
1	auxiliary	pre_B is inappropriate
2	required	fault exists in pre_B, B, or $post_B$
2	auxiliary	pre_B or $post_B$ are inappropriate
3	required	unknown, if a fault exists
3	auxiliary	unknown, if a fault exists

Abbreviations

pre — precondition of the target program to be verified

A — code between the beginning of the target program and the method call or loop to be substituted by a contract

pre_B — precondition of the contract, i.e., pre_m or I

B — code of the method that is called or the loop that is executed

$post_B$ — postcondition of the contract, i.e., $post_m$ or $I \wedge c^*$

C — code that is executed after the method call or loop execution

$post$ — postcondition of the target program to be verified

Table 5.1. Interpretation of falsifiable premisses of contract rules

— JAVA + JML (5.3) ——————————————————————

```
1  /*@ ... requires x>=0; ...@*/
2  public int useSqrt(int x){
3    int y = x-1;
4    int z = sqrt(y);
5    ...
6  }
```

———————————————————————————— JAVA + JML —

In a verification attempt of the method **useSqrt**, where the contract of the method **sqrt** (see Chapter 3) is used, the first premiss of the method contract rule is falsifiable. This is because if $x \doteq 0$, then $y \doteq -1$ and the precondition of the method **sqrt** requires that the argument y is greater or equal to zero. It is arguable if the fault is in the code or in the specification of **useSqrt** because one could either change the line int y=x-1; or the precondition **requires x>=0;**.

Secondly, if the precondition pre_B is an auxiliary formula and the first rule premiss is falsifiable, then we regard the auxiliary formula as inappropriate. Hence, a different formula for pre_B has to be considered. For instance, when trying to verify the method **sqrtB** (Listing 5.2) with the loop invariant

$$(i - 1) * (i - 1) \leqslant x \tag{5.3}$$

instead of $(i-1)*(i-1) \leqslant x \vee x \doteq 0$, the first premiss of the loop invariant rule is falsifiable. This is because in the state before the execution of the loop, where $i \doteq 0$, the loop invariant evaluates to $(0-1)*(0-1) \leqslant x$ which is not a consequence of the precondition $x \geqslant 0$ of `sqrtB`.

If the first premiss of the contract rule is falsifiable, then the user has the options to change *pre*, *A*, or *pre_B*. For example, in order to prove the first premiss of the loop invariant rule when verifying the method `sqrtB`, one option is to use the loop invariant from Listing 5.1 or to use the loop invariant (5.3) and change the **requires** clause of the method `sqrtB` to, e.g. `x>0`.

A frequent question is also if *pre* and *pre_B* are consistent, i.e., if there is a state which satisfies both conditions. For this purpose the satisfiability of

$$(\bigwedge \Gamma \wedge \neg \bigvee \Delta) \wedge \mathcal{U} pre_B$$

can be checked with the method described in Chapter 6.

Rule Premiss 2

This premiss ensures that the contract of B, i.e., the called method or the loop, is correct. The method contract rule in KeY does not implement this premiss explicitly (see Section 2.4.6.1, page 63). Instead the correctness of a method contract is ensured in a separate proof (not a sub-proof) for which Algorithm 1 can be utilised, or it is justified by other means.

In case of the loop invariant rule the rule Premiss 2 ensures that I is an invariant of the loop and that it *supports* itself inductively, i.e., its satisfaction after the execution of the loop body follows from the assumption that it is satisfied before the execution of the loop body. Following the abbreviations of Table 5.1 the rule Premiss 2 expresses the property

$$pre \rightarrow [\![A]\!] (pre_B \rightarrow [\![B]\!] post_B) \tag{5.4}$$

We interpret the falsifiability of this branch in two ways depending on the verification approach.

If the contract, i.e. $(pre_B, post_B, \ldots)$, is regarded as a requirement specification, then falsifiability of this branch implies the existence of a software fault. The software fault is, however, not in the caller program

ABC but in the callee B. An example for this situation is a verification attempt of the following code.

```
── JAVA + JML ─────────────────────────────────────────
1  /*@ public normal_behavior
2        requires x>=0; ensures x>=0; diverges true @*/
3  public int useSqrt(int x){ return sqrtA(x); }
───────────────────────────────────────── JAVA + JML ──
```

In this example the method `sqrtA` is the callee, which does not satisfy its requirement specification. The contract of `sqrtA` is therefore useless for verification.

If the contract is regarded as an auxiliary and not as a requirement specification, then falsifiability of the second rule premiss means that an inappropriate contract was chosen.

In both cases, whether the contract is a requirement or auxiliary, our general software fault detection approach of Chapter 4 is applied recursively on the second premiss. Hence, a trace and a counterexample can be provided in order help the user understanding the problem. When using the loop invariant rule and the second rule premiss is falsifiable, then a frequent issue is to determine if the loop invariant is violated during the execution of the loop or if the loop invariant does not support itself. In order to disambiguate this problem a similar solution as proposed in [Claessen and Svensson, 2008] can be followed. In order to check if a loop invariant is violated during the execution of the loop, finite loop unwinding is used (see Sections 2.4.5.2 and 4.3.2) where at each iteration the loop invariant is checked. This technique can be simply integrated into the verification and fault detection process by extending the loop invariant rule with a premiss of the form:

$$\Gamma \Longrightarrow \mathcal{U}(I \wedge (c^* \to [\mathbf{b}](I \wedge (c^* \to [\mathbf{b}](\ldots (I \wedge (c^* \to [\mathbf{b}]I))\ldots))))), \Delta$$

The formula following the update $\mathcal{U}$ expresses that I has to hold in the initial state of the loop, subsuming Premiss 1, and I has to hold after each execution of the loop body $\mathbf{b}$ if the loop condition c is satisfied. The length of this formula has to be finite.

Rule Premiss 3

In this premiss the postcondition of the contract is a surrogate for the description of the state transition by the program B. The premiss expresses the following property.

$$pre \rightarrow \langle\!\langle A \rangle\!\rangle \mathcal{V}_M(post_B \rightarrow \langle\!\langle C \rangle\!\rangle post) \qquad (5.5)$$

The anonymising update $\mathcal{V}_M$ (see Figure 5.2, page 104) assigns un-specified values to the locations described by the modifier set M of B while preserving contextual information that stem from pre, A, and pre_B. The values of the location are then restricted by the postcondition $post_B$, i.e. $post_m$ or $I \wedge \neg c^*$. In these states the rest of the target program has to satisfy the postcondition of the target program. This is expressed by the sub-formula $\langle\!\langle C \rangle\!\rangle post$ respectively $[\pi\omega]post$ following the notation of the rules. If the first and the second premiss are valid, and the postcondition of the contract implies $\langle\!\langle C \rangle\!\rangle post$, then the target program satisfies its requirement specification.

If this rule premiss is falsifiable, then it is unclear what implication this has for the correctness of the target program. An example for this situation are the listings in Figure 5.1 (page 102). One possibility is that the target program is not correct (Listing 5.1). The other possibility is that the contract is just too weak to complete the proof. I.e., the target program may be correct, but a stronger contract has to be used to complete the proof (Listing 5.2)[2].

Conclusion.

The relevant question for the approach described in Chapter 4 is whether falsifiability of a contract rule premiss implies the falsifiability of the verification condition at the root of the proof tree. The latter we represented by Formula (5.1) on page 105. Our approach is to prove validity preservation along a proof branch. Whether the falsifiability of Premiss 1 or 2 is caused by a fault depends on whether pre_B and $post_B$ are required properties or auxiliary formulas (see Table 5.1).

If pre_B and $post_B$ are required properties and Premiss 1 or 2 has a counterexample, then validity preservation between Formula (5.1) and the premiss does not have to be computed because it is already known that a fault exists. The knowledge of the falsifiability of these premisses also allows a more precise localizations of the fault than the knowledge of the falsifiability of Formula (5.1) does.

If pre_B and $post_B$ are auxiliary formulas, then the user or an automatic method has to find formulas pre_B and $post_B$ and a modifier set M that satisfies Premiss 1 and 2. It is not the objective of this

---

[2] Note that the contract that we refer to in the example is given by the loop invariant, i.e. $(I, I \wedge \neg c^*, \{\langle \text{true}, i \rangle\}, partial)$.

chapter to generate specifications but rather to check validity preservation. Hence, in this case we assume the existence of other methods that provide correct and applicable specifications or that help to find faults in these situations.

Remark 5.1. Techniques for automatic generation of specifications in KeY are described, e.g., in [Weiß, 2009; Bubel et al., 2009]. In Section 7.6 we describe a specification mining technique based on bounded symbolic execution that was proposed in [Beckert and Gladisch, 2007] for the purpose of test case generation.

Premiss 3 is the only premiss which checks if the postcondition of the target program, which is the actual requirement to be checked in Formula (5.1) on page 105, is satisfied after the execution of the target program. Falsifiability of Premiss 3 has in contrast to Premisses 1 and 2 in both cases, i.e., whether the contract of B is auxiliary or required, an ambiguous meaning. The contract of B may be either too weak to complete the proof or the target program ABC may be incorrect. If the contract is auxiliary, then falsifiability of the premiss can be caused by a fault in any part of the program ABC. Fortunately, a special validity preservation condition can be constructed for the Premiss 3 which we describe in Section 5.5.2 and which allows to check validity preservation very efficiently.

5.3 Notations and Definitions

Quantified Updates.

For a concise notation we abbreviate parallel quantified updates of the form (see Def. 2.16 on page 34 and Sections 2.3.2.1 and 2.4.4)

$$\texttt{for } \bar{x}_1;\ \text{true};\ f_1(\bar{x}_1) := g_1(\bar{x}_1) \,||\, \ldots \,||\, \texttt{for } \bar{x}_1;\ \text{true};\ f_n(\bar{x}_n) := g_n(\bar{x}_n)$$
$$(5.6)$$

where $f_1, \ldots, f_n \in F \subset \text{FSym}_{nr}$, and $g_1, \ldots, g_n \in G \subset \text{FSym}$, by

$$F := G$$

The correspondence between function symbols $F \subset \text{FSym}_{nr}$ and function symbols $G \subset \text{FSym}$ will be clear from the context. The update overrides the interpretation of each function $f \in F$ by the corresponding function $g \in G$ for all argument values of the function f. Therefore an update of the form (5.6) is technically equivalent to the substitution $[f_1/g_1, \ldots, f_n/g_n]$. Substitutions can be used when implementing the technique described in Section 5.4.3 in other tools than KeY. We prefer to use updates because they can be combined with other updates leading to a uniform notation. Furthermore, using updates possibly allows us to generalize the approach where more general guards than true are used in (5.6).

Modifier Sets and Anonymising Updates.

Following the notation in Section 2.4.6.2, M represents a modifier set and $\mathcal{V}_M$ represents the corresponding anonymising update. If the elements of M are restricted to the form $\langle \text{true}, f(t_1, \ldots, t_n) \rangle$ with $f(t_1, \ldots, t_n) \in Terms$, then we use the notation

$$M := M_{sk}$$

to represent an anonymising update for the modifier set M. The update replaces each function symbol f of $\langle \text{true}, f(x) \rangle \in M$ by a fresh (Skolem) function symbol $f_{sk} \in M_{sk} \subset \text{FSym}_r$ of the same type.

Anonymous updates enable us to replace programs by abstractions. Consider the formula $a \leqslant b \to \langle \text{m()}; \rangle (c > 0 \to a < b + c)$. If it is known that the method m terminates and modifies only c, then the modal operator can be replaced by the anonymous update $\{c := c_{sk}\}$ resulting in the formula $a \leqslant b \to \{c := c_{sk}\}(c > 0 \to a < b + c)$. Update application then yields $a \leqslant b \to (c_{sk} > 0 \to a < b + c_{sk})$ which simplifies to true.

Occurrences of Sequents and Formulas in a Proof Tree.

A branch of a proof tree consists of sequents and is represented by the notation

$$S_0, \ldots, S_n$$

where S_0 is the root of the proof tree, S_n is the leaf of the branch and S_{i+1} is the premiss of a rule applied at S_i, with $i \in \mathbb{N}^0$. We use the notation S_i to refer either (a) to the unique occurrence of the sequent in the proof tree, (b) to the branch on which S_i occurs, or (c) to the formula that the sequent represents. The distinction between these cases will be made clear in the respective context, e.g., by writing "the branch S_i". A sequent S_i represents the formula $\bigwedge \Gamma_i \to \bigvee \Delta_i$ where Γ_i is the antecedent and Δ_i is the succedent of S_i. We use the notation $\bigwedge \Gamma_i$ and

$\bigvee \Delta_i$ also to represent the context formulas at the sequent S_i according to Definition 2.34 (page 46). The context formulas are defined by the rule application at the sequent S_i. The distinction will be made clear in the respective context.

Definition 5.2. *Definition of a contract rule premiss occurrence (PO). Given a branch $S_0, \ldots, S_n$ of a proof tree, let $S_i \in \{S_0, \ldots, S_n\}$ be an occurrence of a sequent on the branch on which a contract rule was applied. Then:*

- *$PO1_{S_i}$, $PO2_{S_i}$, and $PO3_{S_i}$ denote respectively the 1st, 2nd, and 3rd premiss of the contract rule application at the sequent S_i.*
- *$PO12_{S_i}$ is the union $PO1_{S_i} \cup PO2_{S_i}$.*

5.4 Techniques for Validity Preservation Analysis

Proving the validity preservation of a branch is a sub-problem of Algorithm 1. The algorithm tries to show the correctness of a program and in case of verification failure it tries to show program incorrectness and guides the user to find the problem. If a verification condition at the leaf of a proof tree branch is falsifiable, i.e., it has a counterexample, then we check if the branch is validity preserving (Def. 4.4, page 87). In Section 4.4.1 we have explained that contract rules are the critical rules that may destroy validity preservation of a branch. If validity preservation can be proved, then it is sound to conclude that the target program does not satisfy its specification. The user then knows that they could *not* have chosen a better loop invariant or method contract to succeed the verification attempt and instead they should fix the fault in the program or its specification.

Remark 5.3. Checking validity preservation of branches or of rules, which stem from a rule schema that is not validity preserving, is an undecidable problem. Hence, by the term "checking" that we use in the following sections we refer to a proof attempt of a property.

5.4.1 Systematic Analysis of Validity Preservation

A verification attempt of a program with multiple method calls and loops results in multiple applications of contract rules in a proof tree. In such a proof tree, contract rules are applied on subbranches on which contract rules have already been applied. Algorithm 2 is a simple algorithm which systematically checks (see Remark 5.3) validity preservation of a branch. This algorithm is used by Algorithm 1 (page 86).

Algorithm 2 checkValidityPreservation(B)

Require: All applied rules but the contract rules are known to be falsifiability preserving. B is a branch from a failed proof attempt.

1: let $(S_0, \ldots, S_n) = B$
2: **for** $i = n - 1$ to 0 **do**
3:      **if** $i = 0$ /*i.e., the root is reached */ **then**
4:          **return** (**true**, "If S_n has a counterexample, then a fault exists (on the symbolic execution trace of branch B).")
5:      **else if** a contract rule was applied at S_i **then**
6:          **if** $S_{i+1} \in PO12_{S_i}$ /*i.e., 1st or 2nd premiss of contract rule app*/ **then**
7:              **return** (**unknown**, The appropriate description from Table 5.1)
8:          **else if** S_{i+1} is $PO3_{S_i}$ /*i.e., 3rd premiss of contract rule app*/ **then**
9:              Try to prove validity preservation from S_n to S_i, i.e. $VP_{S_i}^{S_n}$
10:             **if** proof of $VP_{S_i}^{S_n}$ does not succeed **then**
11:                  **return** (**unknown**, "Contract at node (i) is too weak to deduce program incorrectness.")
12:          **end if**
13:      **end if**
14:      **end if**
15: **end for**

The input to Algorithm 2 is an open proof branch B that is provided by Algorithm 1 (Line 7). The output of Algorithm 2 is a tuple, where the first value of the tuple is **true** iff B is validity preserving and the second value of the tuple is a message for the user. The loop (Line 2) iterates from the leaf S_n of the branch B to the root S_0 of the proof tree. If Premiss 1 or 2 of a contract rule is encountered (Line 6), then the algorithm terminates with instructions for the user according to Table 5.1. The main part is the validity preservation analysis of Premiss 3 of a contract rule application in Line 9. In the following section different techniques are described for proving the validity preservation of this premiss. If validity preservation was proved at each contract rule application, then B is validity preserving according to Lemma 4.8 and the algorithm terminates in Line 4. If S_n is a falsifiable sequent, then S_0 is falsifiable and if S_0 has the form (5.1) then the target program is incorrect. Otherwise, if proving $\models VP^{S_n}$ fails, then the algorithm may return further information for the user to proceed.

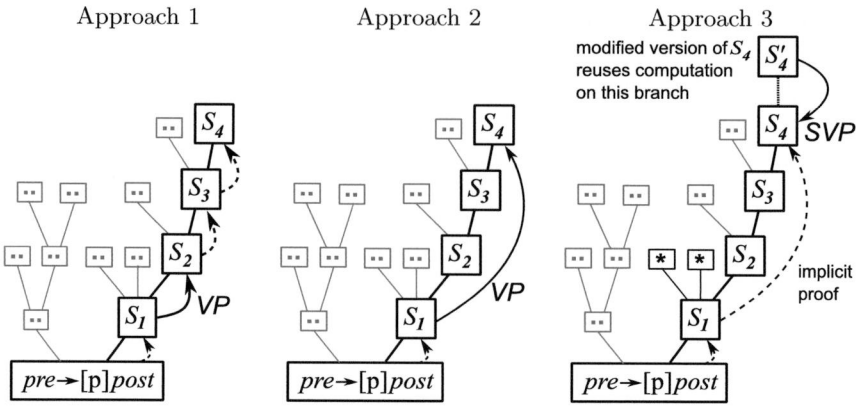

Fig. 5.3. Three approaches for proving the validity preservation of branch S_4; A contract rule was applied at S_1.

5.4.2 Three Approaches for Validity Preservation Analysis

In this section we describe three approaches for validity preservation checking[3], where the second approach is an improvement of the first approach and the third approach is an improvement of the second approach. The first two approaches are applicable for checking the validity preservation of any proof branch while the third is applicable only for branches constructed from the third premiss of a contract rule. In this section we use the abbreviations from Table 5.1 (page 106).

Figure 5.3 illustrates the three approaches. The proof tree represents the proof tree of the verification attempt of the target program. The branch S_n represents an open proof branch. The solid arrows represent the implications of the validity preservation conditions that have to be proven and the dashed arrows represent validity preservation requirements that are established implicitly by Algorithm 2. The approaches are described in the following sections.

Preparing an Example.

For the explanation of the approaches and for explaining why the second and third approach are improvements of their predecessors we use an example that is described in the following. Let the sequent S_i which is defined as

---
[3] see Remark 5.3

$$\underbrace{x' \doteq x, y \geqslant 0}_{pre} \Longrightarrow \underbrace{\langle \texttt{x=x+y;} \rangle}_{ABC} \underbrace{x > x'}_{post} \qquad (5.7)$$

be the current sequent at which a contract rule is applied. The program variables $x', y \in \text{FSym}_r$ and $x \in \text{FSym}_{nr}$ are of type int. The contract rules discussed so far (see Table 5.2, page 104) are applicable only to a method call or a loop, respectively. In order to keep the examples small we omit the introduction of a method $\texttt{m()\{x=x+y;\}}$ and an object to which the method and program variables belong. Instead we introduce the following contract rule which follows the same principles as the rules in Table 5.2.

$$\frac{\begin{array}{l} pre \Rightarrow \mathcal{U}pre_B \\ pre \Rightarrow \mathcal{U}(pre_B \rightarrow \langle \texttt{B} \rangle post_B) \\ pre \Rightarrow \mathcal{U}\mathcal{V}(post_B \rightarrow \langle \texttt{C} \rangle post) \end{array}}{pre \Rightarrow \mathcal{U}\langle \texttt{BC} \rangle post} \qquad (5.8)$$

Note that the contract is applied after the program part A has been symbolically executed. Hence, $\mathcal{U}$ represents the state-change performed by A and A does not occur in the rule.

In the sequent (5.7) the update $\mathcal{U}$ and the program parts A and C are empty. The program B consists of the statement $\texttt{x=x+y;}$ for which we choose the contract

$$(\underbrace{x' \doteq x,}_{pre_B} \underbrace{y > 0 \vee x \doteq x'}_{post_B}, \underbrace{\{\langle \text{true}, x \rangle\}}_{M}, total) \qquad (5.9)$$

Application of the contract rule (5.8) on the sequent (5.7) with the contract (5.9) yields the following three sequents.

$$\overbrace{x' \doteq x, y \geqslant 0}^{pre} \Longrightarrow \overbrace{x' \doteq x}^{\mathcal{U}pre_B} \qquad\qquad PO1_{S_i}$$

$$x' \doteq x, y \geqslant 0 \Longrightarrow (\overbrace{x' \doteq x}^{pre_B} \rightarrow \overbrace{\langle \texttt{x=x+y;} \rangle}^{B} \overbrace{(y > 0 \vee x \doteq x')}^{post_B}) \quad PO2_{S_i}$$

$$x' \doteq x, y \geqslant 0 \Longrightarrow \overbrace{\{x := x_{sk}\}}^{\mathcal{U}\mathcal{V}M} (\overbrace{(y > 0 \vee x \doteq x')}^{post_B} \rightarrow \overbrace{x > x'}^{\langle \texttt{C} \rangle post}) \; PO3_{S_i} = S_{i+1}$$

The sequents $PO1_{S_i}$ and $PO2_{S_i}$ (see Def. 5.2, page 112) can be proven. A proof attempt of $PO3_{S_i}$ fails, however, with the open proof branches[4] S_n^1 and S_n^2 (see Figure 5.4). A counterexample for S_n^1 is, e.g., $\mathcal{I}(x') =$

---

[4] Note that the notation S_i also identifies branches in a proof tree (see Section 5.3).

$$
\overbrace{\begin{array}{c}
\cfrac{}{x' \doteq x, y > 0 \Rightarrow x_{sk} > x}
\end{array}}^{S_n^1}
\qquad
\overbrace{\begin{array}{c}
x' \doteq x, y \doteq 0, x_{sk} \doteq x \Rightarrow x_{sk} > x \\
\dots, y \geqslant 0, x_{sk} \doteq x \Rightarrow y > 0, \dots
\end{array}}^{S_n^2}
$$

$$
\cfrac{\cfrac{\cfrac{\cfrac{\cfrac{\vdots \qquad\qquad\qquad\qquad\qquad \vdots}{\dots, y > 0, y > 0 \vee x_{sk} \doteq x \Rightarrow \dots \qquad \dots, \neg y > 0 \Rightarrow \dots}\;\text{cut}}{x' \doteq x, y \geqslant 0, y > 0 \vee x_{sk} \doteq x \Rightarrow x_{sk} > x}}{x' \doteq x, y \geqslant 0 \Rightarrow (y > 0 \vee x_{sk} \doteq x) \to x_{sk} > x}}{x' \doteq x, y \geqslant 0 \Rightarrow (y > 0 \vee x_{sk} \doteq x') \to x_{sk} > x'}}{x' \doteq x, y \geqslant 0 \Rightarrow \{x := x_{sk}\}((y > 0 \vee x \doteq x') \to x > x') \quad : S_{i+1}}
$$

$$
S_i = (5.7)
$$

with $* \; *$ *and* $\vdots \; \vdots$ at left.

Fig. 5.4. Failed proof attempt of the verification condition S_i

$\mathcal{I}(x) = \mathcal{I}(x_{sk}) = \mathcal{I}(y) = 1$, and for S_n^2, e.g., $\mathcal{I}(x') = \mathcal{I}(x) = \mathcal{I}(x_{sk}) = \mathcal{I}(y) = 0$.

Both branches are provided as input to Algorithm 2 at a time, in order to check their validity preservation. In the following we look at the three approaches to check the validity preservation in Line 9 of the algorithm.

Approach 1: Checking the Validity Preservation of a Rule Premiss

Algorithm 2 iterates through the sequents S_i of a branch and ensures $\vDash VP_{S_i}^{S_n}$ (see Def. 4.4) from the leaf S_n to the root S_0. If $\vDash VP_{S_{i+1}}^{S_n}$ is ensured in iteration $n - i$, then in order to ensure $\vDash VP_{S_i}^{S_n}$ in the next iteration it is sufficient to ensure that $\vDash VP_{S_i}^{S_{i+1}}$ holds. This follows from Lemma 4.8 (see Section 4.4.1) which states that if the sequents of a proof tree branch B are validity preserving rule premisses, then B is validity preserving. Hence, it is sufficient to check for each rule premiss on a branch that it is a validity preserving rule premiss in order to ensure the validity preservation of the branch (see Approach 1 of Figure 5.3, page 114).

This approach is to prove in Line 9 of Algorithm 2 (page 113) the formula $VP_{S_i}^{S_{i+1}}$, i.e.,

$$
S_i \to S_{i+1} \tag{5.10}
$$

This is also the approach that we have followed in Section 4.4.1 (page 92) in order to show that the rules of KeY's calculus are validity preserving except for the contract rules. Applying this technique

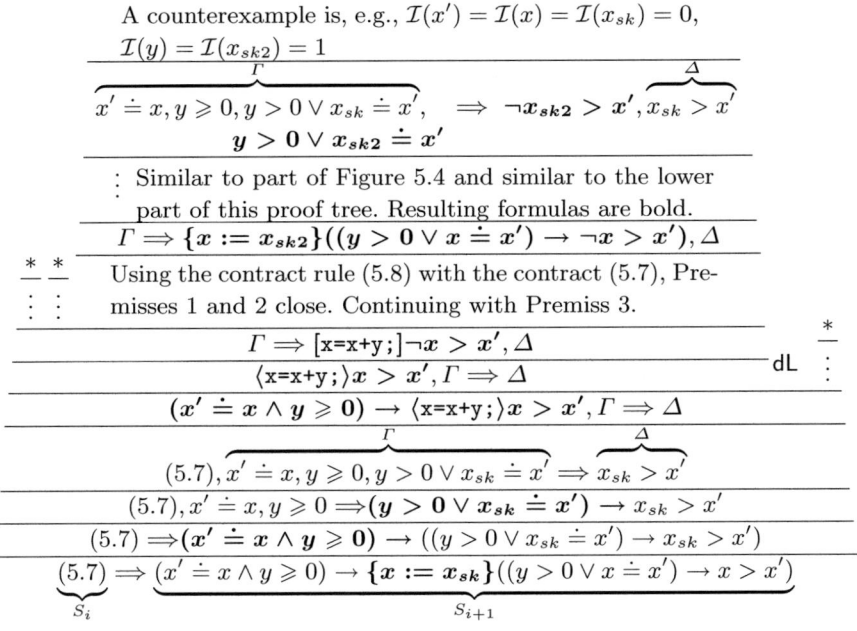

A counterexample is, e.g., $\mathcal{I}(x') = \mathcal{I}(x) = \mathcal{I}(x_{sk}) = 0$, $\mathcal{I}(y) = \mathcal{I}(x_{sk2}) = 1$

$$\overbrace{x' \doteq x, y \geqslant 0, y > 0 \vee x_{sk} \doteq x',}^{\Gamma} \quad \Longrightarrow \quad \neg x_{sk2} > x', \overbrace{x_{sk} > x'}^{\Delta}$$
$$y > 0 \vee x_{sk2} \doteq x'$$

$\vdots$ Similar to part of Figure 5.4 and similar to the lower
part of this proof tree. Resulting formulas are bold.

$$\Gamma \Longrightarrow \{x := x_{sk2}\}((y > 0 \vee x \doteq x') \rightarrow \neg x > x'), \Delta$$

$$\frac{*}{\vdots} \quad \frac{*}{\vdots}$$ Using the contract rule (5.8) with the contract (5.7), Premisses 1 and 2 close. Continuing with Premiss 3.

$$\frac{\Gamma \Longrightarrow [\text{x=x+y;}]\neg x > x', \Delta}{\langle \text{x=x+y;} \rangle x > x', \Gamma \Longrightarrow \Delta} \quad \mathsf{dL} \quad \frac{*}{\vdots}$$
$$\frac{}{(x' \doteq x \wedge y \geqslant 0) \rightarrow \langle \text{x=x+y;} \rangle x > x', \Gamma \Longrightarrow \Delta}$$

$$\frac{\overbrace{(5.7), x' \doteq x, y \geqslant 0, y > 0 \vee x_{sk} \doteq x'}^{\Gamma} \Longrightarrow \overbrace{x_{sk} > x'}^{\Delta}}{}$$
$$\frac{(5.7), x' \doteq x, y \geqslant 0 \Longrightarrow (y > 0 \vee x_{sk} \doteq x') \rightarrow x_{sk} > x'}{}$$
$$\frac{(5.7) \Longrightarrow (x' \doteq x \wedge y \geqslant 0) \rightarrow ((y > 0 \vee x_{sk} \doteq x') \rightarrow x_{sk} > x')}{\underbrace{(5.7)}_{S_i} \Longrightarrow \underbrace{(x' \doteq x \wedge y \geqslant 0) \rightarrow \{x := x_{sk}\}((y > 0 \vee x \doteq x') \rightarrow x > x')}_{S_{i+1}}}$$

Fig. 5.5. Failed proof attempt of the validity preservation of the third premiss of a contract rule application (Approach 1); dL abbreviates the rule schema diamondLeft shown in Table 2.6.

to the proof branches S_n^1 and S_n^2 of the proof tree in Figure 5.4 reveals, however, a limitation of this technique. The validity preservation condition $VP_{S_i}^{S_{i+1}}$ is not valid and yields the open proof tree shown in Figure 5.5. The reason why validity preservation does not hold in this case is disclosed along the description of Approach 2.

Approach 2: Checking the Validity Preservation of a Sequence of Sequents

The validity preservation condition $VP_{S_i}^{S_{i+1}}$ that was used in the first approach is a general condition of a rule premiss. In this approach (see Approach 2 of Figure 5.3) the formula $VP_{S_i}^{S_n}$ which is

$$S_i \rightarrow S_n \tag{5.11}$$

is proven. The formula is proven *explicitly* rather than implicitly as it is the case in the first approach where the induction principle of Lemma 4.8 (page 92) is used. The advantage is that $VP_{S_i}^{S_n}$ is a weaker condition than $VP_{S_i}^{S_{i+1}}$, i.e. $VP_{S_i}^{S_n}$ implies $VP_{S_i}^{S_{i+1}}$, and it is sufficient to prove $VP_{S_i}^{S_n}$ in Algorithm 2.

An intuitive explanation of the two approaches is the following. Formula (5.10) can be rewritten as

$$\neg S_{i+1} \rightarrow \neg S_i \tag{5.12}$$

This formula can be read as: every counterexample of S_{i+1} is also a counterexample for S_i. The formula S_{i+1} is, however, not simplified and it may have counterexamples resulting from many case distinctions. Proving $\neg S_i$ for all those counterexamples of $\neg S_{i+1}$ is, however, not required because it is sufficient if the implication (5.12) holds only for counterexamples of one branch leaf, i.e., S_n^1 or S_n^2 in Figure 5.5. This weaker property is expressed by Formula (5.11) as it can be rewritten to the equivalent formula

$$\neg S_n \rightarrow \neg S_i$$

Figures 5.6 and 5.7 illustrate the problem of the first approach and the advantage of the second approach. Figure 5.6 shows the failed proof attempt of the validity preservation condition $VP_{S_i}^{S_n^1}$ which is not valid. This condition considers counterexamples of S_n^1 which are not necessarily counterexamples of S_i. In contrast, Figure 5.7 shows a successful proof of the validity preservation condition $VP_{S_i}^{S_n^2}$. Hence, the counterexamples of S_n^2 are also counterexamples of S_i. Approach 1 could not succeed because it *tried* to proof validity preservation for both cases. As it is sufficient to prove the validity preservation of one branch Approach 2 is superior to Approach 1.

The condition $VP_{S_i}^{S_n}$ expresses that all counterexamples of S_n are counterexamples of S_i. It seams that an even weaker condition is to show that for a single counterexample X represented as a formula it holds that $\models X \rightarrow \neg S_i$. However, as mentioned in Section 4.3.2 (page 89), the leaves of a proof tree in KeY already represent counterexamples, or models of the negated sequent, if they are falsifiable (see [Rümmer, 2007]). Therefore, if the proof tree is expanded sufficiently, then $\models \neg S_n \rightarrow \neg S_i$ is equivalent to $\models X \rightarrow \neg S_i$.

Remark 5.4. Validity preservation of the third contract rule premiss checks the strength property of the contract. For instance, when using the contract

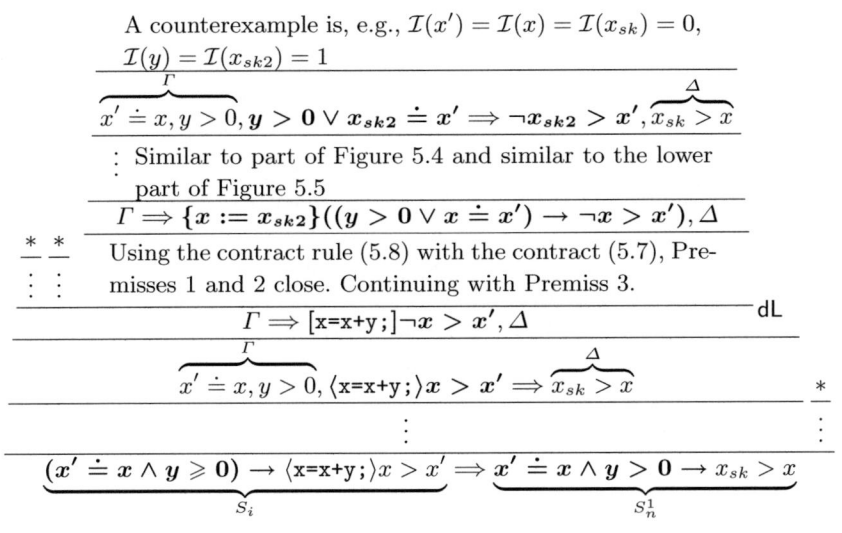

A counterexample is, e.g., $\mathcal{I}(x') = \mathcal{I}(x) = \mathcal{I}(x_{sk}) = 0$, $\mathcal{I}(y) = \mathcal{I}(x_{sk2}) = 1$

$$\overbrace{}^{\Gamma}$$
$$x' \doteq x, y > 0, y > 0 \vee x_{sk2} \doteq x' \Longrightarrow \overbrace{\neg x_{sk2} > x', x_{sk} > x}^{\Delta}$$

⋮ Similar to part of Figure 5.4 and similar to the lower part of Figure 5.5

$$\Gamma \Longrightarrow \{x := x_{sk2}\}((y > 0 \vee x \doteq x') \rightarrow \neg x > x'), \Delta$$

Using the contract rule (5.8) with the contract (5.7), Premisses 1 and 2 close. Continuing with Premiss 3.

$$\Gamma \Longrightarrow [\mathtt{x=x+y;}]\neg x > x', \Delta$$ — dL

$$\overbrace{}^{\Gamma}$$
$$x' \doteq x, y > 0, \langle \mathtt{x=x+y;}\rangle x > x' \Longrightarrow \overbrace{x_{sk} > x}^{\Delta}$$

⋮

$$\underbrace{(x' \doteq x \wedge y \geqslant 0) \rightarrow \langle \mathtt{x=x+y;}\rangle x > x'}_{S_i} \Longrightarrow \underbrace{x' \doteq x \wedge y > 0 \rightarrow x_{sk} > x}_{S_n^1}$$

Fig. 5.6. Failed proof attempt of the validity preservation of the branch S_n^1 (Approach 2); dL abbreviates the rule schema diamondLeft shown in Table 2.6.

$$(x' \doteq x, x \doteq x' + y, \{\langle \mathrm{true}, x\rangle\}, \mathit{total}\ )$$

then validity preservation can be proved for any open proof branch with Approach 1 and 2.

Remark 5.5. The Approaches 1 and 2 can be applied to check the validity preservation of any rule premiss or branch independently of what rules were applied.

Approach 3: Towards a Special Validity Preservation Condition

In Section 5.2 we have argued that it is especially important to check the validity preservation of branches which are extensions of the third premiss of a contract rule. Approach 2 can be further improved for this particular case resulting in the third approach. In the third approach the validity preservation condition $VP_{S_i}^{S_n}$ is replaced by the special validity preservation condition $SVP_{S_i}^{S_n}$ in Line 9 of Algorithm 2. Similarly as in Approach 2, the special validity preservation condition expresses the validity preservation condition of a branch it improves the performance of proving the condition.

The problem of the condition $VP_{S_i}^{S_n}$ is the occurrence of the sequent S_i in the condition (see the Figures 5.5, 5.6, and 5.7). When proving the

$$\frac{\ast}{\dots, \text{false} \Rightarrow \dots} \qquad \frac{\ast}{\Gamma, x_{sk2} \doteq x' \Rightarrow \text{true}, \Delta}$$

$$\frac{\overbrace{\dots, y \doteq 0, y > 0 \Rightarrow \dots}^{\Gamma} \quad \frac{\Gamma, x_{sk2} \doteq x' \Rightarrow \neg x' > x', \Delta}{\Gamma, \boldsymbol{x_{sk2}} \doteq \boldsymbol{x'} \Rightarrow \neg \boldsymbol{x_{sk2}} > x', \Delta}}{\Gamma, \boldsymbol{y} > \boldsymbol{0} \vee \boldsymbol{x_{sk2}} \doteq \boldsymbol{x'} \Rightarrow \neg x_{sk2} > x', \Delta}$$

$$\begin{array}{l} \vdots \quad \text{Similar to part of Figure 5.4 and similar to the lower} \\ \quad \text{part of Figure 5.5} \end{array}$$

$$\frac{}{\Gamma \Rightarrow \{x := \boldsymbol{x_{sk2}}\}((\boldsymbol{y} > \boldsymbol{0} \vee \boldsymbol{x} \doteq \boldsymbol{x'}) \to \neg \boldsymbol{x} > \boldsymbol{x'}), \Delta}$$

$$\frac{\ast}{\vdots} \quad \frac{\ast}{\vdots} \quad \begin{array}{l} \text{Using the contract rule (5.8) with the contract (5.7), Pre-} \\ \text{misses 1 and 2 close. Continuing with Premiss 3.} \end{array}$$

$$\frac{}{\Gamma \Rightarrow [\text{x=x+y;}]\neg \boldsymbol{x} > \boldsymbol{x'}, \Delta} \quad \text{dL}$$

$$\frac{}{\overbrace{x' \doteq x, y \doteq 0, x_{sk} \doteq x}^{\Gamma}, \langle \text{x=x+y;}\rangle \boldsymbol{x} > \boldsymbol{x'} \Rightarrow \overbrace{y > 0}^{\Delta}, x_{sk} > x} \quad \ast$$

$$\vdots \qquad \qquad \qquad \vdots$$

$$\underbrace{(\boldsymbol{x'} \doteq \boldsymbol{x} \wedge \boldsymbol{y} \geqslant \boldsymbol{0}) \to \langle \text{x=x+y;}\rangle \boldsymbol{x} > \boldsymbol{x'}}_{S_i} \Rightarrow \underbrace{(x' \doteq x \wedge y \doteq 0 \wedge x_{sk} \doteq x) \to (x_{sk} > x)}_{S_n^2}$$

Fig. 5.7. Successful proof attempt of the validity preservation of the branch S_n^2 (Approach 2); dL abbreviates the rule schema diamondLeft shown in Table 2.6.

condition $VP_{S_i}^{S_n}$, then all the rule applications that were necessary for deriving the sequent S_n from the sequent S_i may have to be repeated. This includes the contract rule that was applied at S_i, the symbolic execution of the program part C, i.e., the program part following the program abstraction, and first-order reasoning with arithmetics.

The idea behind the special validity preservation condition is to *somehow* reuse information that was computed on the branch S_n and to construct $SVP_{S_i}^{S_n}$ without an explicit occurrence of S_i. Common to the proof trees of Figures 5.5, 5.6, and 5.7 is that the contract rule is used with the contract (5.7) and then a sequence of rule applications follows that is "similar to part of Figure 5.4 and similar to the lower part of Figure 5.5". These proof steps repeat computation that was done during the verification attempt. Regarding the leaf of the open branches in Figures 5.5 and 5.6, as well as the 5th sequent[5] of Figure 5.7, one can see that these proof steps result in the sub-sequent, i.e. subsets of the antecedent and succedent,

$$\dots, y > 0 \vee x_{sk2} \doteq x' \Rightarrow \neg x_{sk2} > x', \dots \qquad (5.13)$$

---

[5] counting from the root of the proof tree

which is derived from the formula

$$\{x := x_{sk2}\}((y > 0 \vee x \doteq x') \rightarrow \neg x > x') \qquad (5.14)$$

This sub-sequent is *in a way* similar to the sub-sequent

$$\dots, y > 0 \vee x_{sk} \doteq x' \Longrightarrow x_{sk} > x', \dots \qquad (5.15)$$

occurring in S_n^2 of the verification attempt (see Figure 5.4, page 116). Formula 5.15 is derived from the formula

$$\{x := x_{sk2}\}((y > 0 \vee x \doteq x') \rightarrow x > x') \qquad (5.16)$$

that occurs in S_{i+1} of the verification attempt. In order to omit the repetition of rule applications the idea is to construct Formula (5.13) from Formula (5.15). Seemingly, the Skolem functions, e.g. x_{sk}, have to be replaced by new Skolem functions, e.g. x_{sk2}. A problem is, however, that the respective sub-formula $x_{sk} > x'$ in (5.15), which stems from the postcondition, occurs negated in (5.13). In general case this formula cannot be syntactically determined in S_n, because it may be replaced by combinations with other formulas. The reason for this negation is that in $VP_{S_i}^{S_n}$, i.e. $S_i \rightarrow S_n$, the sequent S_i occurs negated w.r.t. S_n because $(S_i \rightarrow S_n) \equiv (\neg S_i \vee S_n)$. How to reuse information from a proof attempt of S_i for $\neg S_i$ is a non-trivial question. Checking the condition $S_n \rightarrow S_n$ obviously does not make sense. The solution to this problem is presented in the following section.

5.4.3 Special Validity Preservation Condition

5.4.3.1 The Approach

This section describes our main contribution of this chapter. We check with a special validity preservation condition whether contracts that are used in contract rule applications on a given branch are strong enough to reveal a software fault. A *conventional* proof of the formula $VP_{S_i}^{S_n}$, i.e. $S_i \rightarrow S_n$, that ensures validity preservation of branch S_n, would require a transformation of the program in S_i into a first-order logic formula requiring, e.g., symbolic execution. Instead, we regard the (sub) branch $S_i, \dots, S_n$ that is created by the verification attempt as a *test run* of the target program with symbolic values and we reuse information contained in this branch to prove its validity preservation.

In this way verification and software fault detection are truly unified in one computation. This is achieved by replacing in Line 9 of Algorithm 2 (page 113) the formula $VP_{S_i}^{S_n}$ with the more sophisticated formula $SVP_{S_i}^{S_n}$ that is defined next. This section makes extensive use of abbreviations described in Section 5.3 (page 110).

Definition 5.6. *Let $(S_0, \ldots, S_n) = B$ be a branch and S_i with $0 \leqslant i < n$ be a sequent that has either the form (case 1):*

$$\Gamma_i \Longrightarrow \mathcal{U}\langle \pi p \omega \rangle \varphi, \Delta_i$$

or the form (case 2):

$$\Gamma_i \Longrightarrow \mathcal{U}[\pi p \omega] \varphi, \Delta_i$$

and on S_i a contract rule is applied with the contract $(pre_p, post_p, M, total)$ in case 1 and $(pre_p, post_p, M, partial)$ in case 2 (see Table 5.2, page 104). Let $M \supseteq Mod(p)$ (see Def. 2.50, page 66). S_{i+1} is the 3rd branch of the contract rule, i.e. $S_{i+1} = PO3_{S_i}$. Let $M^1 \subset \mathrm{FSym}_{nr}$ denote the new Skolem functions that are introduced in the anonymising update at S_{i+1} for the modified locations M. Let $M^2 \subset \mathrm{FSym}_{nr}$ denote new Skolem functions for the modified locations M.

The special validity preservation condition $SVP_{S_i}^{S_n}$ is the conjunction of

$$((\{M^1 := M^2\} S_n) \wedge \mathcal{U}\{M := M^2\} post_p) \to S_n \qquad (5.17)$$

$$\neg S_n \to \mathcal{U}\langle \pi p \omega \rangle true \quad \text{(only in case 2)} \qquad (5.18)$$

Theorem 5.7. *Assuming that R is the contract rule applied at S_i with $0 \leqslant i < n$; the 1st and 2nd premisses of R are proven; and $\vDash VP_{S_{i+1}}^{S_n}$ holds, then*

$$\vDash SVP_{S_i}^{S_n} \text{ implies } \vDash VP_{S_i}^{S_n}$$

Theorem 5.7 is the key for using the formula SVP to prove the validity preservation of a branch that contains occurrences of the third premiss of contract rules. The implication of the theorem is that the formula $SVP_{S_i}^{S_n}$, or even just Formula (5.17) as described below, can replace the formula $VP_{S_i}^{S_n}$, i.e. $S_i \to S_n$, in Line 9 of Algorithm 2. In contrast to $VP_{S_i}^{S_n}$, the formula $SVP_{S_i}^{S_n}$ contains no program parts, or it contains only program parts that have not yet been symbolically executed on the branch with the leaf S_n. This is achieved because $SVP_{S_i}^{S_n}$ has no occurrence of $\langle \pi \omega \rangle \varphi$ containing the rest of the program following

p. Since $SVP_{S_i}^{S_n}$ is mainly built from formulas occurring in S_n, all the symbolic execution and first-order logic reasoning that took place up to S_n (by a verification attempt) is *reused*. These properties of $SVP_{S_i}^{S_n}$ support the idea of unified verification and software fault detection. This approach is depicted as Approach 3 in Figure 5.3 (page 114) with $n = 4$.

The main sub-formula of $SVP_{S_i}^{S_n}$ is (5.17). This formula extends the leaf S_n of a branch B with the conjunction $((\{M^1 := M^2\}S_n) \wedge \mathcal{U}\{M := M^2\}post_p)$ that is mainly built from an updated version of S_n and the postcondition from the contract rule applied at S_i. In Figure 5.3 this formula is represented by S_4'. Intuitively speaking, the two updates create copies of the result of the computation that was performed on B such that the conjunction replaces in $VP_{S_i}^{S_n}$ the sequent S_i.

Example. We construct the special validity preservation condition based on the verification attempt shown in Figure 5.4 (page 116). Similarly as in the case of Approach 2, a proof of validity preservation using SVP succeeds for the branch S_n^2 but not for the branch S_n^1. From the branch S_n^2 we get

$$\{M^1 := M^2\}S_n^2 = \{x_{sk} := x_{sk2}\}((x' \doteq x \wedge y \doteq 0 \wedge x_{sk} \doteq x) \rightarrow x_{sk} > x)$$
$$= (x' \doteq x \wedge y \doteq 0 \wedge x_{sk2} \doteq x) \rightarrow x_{sk2} > x$$

where $x_{sk2} \in \mathrm{FSym}_{nr}$ is a new symbol of type *int* and

$$\mathcal{U}\{M := M^2\}post_p = \{x := x_{sk2}\}(y > 0 \vee x \doteq x')$$
$$= y > 0 \vee x_{sk2} \doteq x'$$

Hence, the special validity preservation condition $SVP_{S_i}^{S_n^2}$ is given by

$$((x' \doteq x \wedge y \doteq 0 \wedge x_{sk2} \doteq x) \rightarrow x_{sk2} > x) \wedge (y > 0 \vee x_{sk2} \doteq x')$$
$$\Longrightarrow$$
$$(x' \doteq x \wedge y \doteq 0 \wedge x_{sk} \doteq x) \rightarrow x_{sk} > x$$

and is proven in Figure 5.8. As one can see the contract rule applications and the repetitive parts in the proof trees of Figures 5.5, 5.6, and 5.7 do not exist in the proof tree of Figure 5.8. The reason is that the information that was obtained through similar proof steps in the verification attempt has been reused by the construction of $SVP_{S_i}^{S_n^2}$.

$\square$

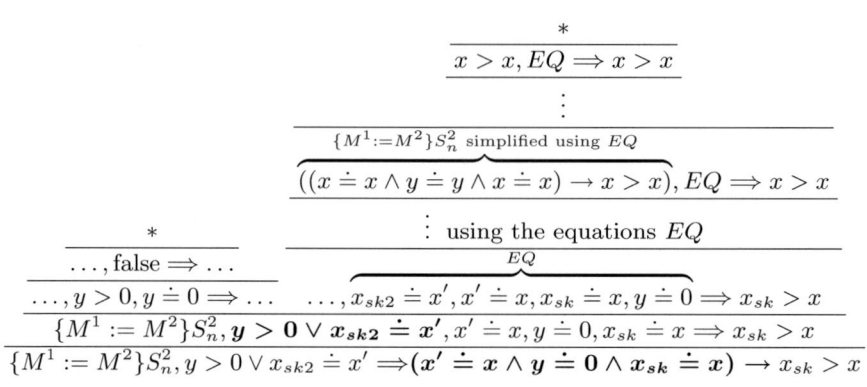

Fig. 5.8. Proof of the special validity preservation condition for branch S_n^2 (Approach 3)

Formula (5.18) in Definition 5.6 ensures that in case of a verification attempt for showing partial correctness of a program *non-terminating* programs are recognized as *correct* programs (see Lemma 2.26, page 42). In practice, however, even if a partial correctness proof is created non-terminating programs are regarded usually as incorrect. Partial correctness proofs are often created for simplicity, i.e., to omit proving of program termination. By ignoring the formula, non-terminating programs in partial correctness proofs are regarded as incorrect which is not sound but usually a welcome behavior. Formula (5.18) can therefore be regarded as optional.

We regard the requirement that the 1st and 2nd branch of the respective contract rule application, i.e. *PO12$_S$*, must be closed, as a minor problem. This is because trying to close these branches is part of the verification process in Algorithm 1 so that no additional work is done for software fault detection. If the branches *PO12$_S$* are not proven, then Algorithm 2 provides hints for the user on how to proceed. The second requirement, i.e. $\vDash VP_{S_{i+1}}^{S_n}$, is ensured by an induction principle of the loop in the algorithm: as the loop iterates the program variable i is decreased and the validity of $VP_{S_{n-1}}^{S_n}, VP_{S_{n-2}}^{S_n}, \ldots, VP_{S_{i+1}}^{S_n}$ is ensured.

5.4.3.2 Soundness Proof

In this section we prove the correctness of Theorem 5.7. Before proceeding to the proof some lemmas are prepared for the proof.

Lemmas

Lemma 5.8. *Let $F, G, H \in$ Formulae. The following statement holds*

$$\vDash F \to G \ \text{ implies } (\vDash G \to H \ \text{ implies } \vDash F \to H) \qquad (5.19)$$

Proof. The statement 5.19 can is equivalent to the statement

$$(\vDash F \to G \text{ and } \vDash G \to H) \text{ implies } \vDash F \to H \qquad (5.20)$$

which expresses the transitivity of implication which is a propositional fact.

∎

Lemma 5.9. *Let $F, G, H \in$ Formulae. The following statement holds*

$$\vDash F \to G \ \text{ implies } \ \vDash (F \wedge H) \to (G \wedge H) \qquad (5.21)$$

Proof. We consider two cases. If $H \equiv$ true (case 1), then statement 5.21 simplifies to

$$\vDash F \to G \text{ implies } \vDash F \to G \qquad (5.22)$$

which is true. Otherwise, if $H \equiv$ false (case 2), then statement 5.21 simplifies to

$$\vDash F \to G \text{ implies true} \qquad (5.23)$$

which is true as well.

∎

Lemma 5.10. *Following the notation of Definition 5.6, if $\vDash VP^{S_n}_{S_{i+1}}$, then the following formula is valid.*

$$\neg S_n \to (\bigwedge \Gamma_i \wedge \neg \bigvee \Delta_i) \qquad (5.24)$$

Note that Γ_i and Δ_i are the context formulas of S_i (see Table 5.2 on page 104).

Proof. According to Table 5.2, $\Gamma_i = \Gamma_{i+1}$, $\Delta_i = \Delta_{i+1}$, and

$$S_{i+1} \equiv (\bigwedge \Gamma_{i+1} \to (\phi \vee \bigvee \Delta_{i+1})) \qquad (5.25)$$

where $\phi \in$ Formulae.

Starting with the assumption $\vDash VP^{S_n}_{S_{i+1}}$ the validity of Formula (5.24) is derived.

$$S_{i+1} \rightarrow S_n \qquad\qquad \text{Assumption} \models VP_{S_{i+1}}^{S_n}$$
$$\neg S_n \rightarrow \neg S_{i+1} \qquad\qquad \text{Contraposition}$$
$$\neg S_n \rightarrow \neg(\textstyle\bigwedge\Gamma_{i+1} \rightarrow (\phi \vee \textstyle\bigvee\Delta_{i+1})) \qquad\qquad \text{Formula (5.25)}$$
$$\neg S_n \rightarrow (\textstyle\bigwedge\Gamma_{i+1} \wedge \neg(\phi \vee \textstyle\bigvee\Delta_{i+1})) \qquad\qquad \text{Negation of an implication}$$
$$\neg S_n \rightarrow (\textstyle\bigwedge\Gamma_{i+1} \wedge \phi \wedge \neg \textstyle\bigvee\Delta_{i+1}) \qquad\qquad \text{Negation of a disjunction}$$
$$\neg S_n \rightarrow (\textstyle\bigwedge\Gamma_{i+1} \wedge \neg \textstyle\bigvee\Delta_{i+1}) \qquad\qquad \text{Weakening}$$
$$\neg S_n \rightarrow (\textstyle\bigwedge\Gamma_i \wedge \neg \textstyle\bigvee\Delta_i) \qquad\qquad \Gamma_i = \Gamma_{i+1},\ \Delta_i = \Delta_{i+1},\ \text{(Table 5.2)}$$

■

Proof of Theorem 5.7

In this proof the formula $SVP_{S_i}^{S_n}$ (see Def. 5.6) is constructed from a formula that is equivalent to $VP_{S_i}^{S_n}$ while making use of the assumptions in Theorem 5.7. The construction of $SVP_{S_i}^{S_n}$ ensures that $SVP_{S_i}^{S_n}$ implies $VP_{S_i}^{S_n}$. The proof is divided into two parts. In the first part we use a contract rule in order to derive conditions from $VP_{S_i}^{S_n}$. In the second part an alternative formula for the main condition is constructed.

Part I By Definition 4.4, $VP_{S_i}^{S_n}$ is equivalent to $S_i \rightarrow S_n$ which is equivalent to

$$\neg S_n \rightarrow \neg S_i \qquad\qquad (5.26)$$

The assumption of the theorem, that the rule R that is applied at S_i with $0 \leqslant i < n$ is a contract rule, implies that S_i has the syntactical form

$$\Gamma_i \Longrightarrow \mathcal{U}\langle\!\langle \pi p \omega \rangle\!\rangle \varphi, \Delta_i$$

Thus, $VP_{S_i}^{S_n}$ is equivalent to

$$\neg S_n \rightarrow \neg(\overbrace{\textstyle\bigwedge\Gamma_i \rightarrow (\mathcal{U}\langle\!\langle \pi p \omega \rangle\!\rangle \varphi \vee \textstyle\bigvee\Delta_i)}^{S_i}) \qquad\qquad (5.27)$$
$$\neg S_n \rightarrow (\textstyle\bigwedge\Gamma_i \wedge \neg(\mathcal{U}\langle\!\langle \pi p \omega \rangle\!\rangle \varphi \vee \textstyle\bigvee\Delta_i)) \qquad\qquad (5.28)$$
$$\neg S_n \rightarrow (\textstyle\bigwedge\Gamma_i \wedge \neg\textstyle\bigvee\Delta_i \wedge \neg (\mathcal{U}\langle\!\langle \pi p \omega \rangle\!\rangle \varphi)) \qquad\qquad (5.29)$$

Since $\neg\langle\!\langle \pi p \omega \rangle\!\rangle \varphi \equiv [\langle \pi p \omega \rangle]\neg\varphi$ (Lemma 2.26, page 42) and $\neg\mathcal{U}\phi \equiv \mathcal{U}\neg\phi$ (Lemm 2.45, page 56), we obtain by a equivalence transformations

$$\neg S_n \rightarrow ((\textstyle\bigwedge\Gamma_i \wedge \neg \textstyle\bigvee\Lambda_i) \wedge \mathcal{U}[\langle \pi p \omega \rangle]\neg\varphi) \qquad\qquad (5.30)$$

This formula is equivalent to the conjunction of the following two formulas

$$\neg S_n \to (\bigwedge \Gamma_i \land \neg \bigvee \Delta_i) \tag{5.31}$$

$$\neg S_n \to \mathcal{U}[\langle \pi p \omega \rangle] \neg \varphi \tag{5.32}$$

Due to the assumption $\models VP_{S_{i+1}}^{S_n}$ of the theorem, Lemma 5.10 implies that the Formula (5.31) is valid.

There are syntactically two cases of Formula (5.32) depending on the concrete modality $[\langle \pi p \omega \rangle]$. If in (5.27) the modal operator $[\pi p \omega]$ was used, which is the case 2 in Definition 5.6, then the modal operator in Formula (5.32) is $\langle \pi p \omega \rangle$. In this case we use Lemma 2.26 to separate the program termination problem from the rest of the condition and obtain

$$\neg S_n \to \mathcal{U}(\langle \pi p \omega \rangle \text{true} \land [\pi p \omega] \neg \varphi) \tag{5.33}$$

which is equivalent to the conjunction of the following two formulas.

$$\neg S_n \to \mathcal{U}\langle \pi p \omega \rangle \text{true} \tag{5.34}$$

$$\neg S_n \to \mathcal{U}[\pi p \omega] \neg \varphi \tag{5.35}$$

Formula (5.34) is the condition (5.18) in Definition 5.6. If in (5.27) the modal operator $\langle \pi p \omega \rangle$ was used, which is the case 1 in the definition, then the modal operator in Formula (5.32) is $[\pi p \omega]$ and therefore in this case (5.32) and (5.35) are identical and the condition (5.18) in Definition 5.6 is not required.

According to the assumption in Theorem 5.7 the contract rule R was applied on S_i. The appropriate contract rule of Figure 5.2 is now applied on (5.35) with the same contract $(pre_p, post_p, M, term)$, where $term \in \{total, partial\}$, that was applied on the sequent S_i. This results in three proof obligations written as formulas rather than sequents:

1: $\neg S_n \to \mathcal{U} pre_p \tag{5.36}$
2: $\neg S_n \to \mathcal{U} \mathcal{V}_M^2 (pre_p \to [p] post_p) \tag{5.37}$
3: $\neg S_n \to \mathcal{U} \mathcal{V}_M^2 (post_p \to \neg [\pi \omega] \varphi) \tag{5.38}$

The assumption that $PO1_{S_i}$ is proven means that $\bigwedge \Gamma_i \to (\mathcal{U} pre_p \lor \bigvee \Delta_i)$, or equivalently

$$(\bigwedge \Gamma_i \land \neg \bigvee \Delta_i) \to \mathcal{U} pre_p \tag{5.39}$$

is valid. Formula (5.31) is valid as well (Lemma 5.10). From the validity of Formulas (5.31) and (5.39) and the transitivity of implication we conclude that Formula (5.36) is valid.

Similarly, the assumption that $PO2_{S_i}$ is proven means that

$$\bigwedge \Gamma_i \rightarrow (\mathcal{UV}_M^1(pre_p \rightarrow [p]post_p) \vee \bigvee \Delta_i) \qquad (5.40)$$

is valid. This is equivalent to the validity of

$$(\bigwedge \Gamma_i \wedge \neg \bigvee \Delta_i) \rightarrow \mathcal{UV}_M^1(pre_p \rightarrow [p]post_p) \qquad (5.41)$$

where $\mathcal{V}_M^1$ is the anonymising update (Def. 2.52, page 68) for the modifier set M that was introduced at $PO2_{S_i}$ during the verification attempt. From the validity of Formula (5.31) by Lemma 5.10, the validity of Formula (5.41), and the transitivity of implication we conclude that

$$\neg S_n \rightarrow \mathcal{UV}_M^1(pre_p \rightarrow [p]post_p) \qquad (5.42)$$

is valid. Formula (5.42) differs from Formula (5.37) only by the Skolem functions in the anonymising updates introduced for M, i.e. $\mathcal{V}_M^1$ versus $\mathcal{V}_M^2$. Hence Formula (5.37).

We conclude that under the assumptions of the theorem the conjunction of (5.34) and (5.38) implies $VP_{S_i}^{S_n}$. This argument uses the correctness of the rule R (see Rule 5.8 on page 115), which is a generalization of the loop invariant and method contract rules (Section 2.4.6.3).

Part II In (5.38) the sub-formula φ may contain program parts, i.e. modal operators, that are already symbolically executed on the current branch. The goal in the second part of the proof is to construct an equivalent formula to (5.38) that is based on the sequent S_n and does not contain the formula φ.

Equivalence transformations of (5.38) yield:

$$(\neg \mathcal{UV}_M^2(post_p \rightarrow \neg[\pi\omega]\varphi)) \rightarrow S_n \qquad (5.43)$$

$$\overbrace{(\mathcal{UV}_M^2(post_p \wedge [\pi\omega]\varphi))}^{\Phi} \rightarrow S_n \qquad (5.44)$$

Next we replace the sub-formula Φ in (5.44) by an equivalent or weaker formula Φ'. This replacement is sound because the substitution is performed on the premiss of the implication so that the resulting formula is stronger or equivalent to (5.44), i.e.,

$$\models \Phi \rightarrow \Phi' \text{ implies } (\models \Phi' \rightarrow S_n \text{ implies } \models \Phi \rightarrow S_n) \qquad (5.45)$$

The correctness of this statement is proved as Lemma 5.8. In the following steps we construct the formula $\Phi \rightarrow \Phi'$. The construction starts with the assumption of Theorem 5.7 that the statement

$$\models VP_{S_{i+1}}^{S_n} \qquad (5.46)$$

holds. The validity of the following statements is based on this assumption. By Definition 4.4 the statement (5.46) is equivalent to (we use sequents for a compact notation):

$$\models S_{i+1} \Longrightarrow S_n \qquad (5.47)$$

The sequent S_{i+1} has the form $\Gamma_{i+1} \Longrightarrow \mathcal{UV}_M^1(post_p \rightarrow [\pi\omega]\varphi), \Delta_{i+1}$ as it is the 3rd premiss of the contract rule application at S_i, i.e. $PO3_{S_i}$. Note that according to Figure 5.2 (page 104), $\Gamma_i = \Gamma_{i+1}$ and $\Delta_i = \Delta_{i+1}$.

The implication $S_{i+1} \Longrightarrow S_n$ can be rewritten by equivalence transformation as

$$\neg S_n \Longrightarrow \neg S_{i+1}$$
$$\neg S_n \Longrightarrow \neg(\bigwedge \Gamma_{i+1} \rightarrow (\mathcal{UV}_M^1(post_p \rightarrow [\pi\omega]\varphi) \vee \bigvee \Delta_{i+1}))$$
$$\neg S_n \Longrightarrow \neg(\bigwedge \Gamma_i \rightarrow (\mathcal{UV}_M^1(post_p \rightarrow [\pi\omega]\varphi) \vee \bigvee \Delta_i))$$
$$\neg S_n \Longrightarrow (\bigwedge \Gamma_i \wedge \neg \bigvee \Delta_i) \wedge \neg\mathcal{UV}_M^1(post_p \rightarrow [\pi\omega]\varphi)$$
$$\neg S_n \Longrightarrow \neg\mathcal{UV}_M^1(post_p \rightarrow [\pi\omega]\varphi) \qquad \text{(see Lemma 5.10)}$$
$$\mathcal{UV}_M^1(post_p \rightarrow [\pi\omega]\varphi) \Longrightarrow S_n$$

Statement (5.47) is therefore equivalent to the statement

$$\models \mathcal{UV}_M^1(post_p \rightarrow [\pi\omega]\varphi) \Longrightarrow S_n \qquad (5.48)$$

Let $M^1 \subset$ FSym be the Skolem functions that were introduced with the anonymising update $\mathcal{V}_M^1$ in sequent S_{i+1}. Let $M^2 \subset$ FSym be the Skolem functions that were introduced with the anonymising update $\mathcal{V}_M^2$ in (5.37) and (5.38). The anonymising updates are defined as

$$\mathcal{V}_M^1 = \{M := M^1\} \text{ and } \mathcal{V}_M^2 = \{M := M^2\}$$

By extending both sides of the sequent (5.48) with the update $\{M^1 :=$ $M^2\}$ (see Lemma 2.27) we obtain:

$$\vDash \{M^1 := M^2\}\mathcal{U}\mathcal{V}_M^1(post_p \to [\pi\omega]\varphi) \Rightarrow \{M^1 := M^2\}S_n \qquad (5.49)$$

Recall that the validity of the statements is based on the assumption that $\vDash VP_{S_{i+1}}^{S_n}$ holds. The statement (5.48) which is equivalent to the assumption (5.46) on page 129 implies the statement (5.49).

The rule R ensures that the Skolem functions in M^1 cannot occur in $\mathcal{U}$ and they cannot occur in $post_p \to [\pi\omega]\varphi$. This is because M^1 is introduced by the rule application while $\mathcal{U}$ and $post_p \to [\pi\omega]\varphi$ exist already before the rule application. Thus, the following are equivalence transformations

$$\{M^1 := M^2\}\mathcal{U}\overbrace{\{M := M^1\}}^{\mathcal{V}_M^1}(post_p \to [\pi\omega]\varphi) \Rightarrow \{M^1 := M^2\}S_n$$
$$\mathcal{U}\{M^1 := M^2\}\{M := M^1\}(post_p \to [\pi\omega]\varphi) \Rightarrow \{M^1 := M^2\}S_n$$
$$\mathcal{U}\{M^1 := M^2 \,\|\, M := M^2\}(post_p \to [\pi\omega]\varphi) \Rightarrow \{M^1 := M^2\}S_n$$
$$\mathcal{U}\underbrace{\{M := M^2\}}_{\mathcal{V}_M^2}(post_p \to [\pi\omega]\varphi) \Rightarrow \{M^1 := M^2\}S_n$$

The last step is an equivalence transformation according to Lemma 2.42 (page 52) because M^1 does not occur in $post_p \to [\pi\omega]\varphi$. Hence, statement (5.49) is equivalent to

$$\vDash \mathcal{U}\mathcal{V}_M^2(post_p \to [\pi\omega]\varphi) \Rightarrow \{M^1 := M^2\}S_n \qquad (5.50)$$

Let $\{M^1 := M^2\}S_n = S_n'$. Extending the sequent with the formula $\mathcal{U}\mathcal{V}_M^2 post_p$ yields

$$\vDash (\mathcal{U}\mathcal{V}_M^2(post_p \to [\pi\omega]\varphi)) \wedge (\mathcal{U}\mathcal{V}_M^2 post_p) \Rightarrow S_n' \wedge \mathcal{U}\mathcal{V}_M^2 post_p \qquad (5.51)$$

which is sound according to Lemma 5.9. Simplification of (5.51) yields

$$\vDash (\mathcal{U}\mathcal{V}_M^2((post_p \to [\pi\omega]\varphi) \wedge post_p)) \Rightarrow S_n' \wedge \mathcal{U}\mathcal{V}_M^2 post_p \qquad (5.52)$$

$$\vDash \mathcal{U}\mathcal{V}_M^2(post_p \wedge [\pi\omega]\varphi) \Rightarrow S_n' \wedge \mathcal{U}\mathcal{V}_M^2 post_p \qquad (5.53)$$

The formula $\mathcal{U}\mathcal{V}_M^2(post_p \wedge [\pi\omega]\varphi)$ is equivalent to Φ. Thus, the sought-after formula Φ' is $S_n' \wedge \mathcal{U}\mathcal{V}_M^2 post_p$ (see the statement (5.45)). By substituting Φ' for Φ in (5.44) and expanding the abbreviations S_n' and $\mathcal{V}_M^2$ the formula $\Phi' \to S_n$ is given by

$$(\{M^1 := M^2\}S_n \wedge \mathcal{U}\{M := M^2\}post_p) \,\to\, S_n \qquad (5.54)$$

We conclude that under the assumptions of the theorem, validity of the conjunction of (5.34) and (5.54), which is the $SVP_{S_i}^{S_n}$ according to Definition 5.6, implies the validity of $VP_{S_i}^{S_n}$.

∎

5.5 Example

In this section we prove that the method `sqrtA` from Figure 5.1 (page 102) does not satisfy its specification. This section is divided into a verification attempt and validity preservation checking according to Algorithm 1. For checking the validity preservation of an open proof branch S_n the special validity preservation condition $SVP_{S_i}^{S_n}$ (see Section 5.4.3) is used which is constructed from S_n and a sequent S_i on which a contract rule was applied.

5.5.1 Verification Attempt

We use the same simplified translation of the JML specification of the method `sqrtA` as in Section 4.3.2 on page 89 (let X^2 denote $X * X$):

$$\overbrace{x \geqslant 0, 0 \neq \texttt{null}}^{\Gamma} \implies \{\}[\texttt{r=o.sqrtA(x)}]\overbrace{(r^2 \leqslant x \wedge (r+1)^2 > x)}^{\varphi} \quad : S_0$$

Applying symbolic execution rules results in the sequents

$$\Gamma \implies [\pi\ \texttt{i=0;while}\overbrace{(\texttt{i*i<=x})}^{c}\texttt{\{i=i+1;\}return i;}\ \omega]\varphi \qquad : S_1$$

$$\Gamma \implies \{i := 0\}[\pi\ \texttt{while(c)\{i=i+1;\}return i;}\ \omega]\varphi \qquad : S_2$$

Applying the loop invariant rule with the contract

$$\overbrace{((i-1)^2 \leqslant x \vee i \doteq 0}^{I}, \overbrace{((i-1)^2 \leqslant x \vee i \doteq 0) \wedge i^2 > x}^{I \wedge \neg c^*}, \overbrace{\{\langle \texttt{true}, i \rangle\}}^{M}, partial)$$

yields the following three premises

$$\textbf{1:}\ \Gamma \implies \overbrace{\{i := 0\}}^{U}\overbrace{(i-1)^2 \leqslant x \vee i \doteq 0}^{I} \qquad\qquad (PO1_{S_2})$$

$$\textbf{2:}\ \Gamma \implies \{i := 0\}\{i := i_{sk^1}\}(I \wedge c^* \to [\texttt{i=i+1}]I) \qquad (PO2_{S_2})$$

$$\textbf{3:}\ \Gamma \implies \{i := 0\}\{i := i_{sk^1}\}(I \wedge \neg c^* \to [\pi\ \texttt{return i;}\ \omega]\varphi) \quad (PO3_{S_2} = S_3)$$

$$x \geqslant 1 + i_{sk1} * (-2),$$
$$(i_{sk1})^2 \geqslant 0,$$
$$i_{sk1} \geqslant 1,$$
$$(i_{sk1})^2 \geqslant 1 + x,$$
$$(i_{sk1})^2 \leqslant i_{sk1} * 2 + x - 1,$$
$$x \geqslant 0$$
$$\Longrightarrow$$

Fig. 5.9. Open branch S_n resulting from a verification attempt of the method `sqrtA`; A counterexample of this sequent is, e.g., $\mathcal{I}(x) = 1, \mathcal{I}(i_{sk1}) = 2$.

The abbreviations $PO1_{S_2}$, $PO2_{S_2}$, and $PO3_{S_2}$ are defined in Definition 5.2 (page 112). The premises $PO1_{S_2}$ and $PO2_{S_2}$ are provable.

Running this example with the KeY tool yields one open branch S_n, with $n > 3$, that extends the branch S_3. The sequent S_n is shown in Figure 5.9 and is copied directly from the KeY tool with adapted notation. Note that the succedent of S_n is empty. A counterexample of this sequent is, e.g., $\mathcal{I}(x) = 1, \mathcal{I}(i_{sk1}) = 2$. The verification attempt has failed at this point and the user does not know the reason for the failure. The description of the example continues in the following section.

5.5.2 Checking Validity Preservation

The sequent S_n cannot be proved by the verification system. The next step is to check if S_n is actually falsifiable which can be done by the user, an SMT solver, or the method described in Chapter 6. The sequent S_n turns out to be falsifiable.

According to Definition 5.6, $SVP_{S_2}^{S_n}$ is the conjunction of the Formulas (5.17) and (5.18) (see page 122). Note that also the side condition that $PO1_{S_2}$ and $PO2_{S_2}$ are proven must be checked. This was, however, done as part of the verification attempt (see Section 5.5.1).

The role of Formula (5.18) is to prevent the provability of $SVP_{S_2}^{S_n}$ in case the target program does not terminate because non-termination implies program correctness when using the modal operator [], (case 2 in the definition). In practice the reason for using the modal operator [] is, however, often to simplify a verification attempt. Even when using the modal operator [] the user may implicitly regard non-terminating programs as incorrect. For terminating programs this formula causes a computationally expensive proof obligation. For these reasons the user may ignore Formula (5.18) if they understand the difference.

The important formula to be proven is (5.17), which has the form

$$\left(\overbrace{\{i:=0\}}^{U}\overbrace{\{i:=i_{sk^2}\}}^{M:=M^2}\overbrace{\left((i-1)^2 \leqslant x \vee i \doteq 0\right) \wedge i^2 > x)}^{I\wedge\neg c^*} \wedge \overbrace{\{i_{sk^1} := i_{sk^2}\}}^{M^1:=M^2} S_n\right)$$
$$\rightarrow S_n$$

in our example. The sequent S_n has the form $\Gamma_n \Longrightarrow$, which is equivalent to $\neg\Gamma_n$. The formula can therefore be rewritten by equivalence transformations as

$$(\{i_{sk^1} := i_{sk^2}\}\neg\Gamma_n \wedge \{i := i_{sk^2}\}((i-1)^2 \leqslant x \vee i \doteq 0) \wedge i^2 > x) \rightarrow \neg\Gamma_n$$

$$(\Gamma_n \wedge ((i_{sk^2}-1)^2 \leqslant x \vee i_{sk^2} \doteq 0) \wedge (i_{sk^2})^2 > x) \rightarrow \Gamma_n' \qquad (5.55)$$

where Γ_n' is obtained by applying the update $\{i_{sk^1} := i_{sk^2}\}$ on Γ_n. $SVP^{S_n}_{S_2}$ simplifies therefore to a first-order logic formula that is built based on the leaf node S_n and the post condition of the contract. The approach is implemented in KeY which proves Formula (5.55) automatically in approximately 230 proof steps.

The user now knows that choosing a different contract would not have lead to a successful verification attempt because the program or the requirement specification has to be fixed. By looking at the used symbolic execution rules the trace can be read as the program execution trace that reveals the software fault.

5.6 Evaluation

For experiments and evaluation of the techniques described in this thesis we have used examples from a banking software. The banking software was used in case studies on verification [Burdy et al., 2003] and JML-based validation [du Bousquet et al., 2004]. In this system the bank customer can check his or her accounts as well as make money transfers between accounts. The customer can also set some rules for periodical money transfer. Figure 5.10 (page 138) shows a part of the case study source code. The source code contains JML annotations such as method contracts, class invariants, and loop invariants and is therefore suitable for our experiments.

The goals of the experiments were to check how often validity preservation can be proved in practice, and how big is the computational overhead of validity preservation checking with respect to the verification attempt. We have implemented the Approaches 2 and 3 of Figure 5.3 (page 114) in the KeY tool. In addition we have implemented the possibility to prove the validity preservation of a branch directly without any optimizations. The latter approach, which we call Approach X in the following, is to prove the formula $S_0 \to S_n$, where S_0 is the root and S_n is the leaf of the selected branch (see Def. 4.4). The approach of the evaluation is to compare the number of rules applied during a verification attempt (VA Rules) with the additional number of rule applications required to prove validity preservation (Approach Rules). We are interested only in unsuccessful verification attempts because branches of closed proofs are trivially validity preserving.[6] Since the original methods can be verified with KeY, we have introduced faults into the methods or their specifications. In the following the modified methods are annotated with '*'. The results of our experiments are shown in Table 5.2.

The columns entitled *Overhead* compare the number of rule applications of the respective approach with the number of rule applications of the verification attempt. All rules were applied automatically. Approach X requires in average 106% rule applications compared to the verification attempt. Approach 2, with 45%, requires less than half of the computational resources required by Approach X. Approach 3 checks the special validity preservation (*SVP*) condition and reuses most of the information that was computed during the verification attempt. In Line 13 of Table 5.2 the proof attempt with Approach 3 did not succeed. This is because the *SVP* condition is not equivalent to the validity preservation condition of a branch (see Theorem 5.7). However, in most cases the *SVP* condition was proved and required only 10% of the resources that were used during the verification attempt.

In addition to this main result, Table 5.2 confirms also another expectation we had. First we explain the rows of the table in more detail. The verification attempts in Lines 1, 3, 7, 11, 13 were stopped by the automatic proof search strategy of KeY when using the standard settings. This strategy applies quantifier instantiation rules until (i) a certain instantiation criteria is met and (ii) no other rules can be applied except

---

[6] If the leaf of a branch S_n is true, then the validity preservation condition $VP_{S_0}^{S_n}$ is $S_0 \to true$, which is a valid.

Method	VA			Approach X		Approach 2		Approach 3	
	Ln.	P	Rules	Rules	Overhead	Rules	Overhead	Rules	Overhead
isValidBank*	1		1022	1572	154%	677	66%	204	20%
	2	1	1122	1578	141%	682	60%	200	18%
isValACC*	3		1972	3411	173%	1139	57%	256	13%
	4	3	2072	2694	130%	817	39%	178	8%
	5	3	2072	3470	167%	1177	56%	267	13%
	6	5	2172	2738	126%	805	37%	178	8%
getRef* (see Fig. 5.10)	7		1447	1986	137%	1075	74%	310	21%
	8	7	1547	1482	95%	424	27%	139	9%
	9	7	1547	2134	138%	1081	69%	336	22%
	10	9	1647	2102	127%	770	46%	301	18%
BOcreate*	11		4706	2073	44%	854	18%	117	2%
	12	11	4806	2055	43%	848	17%	114	2%
BOcreate**	13		4396	5190	118%	3428	77%	-	-
Avg. Overhead					106%		45%		10%

Table 5.2. Overhead of validity preservation checking with respect to verification; VA: verification attempt; Ln.: line number or experiment id; P: predecessor, i.e., the verification attempt that was extended; Approach X: direct proof of the formula $S_0 \to S_n$; Rules: number of calculus rules applied; Overhead: number of rules applied by the approach with respect to the number of rules applied during the verification attempt; two different faults were introduced into BOcreate* and BOcreate**

for unrestricted quantifier instantiations and the *cut* rule. The *cut* rule introduces case distinctions into the proof tree and in this way the critical state space of proof obligations is narrowed. Intuitively this means that more concrete initial program states are regarded. KeY's *model search* strategy [Rümmer, 2008] uses the cut rule and automatically chooses case distinctions. By continuing the verification attempts with the model search strategy the other lines in the table were obtained. The column P shows the predecessor relationship, e.g., the proof tree generated by the verification attempt in Line 1 is extended in Line 2 by 100 rule applications. Our observation is that using the model search strategy, i.e., introduction of case distinctions with the *cut* rule, the efficiency of the approaches is increased. This can be seen when comparing the results in one line with the results in the predecessor line. The model search strategy yields in several cases a payoff in the total number of rules applied during the verification attempt and validity preservation proving. For instance, extending the proof tree of Line 7 with 100 rules yields the situation in Line 8, where Approach X needs

1482 instead of 1986 rule applications, Approach 2 needs 424 instead of 1075 rule applications, and Approach 3 needs 139 instead of 310 rule applications.

5.7 Related Work

The techniques described in this chapter are an extension of [Gladisch, 2008a] where we describe a test case generation technique for full feasible (program) branch coverage. In [Gladisch, 2008a] branch coverage is ensured if contracts satisfy a *strength condition*. In this work we have extended this idea resulting in the *special validity preservation condition (SVP)*. Checking validity preservation for contract rules is also possible with the *strength condition* of a contract. However, the *SVP* can be viewed as a *customized* strength condition for a contract that is weaker and therefore valid in far more cases than the more general strength condition given in [Gladisch, 2008a]. Furthermore, in contrast to the strength condition defined in [Gladisch, 2008a], *SVP reuses* symbolic execution that has already been performed. The latter property is the reason why we argue that our approach unifies verification and software fault detection.

While our approach starts with a verification attempt, the approach in [Rümmer and Shah, 2007] tries to show program incorrectness by starting at the root of the proof tree with a formula that express program incorrectness. Thus, in contrast to our approach the approach in [Rümmer and Shah, 2007] can only show program incorrectness.

Another related work that unifies verification and fault detection very closely is Synergy [Gulavani et al., 2006] that is an extensions of the Lee-Yannakakis algorithm [Lee and Yannakakis, 1992] and is an improvement to SLAM [Ball and Rajamani, 2001] and BLAST [Henzinger et al., 2002]. While these approaches are based on abstraction and refinement, our approach is optimized for underlying verification techniques that are based on symbolic execution or weakest precondition computation. Furthermore, the approaches [Gulavani et al., 2006], [Henzinger et al., 2002], and [Leino and Logozzo, 2005] are more concerned with the automatic generation of annotations while in our work theorem proving and the challenges with user-provided loop invariants and method contracts are in focus. The latter applies also to [Claessen and Svensson, 2008] where in contrast to our work explicit program execution is used and also other reasons for proof failure than program error are considered. The main concern in [Claessen and Svensson, 2008] is, however, finding the right program input to detect a fault while in our approach we reason about the existence of such an input.

Approaches that start with a verification attempt and in case of failure generate counterexamples for the unproved verification conditions are e.g. Spec# [Barnett et al., 2005], VCC [Schulte et al., 2007], Caduceus/Krakatoa [Filliâtre and Marché, 2007], Bogor/Kiasan [Deng et al., 2006a]. These approaches have the problem that a counterexample for a verification condition has an ambiguous meaning, i.e., the used contracts can be too weak or the target program has an error. Our contribution in contrast deals with this problem and therefore extends the existing approaches.

5.8 Summary and Conclusion

The techniques described in this chapter extend existing approaches that try to verify a program and in case of verification failure generate counterexamples for verification conditions. In contrast to existing approaches our approach allows us to conclude the existence of a software fault from falsifiable verifications even if contract rules were used during the verification attempt. Furthermore, checking the existence of a software fault after the verification attempt does not require explicit program testing, symbolic execution, or weakest precondition computation. Instead we *reuse* information obtained from the verification attempt to reason about the existence of a software fault. In this way our technique unifies verification and software fault detection. We have implemented and successfully tested three of the described approaches on some methods of a small banking software. For proving the validity preservation of a branch Approach 2 added 45% and Approach 3 added only 10% of computational overhead after a failed verification attempt.

```
1   /* Copyright (c) 2002 GEMPLUS group. */
2   public class AccountMan_src {
3    private /*@ spec_public @*/ Vector LocalVector;
4    /*@ private invariant LocalVector != null;
5        private invariant LocalVector.elementCount >= 0;
6        private invariant
7          (\forall int i;0 <= i && i <= LocalVector.elementCount;
8                (LocalVector.elementData[i] instanceof Account) &&
9                      (LocalVector.elementData[i]!=null)); @*/
10   ... // field and method declarations
11   /*@ public normal_behavior
12     requires true;
13     ensures (\exists int i; i >= 0 && i< LocalVector.elementCount &&
14        ((Account)(LocalVector.elementData[i])).accountnum == Acc)
15            ==> (\result != null && \result.accountnum == Acc);
16     ensures (!(\exists int i; i >= 0 && i<LocalVector.elementCount &&
17        ((Account)(LocalVector.elementData[i])).accountnum == Acc))
18        ==> \result == null;
19     modifies \nothing;
20     nullable
21   @*/
22   protected Account getRef(int Acc) {
23    int i = 0;
24    Account accn = null;
25    Account temp = null;
26    /*@ modifies i, accn, temp ;
27      loop_invariant (\exists int k ; k >=0 && k <i &&
28          ((Account)(LocalVector.elementData[k])).accountnum == Acc)
29        ==> (accn != null && accn.accountnum == Acc);
30      loop_invariant (!(\exists int i; i >= 0 &&
31                    i < LocalVector.elementCount &&
32          ((Account)(LocalVector.elementData[i])).accountnum == Acc))
33        ==> accn == nul;
34      loop_invariant i >=0 && i <= LocalVector.elementCount;  @*/
35      while (i < LocalVector.size()) {
36          temp = (Account) LocalVector.elementAt(i);
37          if (temp.getAccountnum() == Acc){ accn = temp; }
38          i++;
39      }
40    return accn;
41   }}
```

Fig. 5.10. Excerpt from the banking case study showing the declaration and the specification of the field LocalVector and the method getRef

6

Counterexample Generation for Verification Conditions with Quantifiers

6.1 Introduction

Showing the satisfiability of a first-order logic (FOL) formula means to show the existence of an interpretation in which the formula evaluates to true. This is an important and long studied problem in different application domains such as formal software verification, software testing, and artificial intelligence. In software verification and testing the models, i.e. interpretations, are used as counterexamples to debug programs and specifications and to generate test data, respectively. The approach that we suggest is to use programs to represent partial models and to use formal verification in order to evaluate quantified formulas to true.

The technique described in this chapter is a model generation technique which is a sub-component of our software-fault detection approach described in Chapter 4. This technique is required in order to generate counterexamples for verification conditions that could not be proved during a verification attempt. If a verification condition has a counterexample and the branch of the proof tree on which the verification condition occurs is validity preserving (see Chapters 4 and 5), then the target program does not satisfy its specification. Hence, a software fault is detected and the counterexample helps finding the fault because it represents the initial state of the program run that reveals the fault. The generation of counterexamples is further important in counterexample guided abstraction refinement (CEGAR) [Clarke et al., 2000] and for checking the consistency, i.e. contradiction-freeness, of axioms and of preconditions in specifications.

Satisfiability modulo theory (SMT) solvers are considered as the state-of-the-art techniques for showing satisfiability of FOL formulas

——— JAVA + JML ————————————————————————————

```
1   /*@ public normal_behavior
2    @ requires next!=null && prev!=null && next!=prev
3    @ && (\forall int k; true ; 0<=next[k] && next[k] < prev.length)
4    @ && (\forall int l; 0<=l && l<next.length; next[l]==l);
5    @ ensures (\forall int j; 0<=j && j<next.length; prev[next[j]]==j);
6    @ modifies prev[*]; @*/
7   public void link(){
8   /*@ loop_invariant (\forall int x; 0<=x && x <= i; prev[next[x]]==x)
9                  && (0<=i && i<=next.length) ; modifies prev[*],i; @*/
10   for(int i=0;i<next.length;i++){ prev[next[i]]=i; }
11  }
```

————————————————————————————————— JAVA + JML ———

Fig. 6.1. An example of a JAVA method (of class `MyCls`) with a JML specification that is not verifiable because the underlined formula should be $x < i$ instead of $x \leqslant i$

and to generate models for FOL formulas. A major bottleneck is, however, the handling of quantifiers (see, e.g., [Déharbe and Ranise, 2009; Moskal et al., 2008; Ge et al., 2009; Nieuwenhuis et al., 2007]). SMT solvers can often create models for quantified formulas if *one* theory is involved. Verification conditions, however, usually include quantified formulas belonging to the combinations of multiple theories. Such verification conditions lead to problems that are not in the decidable fragments of the solvers. In such cases an SMT solver returns the result *unknown*, which means that the solver cannot determine if the formula is satisfiable or not.

As a motivating example, assume we want to show the satisfiability of the formula

$$\forall x.(x \geqslant 0 \rightarrow prev(next(x)) = x) \tag{6.1}$$

where *prev* and *next* are uninterpreted function symbols. The formula stems from an unproved verification condition. Some state-of-the-art SMT solvers – concretely we have tested Z3 [de Moura and Bjørner, 2008], CVC3 [Barrett and Tinelli, 2007], Yices [Dutertre and de Moura, 2006b,a] – are in contrast to the here described technique not capable of to solve this formula. The reason is that this formula is not in the decidable fragment of the solvers because it combines arithmetics, uninterpreted functions, and quantification. We will use this example to demonstrate our approach in this chapter.

$\forall x : \texttt{int}.(x \leqslant -1 \lor x \geqslant 1 + i_0 \lor \texttt{get}_0(\texttt{prev}(\texttt{self}), \texttt{acc}_{[]}(\texttt{next}(\texttt{self}), x) \doteq x),$

$\forall x : \texttt{MyCls}.(\texttt{prevAtPre}(x) \doteq \texttt{prev}(x)),$

$\forall x : \texttt{MyCls}.(x \doteq \texttt{null} \lor \neg\texttt{created}(x) \lor \neg\texttt{a}(x) \doteq \texttt{null}),$

$\forall x : \texttt{MyCls}.(x \doteq \texttt{null} \lor \neg\texttt{created}(x) \lor \neg\texttt{next}(x) \doteq \texttt{null}),$

$\forall x : \texttt{MyCls}.(x \doteq \texttt{null} \lor \neg\texttt{created}(x) \lor \neg\texttt{prev}(x) \doteq \texttt{null}),$

$\forall x : \texttt{int}.\texttt{acc}_{[]}(\texttt{next}(\texttt{self}), x) \geqslant 0),$

$\forall x : \texttt{int}.\texttt{acc}_{[]}(\texttt{next}(\texttt{self}), x) \leqslant -1 + \texttt{length}(\texttt{prev}(\texttt{self}))),$

$\forall x : \texttt{int}.(l \leqslant -1 \lor l \geqslant \texttt{length}(\texttt{next}(\texttt{self})) \lor \texttt{acc}_{[]}(\texttt{next}(\texttt{self}), x) \doteq x),$

$\ldots \Longrightarrow \ldots$

Fig. 6.2. Quantified formulas in a sequent resulting from a failed verification attempt of the code in Figure 6.1; 21 additional ground formulas are abbreviated by '...'

Verification conditions with quantified formulas occur frequently as we have already motivated in Section 4.4.2 (page 98). Whenever an object field of a class type is declared in a class C, then according to JML's semantics KeY generates a formula which states that *for all* objects of C the field is not `null`. Hence, a quantified formula is introduced into verification conditions even if it was not explicitly defined by the user. Similarly, if a class invariant is declared in C, then a formula is generated which states that the invariant holds for all objects of C (see Figure 4.3, page 98).

If in a verification condition a single sub-formula occurs that is not in the decidable fragment of an SMT solver, then the SMT solver cannot be used for counterexample generation of the verification condition. In order to see how severe this problem is in practice consider the example in Figure 6.1. The method `link` initializes the array `prev` such that `prev[next[i]]=i` for all indices `i` of the array `next`, i.e., the method creates a doubly linked list based on arrays. A verification attempt of the method with KeY fails with an open proof branch. Figure 6.2 shows the quantified formulas occurring in the verification condition of the proof branch. Although the verification condition is falsifiable an SMT solver cannot generate a counterexample because it contains quantified formulas with uninterpreted and arithmetic function symbols.

We propose a model generation technique that is not explicitly restricted to a specific class of formulas. Consequently, the technique is not a decision procedure, i.e., it may not terminate. However, it can solve more general formulas than SMT solvers can solve in cases where it terminates. The proposed technique is also capable of generating only partial interpretations that satisfy only the quantified formulas, and return a residue of ground formulas that is to be shown satisfiable. Ground formulas are formulas without quantifiers. In this mode the technique acts as a pre-computation step for SMT solvers to eliminate quantifiers. Quantifier elimination in this sense is sound for showing satisfiability but not for refutational or validity proofs. However, for the handling of quantifiers in refutational and validity proofs powerful instantiation based techniques already exist. These can be combined with the proposed technique in order to create semi-decision procedures.

While model generation is not a new idea, the novelties of our approach are (1) the choice of language to represent (partial) interpretations, (2) the technique for the construction of models, and (3) the means to evaluate (quantified) formulas under these interpretations. Since satisfiability solving and model generation for ground formulas is already well studied, we concentrate on the handling of quantified formulas.

This chapter is a combination of the papers [Gladisch, 2010b] and [Gladisch, 2010a]. The first paper presents the theory of the approach with a soundness proof. The second paper describes the algorithm, applies it to test data generation, and provides an evaluation and comparison of the algorithm to SMT solvers. These contributions are all included in this chapter.

6.1.1 Background and Related Work

One has to distinguish between different quantifiers in different contexts, namely between those that can be Skolemized and those that cannot be Skolemized. For instance, in an attempt to show the validity of the formula $\forall x.\varphi(x)$, the variable x can be Skolemized, i.e. replaced by a fresh constant, because all symbols of the signature are implicitly universally quantified in this context. When showing the validity of $\exists x.\varphi(x)$, Skolemization is not possible. In contrast, when showing satisfiability, Skolemization is allowed for $\exists x.\varphi(x)$ but not for $\forall x.\varphi(x)$. Thus, assuming the formulas being in prenex form, the tricky cases are the handling of (a) existential quantification when showing validity and (b) universal quantification when showing satisfiability. In order to handle case (a) some instantiation(s) of the quantified formulas can be created *hoping* to complete the proof. Soundness is preserved by any instantiation. The situation in case (b) is, however, worse when using instantiation-based methods because these methods are sound only if a complete instantiation of the quantified formula is guaranteed.

A popular instantiation heuristic is E-matching [Moskal et al., 2008] which was first used in the theorem prover Simplify [Detlefs et al., 2005]. E-matching is, however, not complete in general. In general a quantified formula $\forall x.\varphi(x)$ cannot be substituted by a satisfiability preserving conjunction $\varphi(t_0) \wedge \ldots \wedge \varphi(t_n)$ where $t_0 \ldots t_n$ are terms computed via E-matching. For this reason, Simplify may produce unsound answers (see also [Kiniry et al., 2006]) as shown in the following example.

$$\forall h.\forall i.\forall v.select(store(h,i,v),i) = v \tag{6.2}$$

$$\forall h.\forall j.0 \leqslant select(h,j) \wedge select(h,j) \leqslant 2^{32} - 1 \tag{6.3}$$

Formula (6.2) is an axiom of the theory of arrays and (6.3) specifies that all array elements of all arrays have values between 0 and $2^{32} - 1$. The first axiom is used to specify heap memory in [Moskal, 2009]. Formula (6.3) seems like a useful axiom to specify that all values in the heap memory have lower and upper bounds, as it is the case in computer systems. However, the conjunction (6.2) $\wedge$ (6.3) is unsatisfiable, which can be easily seen when considering the following instantiation $[h := store(h_0, k, 2^{32}), j := k]$, (see [Moskal, 2009]). Simplify, however, produces a counterexample for $\neg((6.2) \wedge (6.3))$, which means that it satisfies the *false* formula (6.2) $\wedge$ (6.3). E-matching may be used for sound satisfiability solving when a complete instantiation of quantifiers is ensured. For instance, completeness of instantiation via E-matching has been shown for the Bernays-Schönfinkel class in [Ge and de Moura, 2009]. An important fragment of FOL for program specification which allows a complete instantiation is the Array Property Fragment [Bradley et al., 2006]. E-matching is used in state-of-the-art SMT solvers such as Z3 [de Moura and Bjørner, 2008], CVC3 [Barrett and Tinelli, 2007], Yices [Dutertre and de Moura, 2006b,a], and others (see [de Moura and Bjørner, 2007]). Formula (6.1) which is solvable with our technique is, however, neither in the Bernays-Schönfinkel class nor in the Array Property Fragment.

Another set of approaches for finding instantiations of quantified formulas is based on free-variables (see e.g. [Giese, 2001]). These approaches focus, however, on validity or respectively unsatisfiability proofs and not on satisfiability solving. More precisely, they do not guarantee a complete instantiation of quantifiers.

Satisfiability of a formula can be shown by weakening the formula with existential quantifiers and then showing its validity, instead of satisfiability. This idea is followed in [Rümmer and Shah, 2007] for proving

143

the existence of a state that reveals a software fault. For instance, let $\phi(t)$ be a formula with an occurrence of the term t, then the approach generates the formula $\exists x.\{t := x\}\phi(t)$.[1] This transformation is repeated also for other terms of ϕ. The approach uses then free variables for computing instantiations of the existentially quantified variables.

Model generation theorem provers (MGTP) are similar to SMT solvers as their underlying technique is DPLL lifted to FOL. For instance, the theorem prover Darwin [Baumgartner et al., 2006] is an instantiation-based prover which is sound and complete for the *unsatisfiability* of FOL without theories. For the satisfiability part it decides Bernays-Schönfinkel formulas. In [Ahrendt, 2001] a complete model generator is described but similarly as in the case of the theorem prover Simplify the method is not sound for model generation. The idea is to generate *likely* representations of models and let the user decide if the models are correct or not. Saturation-based provers based on superposition, e.g. SPASS [Horbach and Weidenbach, 2009a,b; Althaus et al., 2009], can be instantiated to decision procedures for some decidable fragments of first-order logic.

Quantified constraint satisfaction problem (QCSP) solvers, e.g., [Gent et al., 2005], primarily regard the finite version of the satisfiability problem, whereas our approach handles infinite domains. Some of the work, e.g. [Benhamou and Goualard, 2000], also considers continues domains, however, these techniques do not handle uninterpreted function symbols other than constants. The finite domain version of the satisfiability problem in first-order logic is handled by finite model finding methods such as [Zhang and Zhang, 2004].

Different model building techniques are described in [Ricardo et al., 2004]. The authors distinguish between enumeration-based methods corresponding to the above mentioned instantiation techniques and deduction-base methods which are in the main focus of their book. Deductive methods produce syntactic representations of models in some logical language. Nitpik which is a counter example generator for Isabelle/HOL uses first-order relational logic (FORL) [Blanchette, 2010]. FORL extends FOL with relational calculus operators and the transitive closure. The approach we propose is a deduction-based method which differs from existing approaches in the representation and generation of models.

---

[1] Assuming that the top-level symbol of t is a non-rigid function symbol

Quantifier elimination techniques, in the *traditional* sense, replace quantified formulas by *equivalent* ground formulas, i.e. without quantifiers. Popular methods are, e.g., the Fourier-Motzkin quantifier elimination procedure for linear rational arithmetic and Cooper's quantifier elimination procedure for Presburger arithmetic (see, e.g., [Ghilardi, 2003] for more examples). These techniques are, in contrast to the proposed technique, not capable of eliminating the quantifier in, e.g., (6.1). Since first-order logic is only semi-decidable, equivalence preserving quantifier elimination is possible only in special cases. The transformation of formulas by our technique is not equivalence preserving. The advantage of our technique is, however, that it is not restricted to a certain class of formulas. Hence, our approach can solve formulas that other approaches cannot solve.

6.2 The Basic Idea of our Approach

The basic idea of our approach is to generate a partial FOL model in which a quantified formula that we want to eliminate evaluates to true. A set of quantified formulas can be eliminated, i.e. evaluated to true, by successive extensions of the partial model. This approach can be continued also on ground formulas to generate complete models. While this basic idea is simple, the interesting questions are: how to represent the interpretations, how to generate (partial) models, and what calculus is suitable in order to evaluate formulas under those (partial) interpretations.

The approach that we suggest is to use programs to represent partial models and to use formal verification in order to evaluate the quantified formulas to true. Our approach is to regard a given quantified formula φ as a postcondition and to generate for φ a program p such that the final states of p satisfies φ. Thus, one of our contributions is a program generation technique.

For example, in order to solve Formula (6.1), we could generate the following program (assuming, e.g., JAVA-like syntax and semantics):

```
for(i=0;true;i++){ next[i]=new T(); next[i].prev=i; }
```
$$(6.4)$$

and then prove the validity of the dynamic logic formula[2]

$$\langle(6.4)\rangle(6.1) \qquad (6.5)$$

---

[2] The formula $\langle(6.4)\rangle(6.1)$ can be read as the weakest precondition wp((6.4),(6.1)).

If Formula (6.5) is valid, then according to Definition 2.25 there is a state S such that the program (6.4) terminates in a state S' in which the Formula (6.1) is true. If the verification calculus is capable to prove this formula, then effectively the quantified formula is eliminated because it is replaced by the formula true and a partial interpretation represented in form of a program is obtained. Hence, the satisfiability problem is replaced by a program generation and verification problem.

A typical programming language such as JAVA is, however, not *directly* suitable for this task. A syntactical problem is that function and predicate symbols are usually not representable in such languages. A more severe problem is that for the verification of programs with loops, loop invariants have to be generated.

We found that a language and a calculus that are suitable for our purpose are KeY's updates and the update simplification calculus built into KeY. Quantified updates can represent models for many quantified formulas. However, since (quantified) updates are less expressive than a turing-complete while-language the updates simplification calculus can fully automatically reduce FOL formulas with updates to pure FOL formulas. Loop invariants do not have to be generated for the verification step. Another important advantage of updates is that updates are syntactically and semantically closer to first-order logic than general programming languages. The latter aspect simplifies the generation of updates from formulas.

6.3 Model Generation by Iterative Update Construction

6.3.1 The Goal and the Challenges

In order to show the satisfiability of a formula ϕ_{in}, our approach is to generate an update u, such that $\models \{u\}\phi_{in}$. If such an update exists, then ϕ_{in} is satisfiable and the update represents a set of models of ϕ_{in}.

The main contribution of this chapter is a technique for generating (partial) models for quantified formulas. As this work was developed in the context of KeY we regard the model generation problem of a quantified formula $\forall x.\phi(x)$ in a sequent $\varphi = (\Gamma, \forall x.\phi(x) \implies \Delta)$. The formula $\phi(x) \in \mathrm{Fml}^{FOL}$ denotes a formula with an occurrence of the variable $x \in \mathrm{VSym}$ and $\Gamma, \Delta \subset \mathrm{Fml}^{FOL}$.[3] Such sequents occur frequently as

---

[3] Note that KeY can transform all DL formulas that contain no programs into FOL formulas.

open branches of failed proof attempts after symbolic execution and update simplification have been applied. The reason for proof failure is often unclear and it is desired to determine if φ has a counterexample, i.e., if a model exists for $\neg\varphi$. The goal is therefore given by the following problem description.

Remark 6.1. In this chapter we often use the sequent notation to represent the equivalent formulas according to Definition 2.29.

Problem 6.2. Given a sequent $(\Gamma, \forall x.\phi(x) \Longrightarrow \Delta)$ the goal is to generate an update u such that (see Remark 6.1):

$$(\{u\}(\Gamma, \forall x.\phi(x) \Longrightarrow \Delta)) \equiv (\Gamma', \text{true} \Longrightarrow \Delta') \qquad (6.6)$$

where Γ' and Δ' are obtained by applying $\{u\}$ on the formulas of the sets Γ and Δ, respectively.

If this problem is solved by a technique for given formulas, then this technique can be applied iteratively to all quantified formulas occurring in Γ and Δ resulting in a sequent $\Gamma'' \Longrightarrow \Delta''$ that consists only of ground formulas. Note that this problem is undecidable in the general case because otherwise the satisfiability problem of first-order logic formulas would be decidable. A technique for solving this problem can also be used to build models for ground formulas but we concentrate mainly on the harder problem – the removal of quantified formulas from a sequent. Note that non-Skolemizable quantified formulas occurring in the succedent Δ are those with existential quantifiers and they can be *moved* to the antecedent Γ using the following equivalence:

$$(\Gamma \Longrightarrow \exists x.\phi(x), \Delta) \equiv (\Gamma, \forall x.\neg\phi(x) \Longrightarrow \Delta)$$

We have implemented different algorithms that follow this approach. Unfortunately, only in rare cases the Problem 6.2 was solved by early algorithms we have developed. Based on experiments with these algorithms we have identified two important problems that we state in form of the following informal proposition.

Proposition 6.3. *a) In general cases of* $\forall x.\phi(x)$, *it is necessary to somehow analyze the semantic properties about the matrix* $\phi(x)$ *and to construct the update u based on this information in order to satisfy* $\models \{u\}\forall x.\phi(x)$.

b) *The KeY theorem prover is often not sufficiently powerful to au-tomatically simplify* $(\Gamma', \{u\}\forall x.\phi(x) \Longrightarrow \Delta')$ *to* $(\Gamma', \text{true} \Longrightarrow \Delta')$ *if* $\vDash \{u\}\forall x.\phi(x)$ *and* u *is a quantified update.*

The problem (a) of Proposition 6.3 requires some systematic method that analyzes the semantic properties of the matrix $\phi(x)$. This is because the formula $\phi(x)$ can have an arbitrary propositional structure or contain literals with semantic dependencies. For instance, in the formula $\forall x.(f(x) > x \wedge g(x) < f(x))$ the function g depends on the function f, and the function f depends on the variable x. Some possibilities to analyze the semantic properties of $\phi(x)$ are to test instances of $\phi(x)$ or to use free variables (see, e.g., [Giese, 2001]). We have experimented with the latter approach and could solve problem (a) in some cases.

The reason for problem (b) is that in order to simplify the matrix $\phi(x)$ the sequent calculus requires semantic information about $\phi(x)$ to be available on the sequent level, i.e., in the formulas $\Gamma \cup \Delta$. For instance, the calculus presented in Section 2.4 is not capable to evaluate the quantified formula in the sequent $\forall x.(A \rightarrow (A \vee B)) \Longrightarrow$ to true[4]. This is because propositional rules are not applicable on the quantified formula and the only applicable rule is quantifier instantiation, which does not eliminate the quantified formula either.

6.3.2 The Solution

We have implemented an algorithm that solves both problems of Proposition 6.3 and is capable to solve Problem 6.10 in many cases. The algorithm is described in Section 6.4. In this section we provide a theorem that formalizes the crucial problem simplification technique of the algorithm. The simplification technique is the core of the algorithm and we therefore prove the soundness of this simplification.

For the construction of the updates it is sometimes necessary to introduce and axiomatize fresh function symbols. For instance, it may be desired to introduce a fresh function $notZero \in \text{FSym}_{nr}$ with the axiom $\neg(notZero \doteq 0)$. With this axiom it is, e.g., possible to write

---

[4] The KeY tool implements a more powerful calculus than presented in this thesis and it is capable of evaluating the quantified formula to true. It reaches, however, its limitations when more complex matrices are encountered because this kind of evaluation does not follow the idea of the sequent calculus.

an update $a := b + notZero$, with $a, b \in \text{Trm}^{FOL}$, expressing a general assignment to a with a value different from b. Each update u_i is therefore associated with an axiom α_i. Note that several axioms can be combined to one axiom by using a conjunction.

Definition 6.4. *Given a sequent* $\varphi = (\Gamma, \forall x.\phi(x) \implies \Delta)$*, where* $\Gamma, \Delta \subset \text{Fml}^{FOL}$ *and* $\phi(x) \in \text{Fml}^{FOL}$ *is a formula with an occurrence of* $x \in$ *VSym. Let* $m \in \mathbb{N}$, $u_0, \ldots, u_m \in$ *Updates; and formulas* $\alpha_0, \ldots, \alpha_m \in \text{Fml}^{FOL}$*. The formulas* $\psi_m, \varphi'_m, \varphi_m \in$ *Formulae, for* $m \in \mathbb{N}$*, are defined recursively as:*

- $\varphi_0 = (\Gamma, \forall x.\phi(x) \implies \Delta)$ $\varphi_{m+1} = \alpha_m \to \{u_m\}\varphi_m$
- $\varphi'_0 = (\Gamma, \underline{\text{true}} \implies \Delta)$ $\varphi'_{m+1} = \alpha_m \to \{u_m\}\varphi'_m$
- $\psi_0 = (\Gamma \implies \underline{\forall x.\phi(x)}, \Delta)$ $\psi_{m+1} = \alpha_m \to \{u_m\}\psi_m$

Definition 6.4 can be seen as an abstract search technique where the sequence of updates $u_m ; \ldots ; u_0$, $m \in \mathbb{N}$, has to be found for solving the Problem 6.2. The updates $u_m ; \ldots ; u_0$ constitute the update u in Problem 6.2 and $\varphi_0 \equiv \varphi$ is the original sequent that is to be shown falsifiable. In the following theorem we assume $\gamma = \underline{\forall x.\phi(x)}$.

Theorem 6.5. *Let* $\mathcal{S}$ *be the set of partial models (see Def. 2.6). Let* $\varphi = (\Gamma, \gamma \implies \Delta)$ *and* $\psi_m, \varphi'_m, \varphi_m \in$ *Formulae be defined according to Definition 6.4, then*

   i. $\models \psi_m \leftrightarrow (\varphi'_m \leftrightarrow \varphi_m)$
   ii. If there is $s_m \in \mathcal{S}$ *such that* $s_m \models \neg\varphi_m$*, then there exists* $s \in \mathcal{S}$ *with* $s = val_{s_m}(u_m; \ldots ; u_1)(s_m)$ *and* $s \models \neg\varphi$*.*

The theorem is proven in Section 6.3.3.

The theorem describes under what condition a sequence (not sequent) of update and axiom pairs $(u_0, \alpha_0), \ldots, (u_m, \alpha_m)$ evaluates a quantified formula to true; and the theorem describes how this sequence represents a partial model.

Formula $\neg\varphi$ is the formula for which a model shall be generated. Statement (*ii*) of Theorem 6.5 states that if there is a model $s_m \in \mathcal{S}$ for a formula $\neg\varphi_m$, according to Definition 6.4, then from s_m a model for $\neg\varphi$ can be derived by evaluation of the updates $u_0, \ldots, u_m$. Hence, $\neg\varphi_m$ can be used to show the satisfiability of $\neg\varphi$.

For instance, let $\varphi \equiv (\neg a = b)$, then a suitable pair (u_0, α_0) to construct φ_1 is, e.g. $(a := b, \text{true})$. In this case φ_1 has the form $\text{true} \to \{a := b\}(\neg a = b)$ which can be simplified to false. Hence, any state $s_1 \in \mathcal{S}$ satisfies $s_1 \models \neg\varphi_1$ which implies that $\neg\varphi$ is satisfiable and a model $s \in \mathcal{S}$ for $\neg\varphi$ is $s = val_{s_1}(a := b)(s_1)$. Note, that choosing an update is a problem for which no general uniform solution exists, e.g., the pair $(b := a, \text{true})$ or the pair $(a := 1 \,\|\, b := 1, \text{false})$ are also suitable candidates. We provide heuristics for finding such updates in Section 6.5.

An important property of the statement (ii) for the construction of an update search procedure is that soundness of the statement is preserved by any pair (u, α). I.e., in principle random updates could be *tried-out* by a search procedure. For instance, consider the pair $(a := 1 \,\|\, b := 2, \text{true})$ or the pair $(a := b, \text{false})$ where neither of them represents a model of φ, with $\varphi \equiv (\neg a = b)$. In both cases φ_1 evaluates to true. Hence, there is no $s_1 \in \mathcal{S}$ such that $s_1 \vDash \neg\varphi_1$ and therefore statement (ii) makes no implication regarding the satisfiability of $\neg\varphi$.

Based on statement (i) an algorithm can be constructed for the generation of models for ground formulas. The challenge is, however, to generate a model that satisfies a quantified formula that cannot be Skolemized. If ψ_m is valid then the model generation problem for $\neg\varphi_m$ can be replaced by the model generation problem for $\neg\varphi'_m$ because φ_m and φ'_m are equivalent. Considering Definition 6.4, the statement (i) is interesting because in φ'_m the quantified formula is eliminated, i.e., it is replaced by true. Together with statement (ii), $\neg\varphi'_m$ can be used to generate a model for $\neg\varphi$.

The problem is to check if $\varphi'_m \equiv \varphi_m$, which is a generalization of Problem 6.2. Theorem 6.5 states that the problem $\varphi'_m \equiv \varphi_m$ can be solved by a validity proof of ψ_m. This allows solving the problems described in Proposition 6.3 because the quantified formula in ψ_m occurs negated with respect to φ_m and can therefore be Skolemized. For instance, let $\varphi_m = (\forall x.\phi(x) \Longrightarrow)$, then $\psi_m = (\Longrightarrow \forall x.\phi(x))$. In contrast to φ_m, the latter can be simplified to $(\Longrightarrow \phi(sk))$, where $sk \in \text{FSym}_r$ is the Skolem function. When ψ_m is Skolemized, then it is (a) easy to analyze the semantics of $\phi(sk)$ and (b) the propositional structure of $\phi(sk)$ can be *flattened* to the sequent level which is necessary to simplify quantified updates. In this way both problems described in Proposition 6.3 are solved. For instance, the calculus described in Section 2.4 is not capable to simplify $(\{u\}\forall x.(A \rightarrow (A \vee B)) \Longrightarrow)$ to $(\text{true} \Longrightarrow)$ but it can simplify $(\Longrightarrow \{u\}\forall x.(A \rightarrow (A \vee B)))$ to $(\Longrightarrow \text{true})$, for any update u. More examples showing these advantages are provided in the following sections such as Example 6.9 on page 157.

The approach can be generalized for the generation of models for ground formulas by using the more general Definition 6.6 instead of Definition 6.4 in Theorem 6.5.

Definition 6.6. *Given a sequent $\varphi = (\Gamma, \gamma \Longrightarrow \Delta)$, where $\gamma \in \mathrm{Fml}^{FOL}$ and $\Gamma, \Delta \subset \mathrm{Fml}^{FOL}$. Let $m \in \mathbb{N}$, $u_0, \ldots, u_m \in Updates$; and the formulas $\alpha_0, \ldots, \alpha_m \in \mathrm{Fml}^{FOL}$. The formulas $\psi_m, \varphi'_m, \varphi_m \in Formulae$, for $m \in \mathbb{N}$, are defined recursively as:*

- $\varphi_0 = (\Gamma, \gamma \Longrightarrow \Delta)$ $\varphi_{m+1} = \alpha_m \to \{u_m\} \varphi_m$
- $\varphi'_0 = (\Gamma, \underline{\text{true}} \Longrightarrow \Delta)$ $\varphi'_{m+1} = \alpha_m \to \{u_m\} \varphi'_m$
- $\psi_0 = (\Gamma \Longrightarrow \gamma, \Delta)$ $\psi_{m+1} = \alpha_m \to \{u_m\} \psi_m$

6.3.3 Soundness Proof of Theorem 6.5

Lemma 6.7. *Let $A, B, C \in Formulae$. The formula following is a valid*

$$(A \to (B \leftrightarrow C)) \leftrightarrow ((A \to B) \leftrightarrow (A \to C)) \qquad (6.7)$$

Proof. Consider the two cases: A evaluates to true and A evaluates to false. The two resulting formulas

$$(B \leftrightarrow C) \ \leftrightarrow \ (B \leftrightarrow C)$$

$$\text{and}$$

$$true \ \leftrightarrow \ (true \leftrightarrow true)$$

are obviously tautologies.   ∎

Proof of Theorem 6.5

The proof of Theorem 6.5 is based on induction on m.

<u>*Induction Base (m = 0)*</u> (i) Validity of

$$(\underbrace{\Gamma \Longrightarrow \forall x.\phi(x), \Delta}_{\psi_0}) \leftrightarrow ((\underbrace{\Gamma, \text{true} \Longrightarrow \Delta}_{\varphi'_0}) \leftrightarrow (\underbrace{\Gamma, \forall x.\phi(x) \Longrightarrow \Delta}_{\varphi_0})) \qquad (6.8)$$

can be shown by using propositional transformation rules. Using the abbreviations $\Phi = \neg\Gamma \vee \Delta$ and $C = \forall x.\phi(x)$, Formula 6.8 rewrites to:

$$(C \vee \Phi) \leftrightarrow (\Phi \leftrightarrow (C \to \Phi)) \qquad (6.9)$$

We consider the two cases: C evaluates to true and C evaluates to false. This results in the following two formulas

$$true \quad \leftrightarrow \quad (\varPhi \leftrightarrow \varPhi)$$

$$and$$

$$\varPhi \quad \leftrightarrow \quad (\varPhi \leftrightarrow true)$$

which are obviously tautologies.

(ii) Since $\varphi_0 = \varphi$ and $s = s_0$ statement (ii) is trivially true.

Induction Step ($m \rightarrow m + 1$) (i) Assuming $\models \psi_m \leftrightarrow (\varphi'_m \leftrightarrow \varphi_m)$, we want to show that $\models \psi_{m+1} \leftrightarrow (\varphi'_{m+1} \leftrightarrow \varphi_{m+1})$. If the statement

$$\models \psi_m \leftrightarrow (\varphi'_m \leftrightarrow \varphi_m) \tag{6.10}$$

holds, then according to Lemma 2.27 (page 43) the following statement holds for any $u_m \in$ *Updates*.

$$\models \{u_m\}(\psi_m \leftrightarrow (\varphi'_m \leftrightarrow \varphi_m)) \tag{6.11}$$

Using Lemma 2.45 this is equivalent to

$$\models \{u_m\}\psi_m \leftrightarrow (\{u_m\}\varphi'_m \leftrightarrow \{u_m\}\varphi_m) \tag{6.12}$$

For any $\alpha \in \mathrm{Fml}^{FOL}$, statement (6.12) implies

$$\models \alpha \rightarrow (\{u_m\}\psi_m \leftrightarrow (\{u_m\}\varphi'_m \leftrightarrow \{u_m\}\varphi_m)) \tag{6.13}$$

Using Lemma 6.7 the following equivalent statements are obtained.

$$\models (\alpha \rightarrow \{u_m\}\psi_m) \leftrightarrow (\alpha \rightarrow (\{u_m\}\varphi'_m \leftrightarrow \{u_m\} \varphi_m)) \tag{6.14}$$

$$\models (\alpha \rightarrow \{u_m\}\psi_m) \leftrightarrow ((\alpha \rightarrow \{u_m\}\varphi'_m) \leftrightarrow (\alpha \rightarrow \{u_m\}\varphi_m)) \tag{6.15}$$

Statement 6.15 is equivalent to $\models \psi_{m+1} \leftrightarrow (\varphi'_{m+1} \leftrightarrow \varphi_{m+1})$.

(ii) Assuming that statement (ii) of the theorem holds for some $m \geqslant 0$ we show that it holds also for $m + 1$. Assume there is $s_{m+1} \in \mathcal{S}$ such that $s_{m+1} \models \neg\varphi_{m+1}$. By propagating the negation of $\neg\varphi_{m+1}$ to the inside of the formula, loosely speaking, we obtain the equivalent formula $\hat{\varphi}_m \in$ *Formulae* that can be recursively defined as

$$\hat{\varphi}_0 = \neg(\varGamma, true \Longrightarrow \varDelta) \qquad \hat{\varphi}_{m+1} = (\alpha_m \wedge \{u_m\}\hat{\varphi}_m)$$

Hence, $s_{m+1} \models \neg\varphi_{m+1}$ is equivalent to $s_{m+1} \models \hat{\varphi}_{m+1}$ which is equivalent to $s_{m+1} \models (\alpha_m \wedge \{u_m\}\hat{\varphi}_m)$. There is $s_m \in \mathcal{S}$ with $s_m =$

$val_{s_{m+1}}(u_m)(s_{m+1})$ such that $s_m \vDash \alpha_m \wedge \hat{\varphi}_m$ and therefore $s_m \vDash \hat{\varphi}_m$. Since $\hat{\varphi}_m$ is equivalent to $\neg\varphi_m$ we have $s_m \vDash \neg\varphi_m$.

According to the induction hypothesis there exists $s \in \mathcal{S}$ with $s = val_{s_m}(u_m; \ldots; u_1)(s_m)$ such that $s \vDash \neg\varphi$. Because of $s_m = val_{s_{m+1}}(u_m)(s_{m+1})$, we conclude that if $s_{m+1} \vDash \neg\varphi_{m+1}$, then there exists $s \in \mathcal{S}$ with $s = val_{s_{m+1}}(u_{m+1}; u_m; \ldots; u_1)(s_{m+1})$ such that $s \vDash \neg\varphi$.

∎

6.4 The Model Search Algorithm

Preliminaries

The basic idea of Algorithm 3 is to generate a partial FOL model in which a quantified formula that we want to eliminate evaluates to true. A set of quantified formulas is eliminated, i.e. evaluated to true, by successive extensions of the partial model. This approach can be continued also on ground formulas to generate complete models. The technique requires a theorem prover for FOL and an implementation of updates and the update simplification calculus. In the following we give general requirements of the theorem prover which are satisfied, e.g., by KeY.

Definition 6.8. *Procedure Th.* *The procedure* Th *represents a theorem prover.*

- *Given a formula $\vartheta \in$ Formulae as input,* Th(ϑ) *returns a set $\Theta \subset$ Fml^{FOL}.*
- *Each $\vartheta' \in \Theta$ is a disjunction consisting of literals and quantified formulas.*
- *$\Theta \vDash_A \vartheta$, where A is the set of new symbols introduced by* Th. *(see Def. 2.12, page 32)*
- *For all $\vartheta' \in \Theta$ the following holds $\vDash (\neg\vartheta') \to (\neg\vartheta)$.*

The requirement that the theorem prover accepts as input DL formulas is an over-approximation because the only extension of FOL needed is the update language. In order to handle FOL formulas with updates, an update simplification preprocessor can be combined with an off-the-shelf theorem prover. The second requirement means that if Th terminates with a set of open proof branches, i.e. unproved proof obligations, then at least the propositional structure of formulas must be simplified. The third and fourth requirements prevent the loss of semantic information during proving. The requirement $\Theta \vDash_A \vartheta$ expresses soundness of Th and implies that if $\Theta = \emptyset$, then $\vDash \vartheta$ holds. The last requirement coincides with the requirement that the branches Θ are validity preserving (see Section 4.4.1).

The KeY tool satisfies these requirements. A sequent can be seen as a disjunction, where the formulas in the antecedent are negated. In the following sections we assume that the set Θ returned by Th consists of sequents and we include sequents into the set Fml^{FOL} as syntactic sugar.

In this chapter two algorithms are described. Algorithm 3, which is described in this section, extracts information from (quantified) formulas for update construction and invokes the theorem prover Th to verify $\{u\}\varphi$. Algorithm 3 queries Algorithm 4 to construct candidate updates based on information obtained from Algorithm 3. Algorithm 4 is described in Section 6.6. In order to keep the pseudo-code small we use indeterministic choice points, marked by the keyword **choose**, and assume a backtracking control-flow w.r.t. to these choice points. In this way we also separate the basic algorithm from concrete search heuristics. If a choice at a choice point cannot be made, e.g., when trying to select an element of an empty set, then the algorithm backtracks or terminates with the result "unknown" resp. "$\emptyset$".

Description of Algorithm 3

Assume we want to generate a model satisfying the input formula ϕ_{in}. The Algorithm 3 reformulates this problem as counterexample generation for $\neg\phi_{in}$ which is represented by φ' (Line 1). In Line 4 the algorithm attempts to show $\vDash \varphi'$. If φ' is valid, then $\Phi = \emptyset$ and the algorithm stops because φ' has no counterexample and ϕ_{in} is unsatisfiable. The other case is that the proof attempt of φ' results in a set of open, i.e. unproved, proof obligations Φ (Line 5). In this case it is unknown if a model of ϕ_{in} exists or not. The proof obligations Φ result from case distinctions in the proof structure created by Th and contain valuable information because they describe situations in which φ' potentially has counterexamples.

In Line 5 the algorithm selects a formula $\varphi \in \Phi$. The goal is to create a counterexample for φ, i.e. to satisfy $\neg\varphi$, in order to satisfy ϕ_{in}. Ground formulas should be preferred at this choice point because they can be efficiently checked by a ground procedure such

---

Algorithm 3 modelSearch(ϕ_{in})

1: $\varphi' := \neg\phi_{in}$
2: solution $:= \bot$
3: **loop**
4:     $\Phi := \mathtt{Th}(\varphi')$
5:     **choose** $\varphi \in \Phi$
6:     **if** φ is ground **then**
7:         **if** GROUNDPROC($\neg\varphi$) = ("sat", groundmodel) **then**
8:             **return** ("sat", groundmodel, solution)
9:         **else**
10:             **backtrack** or **return** ("unknown", $\bot$, $\bot$)
11:         **end if**
12:     **end if**
13:     normalize φ such that all quantified formulas appear in the antecedent of φ
14:     **choose** a quantified formula $\forall x.\phi(x)$ in φ, i.e., let $\varphi = (\Gamma, \underline{\forall x.\phi(x)} \Longrightarrow \Delta)$
15:     $\varphi' := (\Gamma, \underline{\mathrm{true}} \Longrightarrow \Delta)$
16:     $\psi := (\Gamma \Longrightarrow \underline{\forall x.\phi(x)}, \Delta)$
17:     $\Psi := \mathtt{Th}(\psi)$
18:     **while** $\Psi \neq \emptyset$ **do**
19:         **choose** $\psi' \in \Psi$
20:         $\Upsilon := \mathrm{formulaToUpdate}(\psi')$ (see Section 6.6)
21:         **choose** $(u, \alpha) \in \Upsilon$
22:         solution := append (u, α) to solution
23:         $\varphi' := (\alpha \rightarrow \{u\}\varphi')$
24:         $\psi := (\alpha \rightarrow \{u\}\psi)$
25:         $\Psi := \mathtt{Th}(\psi)$
26:     **end while**
27: **end loop**

---

as an SMT solver. Otherwise, we assume φ is not ground. After normalization at Line 13 the antecedent of φ contains at least one universally quantified formula and all formulas of the succedent are ground. This normalization can be easily achieved by the equivalence $(\Gamma \Longrightarrow \exists x.\phi(x), \Delta) \equiv (\Gamma, \forall x \neg\phi(x) \Longrightarrow \Delta)$. A counterexample for φ must satisfy the formulas in the antecedent, i.e. Γ and $\forall x.\phi(x)$. The algorithm selects a quantified formula $\forall x.\phi(x)$ from the antecedent of φ (Line 14) for which a model is generated in the following.

The core idea of this algorithm is to generate an update u, such that $\{u\}\forall x.\phi(x)$ evaluates to true, and in this way to eliminate the quantified formula. The weakest condition under which $\forall x.\phi(x)$ evaluates to true in φ can be expressed as

$$(\underbrace{\Gamma, \forall x.\phi(x) \Longrightarrow \Delta}_{\varphi}) \leftrightarrow (\underbrace{\Gamma, \text{true} \Longrightarrow \Delta}_{\varphi'}) \qquad (6.16)$$

which simplifies by equivalence transformations to

$$\underbrace{\Gamma \Longrightarrow \forall x.\phi(x), \Delta}_{\psi} \qquad (6.17)$$

Any model of (6.17) is also a model of (6.16). This means that in states which satisfy (6.17) the quantified formula $\forall x.\phi(x)$ can be replaced by true. This corresponds to the statement (i) for $m = 0$ of Theorem 6.5 that we show here for convenience.

$$(i) \vDash \psi_m \leftrightarrow (\varphi'_m \leftrightarrow \varphi_m)$$

Hence, in Line 15 the formula φ' is constructed where the quantified formula is replaced by true. Substituting φ by φ' in subsequent computation is sound only if (6.16) or equivalently (6.17) is valid. Therefore formula (6.17) is assigned to ψ in Line 16 and is checked by Th in Line 17. If ψ can be proved, then the algorithm continues in Line 4 where φ' (now without the quantified formula) is used instead of φ. Otherwise, if the proof of (6.17) of does not close (Line 17), then the result is a set of proof obligations Ψ.

The formulas Ψ (Line 19) describe potential states in which $\forall x.\phi(x)$ does not evaluate to true. The goal is therefore to construct an update u (Line 20) such that for each formula $\psi' \in \Psi$, $\vDash \{u\}\psi'$. If this is the case, then also $\vDash \{u\}\psi$ which allows us to eliminate the quantified formula by the equivalence (6.16). Instead of satisfying this condition in one step, our heuristic is rather to extend u iteratively. In each iteration of the inner loop one formula $\psi' \in \Psi$ is selected in Line 19 and Ψ is updated in Line 25 until Ψ *eventually* decreases to $\emptyset$.

The goal of the inner loop is to generate an update u and a formula α (Line 20) and to check if

$$\alpha \to \{u\}\psi \qquad (6.18)$$

evaluates to true. Formula 6.18 (see Line 24) is a weakening of (6.17). The procedure `formulaToUpdate` which is described in Section 6.6 generates candidate pairs (u, a) that are likely to satisfy (6.18).[5] In (6.17),

---

[5] Note that since the procedure `formulaToUpdate` uses only one formula $\psi' \in \Psi$ to construct the pair (u, α), Formula (6.18) may not evaluate to true. In this case the inner loop continues iteration and unsolved formulas $\psi' \in \Psi$ reappear in the next iteration to be solved.

respectively (6.18), the quantified formula occurs negated w.r.t. (6.16). As described in Section 6.3.2 an important consequence of this negation is that in Lines 17 and 25 the theorem prover can Skolemize the quantified formula (6.17) resulting in

$$\Gamma \Longrightarrow \phi(sk), \Delta \tag{6.19}$$

where $sk \in \mathrm{FSym}_r$ is a fresh symbol. In this way the formula $\phi(sk)$ can be simplified by the calculus and information contained in the structure of $\phi(sk)$ is extracted to the sequent level, i.e., the boolean structure of $\phi(sk)$ is flattened (see 1st and 2nd requirement of Def. 6.8). This information occurs in the formulas $\psi' \in \Psi$ (Line 19). The task of generating a pair (u, α) from ψ' for satisfying (6.18) by the procedure `formulaToUpdate` is considerably simpler than generating the pair from the whole unsimplified quantified formula $\forall x.\phi(x)$.

Example 6.9. Let φ be defined as

$$\varphi = (A, \forall x.\underbrace{(f(x) > x \wedge g(x) < f(x))}_{\phi(x)} \Longrightarrow B) \tag{6.20}$$

where $A, B \in Fml_{FOL}$. Generating a model for φ in one step is complicated because the quantified formula cannot be Skolemized. In contrast, in

$$\psi = (A \Longrightarrow \forall x.\phi(x), B)$$

the quantified formula is negated (because $(F \Longrightarrow) \equiv (\Longrightarrow \neg F)$) and can therefore be Skolemized. $\mathrm{Th}(\psi)$ yields

$$\Psi = \{(A \Longrightarrow f(sk) > sk, B), (A \Longrightarrow g(sk) < f(sk), B)\}$$

The structure of each $\psi' \in \Psi$ is simpler than the structure of ψ. The procedure `formulaToUpdate` can then generate, e.g., the following updates with axioms to satisfy the formulas in Ψ respectively:

$$\{((\texttt{for } x; \ \text{true}; \ f(x) := x + 1), \text{true}),$$
$$((\texttt{for } x; \ \text{true}; \ g(x) := f(x) - 1), \text{true})\}$$

Note that the procedure `formulaToUpdate` generates more general updates than are necessary for the satisfaction of Ψ because the goal is to satisfy ψ as described above.

□

Checking Formula (6.18) (on page 156) as described above is important because it is equivalent to

$$(\alpha \rightarrow \{u\}\varphi) \leftrightarrow (\alpha \rightarrow \{u\}\varphi') \qquad (6.21)$$

which in turn is a weakening of (6.16). Accordingly, in Line 23 the formula φ' is updated. If (6.18) is valid, which is checked in Line 25, then the inner loop terminates and the outer loop continues execution. Hence, the original counterexample generation problem for φ is replaced by the counterexample generation problem for $\alpha \rightarrow \{u\}\varphi'$ where the quantified formula is eliminated, i.e. replaced by true. This is sound because if (6.18) is valid, then (6.21) is valid and therefore a counterexample for $\alpha \rightarrow \{u\}\varphi'$ is a counterexample for $\alpha \rightarrow \{u\}\varphi$. The latter implies that φ has a counterexample as well which is formalized by statement (ii) of Theorem 6.5.

6.5 Heuristics for Update Construction from Formulas

While Section 6.3 describes a general sound framework for model generation, in this section we study how to generate a partial model for one selected formula γ in a sequent $\varphi = (\Gamma, \gamma \Longrightarrow \Delta)$. In particular we give an intuition of how quantified updates can be constructed in order to satisfy quantified formulas. The described heuristics can then be used to iteratively extend the partial model for all formulas in the sequent. Important to note is that soundness of Theorem 6.5 is preserved by *any* sequence of update and axiom pairs. Hence, unsoundness cannot be introduced by any of the heuristics.

Definition 6.10. *Update Construction. Let $\gamma \in \mathrm{Fml}^{FOL}$ be the currently selected formula for which a partial model is to be created and which is a sub-formula in a sequent $\varphi = (\Gamma, \gamma \Longrightarrow \Delta)$. Further, let $\psi = (\Gamma \Longrightarrow \gamma, \Delta)$ and $\varphi' = (\Gamma \Longrightarrow \Delta)$.*

The goal of update construction from the formula γ is to create a pair (u, α), with $u \in U$ and $\alpha \in Fml$, such that

- *$\vDash \alpha \rightarrow \{u\}\psi$, and*
- *there is some $s \in \mathcal{S}$ with $s \vDash \neg(\alpha \rightarrow \{u\}\varphi')$*

The first condition ensures that $\vDash (\alpha \rightarrow \{u\}\varphi) \leftrightarrow (\alpha \rightarrow \{u\}\varphi')$ which corresponds to statement (i) of Theorem 6.5. The second condition satisfies, in combination with the first condition, the assumption in the statement (ii) of the theorem. The second condition ensures that, e.g. the trivial pair $(\{\}, \text{false})$ is not used to satisfy the first condition. In this case $\vDash \text{false} \rightarrow \{\}\psi$ but there is no $s \in \mathcal{S}$ satisfying $s \vDash \neg(\text{false} \rightarrow \{\}\varphi')$.

The sequent ψ is equivalent to ψ_0 and φ' is equivalent to φ'_0, according to Definition 6.6 (page 151). In the model search algorithm each time a pair (u_m, α_m) is constructed, new formulas $\varphi'_{m+1}, \varphi'_{m+1}$, and ψ_{m+1} are generated according to Definition 6.6. These formulas must be simplified by Th to φ, ψ and, φ', respectively, such that a new formula $\gamma \in \text{Fml}^{FOL}$ can be selected for update construction. We assume that φ is an open branch of Th, i.e. $\varphi \in \text{Th}$, and it is therefore simplified according to Definition 6.8. Hence, γ is either a literal or a quantified formula. In the following subsections, case distinctions are made on the structure of γ.

6.5.1 Update Construction from Ground Formulas

In the following we ignore the context formulas Γ and Δ, i.e., we assume that $\Gamma = \Delta = \emptyset$. Since $\varphi' \equiv (\emptyset \Longrightarrow \emptyset) \equiv \text{false}$ the second condition of Definition 6.10 is satisfied if $\alpha \not\equiv \text{false}$.

Handling of Equalities

Assume $t_1, t_2 \in \text{Trm}^{FOL}$ are *location terms* (see Def. 2.16, page 34). If γ is of the form

$$t_1 = l \text{ or } l = t_1$$

where l is a literal, then the pair $(t_1 := l, \text{true})$ should be created because it satisfies the first condition of Definition 6.10 as $\vDash \text{true} \rightarrow \{t_1 := l\}(t_1 \doteq l \wedge l \doteq t_1)$. If γ is of the form

$$t_1 = t_2$$

then a choice has to be made between the pairs $(t_1 := t_2, \text{true})$ and $(t_2 := t_1, \text{true})$. In both cases the first condition of Definition 6.10 is satisfied as $\vDash \text{true} \rightarrow \{t_1 := t_2\}(t_1 \doteq t_2)$ and $\vDash \text{true} \rightarrow \{t_2 := t_1\}(t_1 \doteq t_2)$. The particular choice has influence on the rest of the partial model construction.

Equality between terms can in some cases also be established, if the terms share the same top-level function symbol and have location terms as arguments. For instance, let $f(t_1), f(t_2) \in \text{Trm}^{FOL}$ and $f \in \text{FSym}_r$, then $\vDash \alpha \rightarrow \{u\}(f(t_1) = f(t_2))$ can be satisfied by the pair $(t_1 := t_2, \text{true})$ or by $(t_2 := t_1, \text{true})$.

Handling of Arithmetic Expressions

Let $t_1, t_2 \in \mathrm{Trm}^{FOL}$ be arithmetic expressions composed of rigid and non-rigid function symbols. Several solutions exist to satisfy $\vDash \alpha \rightarrow \{u\}(t_1 \doteq t_2)$. Consider for instance the polynomial equation

$$2 * a + b * c = d - e$$

where $a, b, c, d, e \in \mathrm{Trm}^{FOL}$ are location terms. There are five most general updates evaluating this equation to true. These can be obtained by solving the polynomial equation for one of the location terms at a time. Our implementation enumerates those solutions during update search. An example for one of the solutions is

$$(a := (d - e - b * c)/2, \mathrm{true})$$

Note that a, b, c, d, e are not restricted to constants, i.e., terms consisting of a unary function.

Handling of Inequalities

Let $t_1, t_2 \in Trm_{FOL}$ where t_1 is a location term. An inequation

$$\neg t_1 \doteq t_2$$

can be satisfied, e.g., by the pair $(t_1 := t_2 + 1, \mathrm{true})$. A more general update is, however, $t_1 := t_2 + notZero$, where $notZero \in \mathrm{FSym}_{nr}$ is a fresh-symbol representing a value different from 0. This is where the axiom part of a pair comes into play. A more general solution for the formula $t_1 \neq t_2$ is the pair

$$(t_1 := t_2 + notZero, \neg(notZero = 0))$$

This pair satisfies both conditions of Definition 6.10. We allow the constant $notZero$ to be non-rigid, so that during model generation its value can be further concretized.

Inequations of the form

$$t_1 < t_2$$

can be handled by introducing a fresh symbol $gtZero \in \mathrm{FSym}_{nr}$ with the axiom $gtZero > 0$.

6.5.2 Update Construction from Quantified Formulas

Our approach to create models for quantified formulas is to generate quantified updates. For example, the quantified formula

$$\forall x . x > a \rightarrow f(x) = g(x) + x \qquad (6.22)$$

is satisfiable in any state after execution of the quantified update

$$\texttt{for } x; \ x > a; \ f(x) := g(x) + x \qquad (6.23)$$

i.e., $\vDash \{(6.23)\}(6.22)$. Notice the similar syntactical structure between (6.22) and (6.23). Another solution is

$$\texttt{for } x; \ x > a; \ g(x) := f(x) - x \qquad (6.24)$$

for which holds $\vDash \{(6.24)\}(6.22)$. It is easy to see that a translation can be generalized for other *simple* quantified formulas. Furthermore, the heuristics and case distinctions described in Section 6.5.1 can be reused to handle different arithmetic expressions and relations. For instance the formula

$$\forall x . f(x) \geqslant x \rightarrow (g(x) < f(x))$$

evaluates to true after execution of any of the following updates (with axioms)

$$(\texttt{for } x; \ f(x) \geqslant x; \ g(x) := f(x) + gtZero \, , \, gtZero > 0)$$
$$(\texttt{for } x; \ \neg(g(x) < f(x)); \ f(x) := x - gtZero \, , \, gtZero > 0)$$

The update simplification calculus may in some cases introduce new quantified formulas (see Lemma 2.43). In such cases our approach has to be applied either recursively on the new quantified formulas or the heuristic has to choose different updates in a search procedure to prevent the introduction of new quantified formulas.

The initial example of this chapter, i.e. Formula (6.1), can be solved by the following quantified update application which the KeY system simplifies to true.

$$\{(\texttt{for } x_1; \ x_1 \geqslant 0; \ next(x_1) := x_1);$$
$$(\texttt{for } x_2; \ x_2 \geqslant 0; \ prev(next(x_2)) := x_2)\}(6.1)$$

6.5.3 Weakening of Updates

The more locations are assigned specific values by the update u, i.e., the bigger the set of semantic updates $val_s(u)$ is (see Section 2.3.2.1 on page 37), the higher is the probability that the first condition of Definition 6.10 (page 158) is satisfied but not the second.

Example 6.11. In this example we show the effect of different updates on the conditions of Definition 6.10. We do not show the semantic updates, as it is easier to read the *syntactical* updates.

Let

$$\varphi = (\overbrace{g(1) \doteq 1}^{\Gamma}, \overbrace{\forall x. f(x) \doteq g(x)}^{\gamma} \Longrightarrow)$$
$$\varphi' = (g(1) \doteq 1, \text{true} \Longrightarrow)$$
$$\psi = (g(1) \doteq 1 \Longrightarrow \forall x. f(x) \doteq g(x))$$

Attempt 1. Using the pair $(\overbrace{f(1) := g(1)}^{u}, \overbrace{\text{true}}^{\alpha})$ the second condition of Definition 6.10 which is given by

$$\text{there is } s \in \mathcal{S} \text{ with } s \models \neg(\overbrace{\text{true}}^{\alpha} \to \overbrace{\{f(1) := g(1)\}}^{u} \overbrace{\neg(g(1) \doteq 1 \land \text{true})}^{\varphi'}$$

is satisfied. It can be simplified to

$$\text{there is some } s \in \mathcal{S} \text{ with } s \models g(1) \doteq 1$$

However, the first condition of Definition 6.10 which is given by

$$\models \overbrace{\text{true}}^{\alpha} \to \overbrace{\{f(1) := g(1)\}}^{u} \overbrace{(g(1) \doteq 1 \to \forall x. f(x) \doteq g(x))}^{\psi}$$

is not satisfied. The problem is that the update does not ensure that for all values of x the equation $f(x) \doteq g(x)$ holds.

Attempt 2. Now we increase the set of semantic updates $val_s(u)$ by choosing the pair $((\text{for } x; \text{true}; f(x) := g(x)), \text{true})$. In this case both conditions of Definition 6.10 are satisfied. Here we only show the conditions without showing their proofs as their validity is easy to see. The first condition is in this case

$$\models \text{true} \to \{\text{for } x; \text{true}; f(x) := g(x)\}(\psi)$$

It can be proved because $\{\texttt{for } x; \text{ true}; f(x) := g(x)\}\forall x.f(x) \doteq g(x)$ evaluates to true. The second condition is

there is some $s \in \mathcal{S}$ with $s \vDash \neg(\text{true} \to \{\texttt{for } x; \text{ true}; f(x) := g(x)\}\varphi')$

It is easy to see that it holds because $\{\texttt{for } x; \text{ true}; f(x) := g(x)\}\varphi' \equiv \varphi'$ and φ' is satisfiable.

Attempt 3. Making the update more specific may result in the violation of the second condition. For instance, when using the pair

$$\overbrace{((\texttt{for } x; \text{ true}; f(x) := 1 \,\|\, g(x) := 1)}^{u}, \text{true})$$

the first condition of Definition 6.10 is satisfied because the formula $\{\texttt{for } x; \text{ true}; f(x) := 1 \,\|\, g(x) := 1\}\forall x.f(x) \doteq g(x)$ evaluates to true. The semantic update is in this case bigger than in Attempt 2 of this example because it additionally fixes the interpretation of the function symbol g. The second condition of Definition 6.10 is in this case

there is some $s \in \mathcal{S}$ with $s \vDash \neg(\text{true} \to \{u\} \overbrace{\neg(g(1) \doteq 0 \wedge \text{true})}^{\varphi'})$

which simplifies to

there is some $s \in \mathcal{S}$ with $s \vDash 1 \doteq 0$

Hence, it is not satisfied.

A balance has to be kept between the specificity and generality of the update in order to satisfy both conditions.

□

When choosing the update u the goal is to keep the set $val_s(u)$ small such that only the interpretation of locations is fixed that is necessary to satisfy the first condition. Similarly, if α is strong, e.g. false, then the first condition is trivially satisfied but the second condition is false. Hence, the goal is to make α as weak as possible.

A general heuristic to make updates less restrictive is to use the context formulas Γ and Δ in the guard of quantified updates. For instance, let (u, α) be a pair such that, $\vDash \alpha \to \{\texttt{for } x; \text{ guard}; u\}(\Gamma \Longrightarrow \gamma, \Delta)$. The update can be restricted to a smaller set of locations by extending the guard as follows

$$\texttt{for } x; \ guard \wedge (\bigwedge \Gamma \wedge \neg \bigvee \Delta); \ u \qquad (6.25)$$

The formula $\{(6.25)\}(\alpha \rightarrow (\Gamma \Longrightarrow \gamma, \Delta))$, remains valid. The new update is restricted only to the state described by the sequent $\Gamma \Longrightarrow \Delta$ which increases the probability of satisfying the second condition of Definition 6.10. Furthermore, as the update is part of a sequence of updates $u_0, \dots, u_m$ in the model search algorithm, the restriction reduces the global influence of u on the whole sequence $u_0, \dots, u_m$.

6.6 Update Generation for Satisfying Quantified Formulas

Algorithm 4 formulaToUpdate(ψ')

1: let $sk =$ the Skolem function of ψ'
2: let $(\Gamma \Longrightarrow \Delta) = \psi'$
3: let $(\Gamma_{sk} \Longrightarrow \Delta_{sk}) \subset (\Gamma \Longrightarrow \Delta)$ (according to the description)
4: **choose** $\vartheta_{sk} \in (\neg \Gamma_{sk} \cup \Delta_{sk})$ (negation is applied to each element in Γ)
5: **choose** $\vartheta'_{sk} \in \texttt{solve}(\vartheta_{sk})$
6: **choose** $(u, \alpha) \in \texttt{concretize}(\vartheta'_{sk})$
7: **choose** $(u', \alpha) \in \texttt{toQuanUpd}(sk, (u, \alpha), (\Gamma_{sk} \Longrightarrow \Delta_{sk}), \vartheta_{sk})$
8: **choose** $(u'', \alpha') \in \texttt{injectiveSubTerms}((u', \alpha))$
9: **return** (u'', α)

In this section we describe Algorithm 4 which is based on the ideas described in Section 6.5. The algorithm is used by Algorithm 3 (page 155) to construct updates for satisfying quantified formulas. According to Section 6.4 this algorithm receives as input a sequent ψ' that is an open proof obligation of $\texttt{Th}(\psi)$. Algorithm 4 is queried for each open proof obligation and is expected to generate an update with an axiom (u, α) that is *likely* to satisfy the conditions in Definition 6.10.

As each pair (u, α) satisfies one of the open proof obligations $\psi' \in \texttt{Th}(\psi)$, a series of such pairs *eventually* satisfies Formula (6.18) (see page 156) if the inner loop of Algorithm 3 terminates. Algorithm 4 returns a set of alternative solutions for each sequent ψ'. Recall that soundness of the approach is guaranteed by any pair (u, α) because the inner loop of Algorithm 3 does not terminate until a model is generated for ψ.

According to Definition 6.8 the sequent ψ' has been simplified such that all formulas on the sequent level are either quantified formulas or atoms. We are interested in atoms that were derived from $\forall x.\phi(x)$. Therefore our heuristic is to categorize those atoms in ψ' as highly relevant for the construction of the update u that have an occurrence of the Skolem symbol sk, that was introduced in (6.19). Let ψ'_{sk} be defined as

$$\Gamma_{sk} \Longrightarrow \Delta_{sk}$$

such that it coincides with ψ', except that all quantified formulas and formulas that do not contain an occurrence of sk are removed in ψ'_{sk} (Line 3 of Algorithm 4). Hence, all formulas in Γ_{sk} and Δ_{sk} are ground formulas with an occurrence of sk. Following the Example 6.9 (page 157), $(\Gamma_{sk} \Longrightarrow \Delta_{sk})$ is either $(\Longrightarrow f(sk) > sk)$ or $(\Longrightarrow g(sk) < f(sk))$.

The goal is to create an update u such that $\vDash (\{u\}\psi'_{sk})$. Note that $(\{u\}\psi'_{sk}) \rightarrow (\{u\}\psi')$. In order to evaluate $\{u\}\psi'_{sk}$ to true the update u must either evaluate an atom in Γ_{sk} to false, or an atom in Δ_{sk} to true. We refer to the chosen atom, whose interpretation we want to manipulate, as the *core atom* and it corresponds to the formula γ in Definition 6.10. Let ϑ_{sk} denote the chosen core atom (Line 4). The task is to construct a function update u such that $\{u\}\vartheta_{sk}$ evaluates true. This task is divided into two steps realized by the algorithms `solve` (Line 5) and `concretize` (Line 6).

Generation of Updates from Core Atoms

Definition 6.12. *The procedure* `solve` *has the property that given an atom ϑ_{sk}, whose top-level symbol is a relation $R \in \mathrm{PSym}$, it constructs a set of atoms Θ and for each atom $\vartheta'_{sk} \in \Theta$:*

- *$\vartheta'_{sk} = R'(f(t_1, \ldots, t_n), v)$, i.e. syntactic equivalence*
- *$\vartheta'_{sk} \equiv \vartheta_{sk}$, i.e. semantics*

where $R' \in \mathrm{PSym}_r$, $f \in \mathrm{FSym}_{nr}$, $f \neq sk$, and $t_1, \ldots, t_n, v \in \mathrm{Trm}^{FOL}$.

The procedure `solve` creates normal forms from core atoms. For example, for the formula $\vartheta_{sk} = (f(sk) + 3 < g(sk) - sk)$, with "$<$" $\in$ PSym, $f, g \in \mathrm{FSym}_{nr}$, the procedure `solve` may generate, e.g., the following set:

$$\{f(sk) < (g(sk) - sk - 3), g(sk) > (f(sk) + 3 + sk)\} \qquad (6.26)$$

In the first core atom of this set $R' = $ "$<$" and in the second core atom $R' = $ "$>$". Note that the procedure `solve` is part of our heuristic and the resulting set is not strictly defined, it may also be empty. Some core atoms may not be solvable by the procedure but the more results the procedure `solve` produces the better is the chance of generating a suitable update.

Definition 6.13. *The procedure* `concretize` *has the property that given an atom of the form* $R(f(t_1, \ldots, t_n), v)$, *with* $R \in \mathrm{PSym}_r$, $f \in \mathrm{FSym}_{nr}$, *and* $t_1, \ldots, t_n, v \in \mathrm{Trm}^{FOL}$, *it creates a set of pairs* (u, α), *with* $u \in Updates$, $\alpha \in \mathrm{Fml}^{FOL}$, *such that:*

- $u = (f(t_1, \ldots, t_n) := value)$, *where* $value \in \mathrm{Trm}^{FOL}$
- $\alpha \to \{u\}R(f(t_1, \ldots, t_n), v)$ *evaluates to* true

The procedure `concretize` creates for a given normalized core atom ϑ'_{sk} an update u that evaluates $\{u\}\vartheta'_{sk}$ to true. E.g., if the normalized core atom is of the form $t_1 \doteq t_2$, using infix notation, then the result of the procedure `concretize` is simply $((t_1 := t_2), \text{true})$. In some cases it is desired to introduce fresh symbols and to axiomatize them for the construction of the term *value*. Such axiomatizations are collected in the formula α.

For example, using the normalized core atom $\vartheta'_{sk} = (f(sk) < (g(sk) - sk - 3))$ from the solution set of the previous example, the procedure `concretize` may produce, e.g., the following solution:

$$\{\underbrace{(f(sk) := (g(sk) - sk - 3) + sk_2)}_{u}, \underbrace{sk_2 < 0}_{\alpha}\} \qquad (6.27)$$

where $sk_2 \in \mathrm{FSym}_r$ is a fresh constant. Using this solution, we can evaluate $\alpha \to \{u\}\vartheta'_{sk}$ as follows

$$sk_2 < 0 \to \{f(sk) := (g(sk) - sk - 3) + sk_2\}(f(sk) + 3 < g(sk) - sk)$$
$$sk_2 < 0 \to (g(sk) - sk - 3) + sk_2 + 3 < g(sk) - sk$$
$$sk_2 < 0 \to sk_2 < 0$$

Any term $(2 * c - sk - 3) + Z$, where Z is a negative integer literal, is also an admissible solution of the procedure. However, the introduction of the fresh constant sk_2 with the axiom $sk_2 < 0$ is a more general solution than using Z. If the top-level symbol of the core atom is "$\doteq$" and it occurs in the antecedent Γ, i.e., effectively it means "$\neq$", then a fresh symbol $sk_3 \in \mathrm{FSym}_r$ may be introduced with the axiom $\neg(sk_3 \doteq 0)$.

The next step uses the result computed by the procedures `solve` and `concretize` in order to create a quantified update (Line 7).

Update Generalization by Conversion to Quantified Updates

Definition 6.14. *The procedure* toQuanUpd *has the property that given a tuple* (u, α), *with* $u \in$ *Updates and* $\alpha \in$ Fml^{FOL}, *a sequent* $\Gamma_{sk} \Longrightarrow \Delta_{sk}$, *a core atom* ϑ'_{sk}, *and a Skolem function* sk, *it creates the pair* (u', α) *where* $u' \in$ *Updates has the form (let* $z \in$ VSym)

$$\texttt{for } z; \textit{ guard}; u[sk\backslash z]$$

where guard $= \neg((\Gamma_{sk}\backslash\{\vartheta_{sk}\}) \Longrightarrow (\Delta_{sk}\backslash\{\vartheta_{sk}\}))[sk\backslash z].$

The substitution $[sk\backslash z]$ deskolemizes all formulas and terms in order to quantify functions and predicates at those argument positions as they were quantified in the original quantified formula (see (6.17) vs. (6.19) on page 156). The guard $\neg((\Gamma_{sk}\backslash\{\psi_{sk}\}) \Longrightarrow (\Delta_{sk}\backslash\{\psi_{sk}\}))$ restricts the application of the update in order create small models as explained in Section 6.5.3.

For example, assume we want to construct an update that evaluates the formula

$$\forall x.(x > 4 \rightarrow (f(x) + 3 < g(x) - x))$$

to true. Algorithm 3 invokes Algorithm 4 with the following sequent ψ':

$$sk > 4 \Longrightarrow f(sk) + 3 < g(sk) - sk$$

Let $f(sk) + 3 < g(sk) - sk$ be the core atom ϑ_{sk} chosen in Line 4, then according to the previous examples procedures solve and concretize produce the intermediate result (6.27) that serves as input to the procedure toQuanUpd. We obtain the guard

$$\neg((\{sk > 4\}\backslash\{\vartheta_{sk}\}) \Longrightarrow (\{\psi_{sk}\}\backslash\{\psi_{sk}\}))[sk\backslash z]$$

which simplifies to $\neg(z > 4 \Longrightarrow)$ and then to $z > 4$. The final result of the procedure toQuanUpd for this example is the (u, α)-pair:

$$((\texttt{for } z; z > 4; f(z) := (g(z) - z - 3) + sk_2), sk_2 < 0)$$

Updating of Sub-Terms

In order to solve formulas such as (6.1) on page 140, another heuristic is required. If we create an update of the form

$$\texttt{for } x; \textit{ guard}; f(g(x)) := h(x) \tag{6.28}$$

that is supposed to evaluate, e.g., $\forall x.f(g(x)) = h(x)$ to true, then usually the intention is that f is assigned different values at different argument positions. This does not happen, however, if the function g is not injective. For instance if $\forall x.g(x) = 0$, then the update (6.28) just assigns a value to $f(0)$. Our heuristic is to create another update that is applied before (6.28) and that ensures injectivity of the argument of the updated function. In this example the argument is g and the updated function is f.

Definition 6.15. *The procedure* `injectiveSubTerms` *has the property that given an update*

$$\text{for } x; \ guard; \ f(\tau_x) := t_x$$

where $guard \in \text{Fml}^{FOL}$, $f \in \text{FSym}_{nr}$, *and* $\tau_x, t_x \in \text{Trm}^{FOL}$ *are terms with an occurrence of* $x \in \text{FSym}$, *it creates a set of tuples such that every tuple* (u'', α), *with* $\alpha \in \text{Fml}^{FOL}$ *and* $u'' \in \text{Updates}$:

$$\vDash \alpha \to \{u''\}\{\text{for } x; \ guard; \ f(\tau_x) := t_x\}(\forall x.(guard \to f(\tau_x) \doteq t_x))$$

For example, a possible solution of `injectiveArgs` for (6.28) is

$$(\text{for } z; \ guard[x\backslash z]; \ g(z) := z, \text{true})$$

A more general solution is to introduce a fresh function symbol $f_{sk} \in \text{FSym}_{nr}$, axiomatize it with $\forall x.\forall y.x \neq y \to f_{sk}(x) \neq f_{sk}(y)$, and assign it to g, i.e. $\ldots g(z) := f_{sk}(z)$. The axiom introduces a new quantified formula for which another update has to be created in order to evaluate this formula to true. In each step a more specific partial model has to be created until eventually no axioms with quantifiers are introduced. Hence, this technique has to be applied recursively on the arguments of locations.

6.7 From Updates to a Test Preamble

In this section we would like to argue shortly, that the model generation approach described in this chapter is suitable not only for deductive software fault detection but also for test generation. A counterexample for a verification condition represents an initial program state for a program execution that reveals a fault. Hence, such counterexamples are useful for test generation as described in Part III of this thesis.

. . .

$\{\texttt{for } x : \texttt{MyCls}; \ (\texttt{next}(x) \doteq \texttt{null} \land \neg \texttt{a}(x) \doteq \texttt{null} \land \ldots); \ \texttt{created}(x) := \texttt{false}\}$
$\{\texttt{for } x : \texttt{MyCls}; \ (\texttt{a}(x) \doteq 0 \land \neg x \doteq \texttt{null}); \ \texttt{created}(x) := \texttt{false}\}$
$\{\texttt{for } x : \texttt{int}; \ (b \geqslant 1 + x \land x \leqslant -1); \ \texttt{acc}_{[]}(\texttt{next}(\texttt{self})) := -1 + c_2\}$
$\{\texttt{for } x : \texttt{int}; \ x \leqslant -1; \ i := \texttt{acc}_{[]}(\texttt{next}(\texttt{self})) - c_0 * -1 + c_1\}$
$\{\texttt{for } x : \texttt{int}; \ (x \geqslant 0 \land x \geqslant 1 + i_0); \ \texttt{acc}_{[]}(\texttt{next}(\texttt{self})) := \texttt{length}(\texttt{prev}(\texttt{self})) + c_0\}$
$\{\texttt{for } x : \texttt{int}; \ (\texttt{acc}_{[]}(\texttt{next}(\texttt{self}), x) = x \land x \leqslant i_0 \land \ldots); \ \texttt{get}_0(\texttt{prev}(\texttt{self}), x) := x\}$

Fig. 6.3. A subset of generated updates satisfying the quantified formulas in Figure 6.2

The choice of using updates to represent models of quantified formulas is very convenient for test preamble generation. A test preamble is part of a test driver whose goal is to initialize the program under test with a desired program state. Updates can be viewed as a small imperative programming language with some special constructs. An algorithm that converts updates to a test preamble has to follow the semantics of updates. Conversion of function updates to assignments and sequential updates to statements is trivial. Parallel updates were not created by our algorithm. Quantified updates are converted to loops. If a quantified update quantifies over integers, then the integer bounds have to be determined. If the update quantifies over objects, then an approximation of the semantics is to iterate over all objects that were created by the preamble. This solution is, however, only an approximation as it does not initialize objects that are created later on during the execution of the program under test and the ordering $\preceq$ of the Kripke Structure $\mathcal{K}_{\preceq}$ has to be reflected in the test preamble.

6.8 Evaluation

We have implemented our algorithm, i.e., the combination of Algorithms 3 and 4, in an experimental version of the KeY tool. The technique is currently realized as an interactive model generator, i.e., the implementation proposes candidate updates to be selected by the user. The reason for this is two-fold. On the one hand, the interaction with the algorithm enables us to study heuristics for the model generation as well as to identify and understand limitations of the algorithm. On the other hand, it is the paradigm of the KeY tool to combine automation and interaction. A full automation of the model generator is of course possible by making random choices from the list of candidate updates.

Classes with invariants	T	A	B
Account	4	4	4
AccountMan_src	5	5	2
Currency_src	2	2	2
SavingRule	4	2	2
SpendingRule	4	2	2
Transfers_src	3	3	2
Total	22	18	14

Methods with Specifications	T	A	B
AccountMan_src::IsValid()	6	5	2
AccountMan_src::BOdelete()	6	5	2
AccountMan_src::isValidBank()	5	4	2
AccountMan_src::isValAcc()	5	5	2
AccountMan_src::getRef()	5	3	2
Total	27	22	10

Table 6.1. Evaluation of the model generation algorithm applied to a banking software with JML specifications; T: total number of quantified formulas in one conjunction that occurred as test data constraints; A, B: maximum number of quantified formulas solved in a conjunction; A: our model generation algorithm; B: SMT solvers

In order to test the algorithm we have used several examples from different sources. In the beginning, we have used hand-crafted formulas in order to test and develop the algorithm. A crucial improvement was achieved by utilising statement (i) of Theorem 6.5 that allows Skolemization of the quantified formulas by reformulation of the problem (see Sections 6.3.2 and 6.4). Earlier approaches to generate models without the statement were not successful.

Table 6.1 shows a JAVA method with a JML specification. A verification attempt of the method results in a set of open proof obligations. One of them is shown in Figure 6.2 that we abbreviate as φ. Figure 6.3 shows a part of an iterative update application, i.e., the updates are applied in a sequence, that describes a model for $\neg\varphi$ and was generated by the implementation of our approach.

To test our algorithm on more realistic tests, we applied it to the banking software described in Section 5.6 (page 133). The banking software contains JML specifications with quantified formulas. When applying our deductive software fault detection approach, then verification conditions with the quantified formulas are encountered in the proof tree. Our goal was to test for how many of these formulas our algorithm can generate models. Table 6.1 shows some of the results.

The left sub-table of Table 6.1 shows numbers of quantified formulas that stem from class invariants of the respective classes and the right sub-table shows numbers of quantified formulas that stem from method preconditions and loop invariants. Note that additional quantified formulas are generated for declared fields in a class and for class invariants as described in Sections 6.1 and 4.4.2. The column T shows the total number of quantified formulas that occurred in the verification conditions in a *conjunction*, i.e., a complete model must satisfy the whole conjunction. Columns A and B show the maximum number of quantified formulas that we found solvable in one conjunction. We have tested our algorithm and SMT solvers with different combinations of the quantified formulas in one conjunction, where goal was to solve the biggest conjunction. Column A shows the results of our algorithm and column B shows respectively the best result achieved by any of the SMT solvers Z3, CVC3, and Yices. The evaluation shows that our algorithm can solve quantified formulas that state-of-the-art SMT solvers cannot solve. Furthermore, our algorithm was able to generate models for almost all of the quantified formulas when it was applied to the quantified formulas in separation, i.e., not in a conjunction. This simplification did not make an improvement on the SMT side.

6.9 Conclusions and Future Work

We have proposed a model generation approach for quantified first-order logic (FOL) formulas that is based on update construction and verification. The language we propose for representing models is KeY's update language. The advantage of using updates is the possibility to express models for quantified formulas via quantified updates, and the availability of a powerful calculus for simplifying formulas with updates to FOL formulas. In particular, no loop invariants have to be generated in order to simplify quantified updates.

We have identified problems (Proposition 6.3) that occur, when the approach is implemented according to the *basic* description. Theorem 6.5 provides a solution to these problems. The theorem allows us to reformulate the basic model generation approach for quantified formulas into a semantically equivalent approach without the problems described in Proposition 6.3.

Based on Theorem 6.5 and Definitions 6.4 and 6.6 we have derived Algorithm 3 for model generation. The technique can be used in two ways. On the one hand, it can be used as a pre-computation step to SMT solvers by restricting the computation of the formulas ψ_m, φ'_m, and φ_m to Definition 6.4. In this case the technique eliminates quantified formulas and leaves a residue of ground formulas or alternative quantified formulas to be solved by a different method, e.g. an SMT solver. On the other hand, the technique can be used stand-alone for model generation by using the general Definition 6.6 and modifying the algorithm accordingly.

The technique described in this chapter is a necessary ingredient of our general approach described in Chapter 4. The general approach requires to generate counterexamples for verification conditions. SMT solvers are, however, not powerful enough to generate counterexamples from verification conditions generated by KeY. The problem is the combination of quantifiers, arithmetic functions, and uninterpreted function. The technique described in this chapter addresses this problem successfully. Our experiments show that it can generate counterexamples for formulas that SMT solvers cannot solve.

What formulas can be solved by our general approach depends on the chosen language for model representation, the theorem prover in use, and the heuristics for model construction. Quantified formulas are suitable to represent models for certain kinds of quantified formulas. They are, however, not sufficient to represent models of inductively defined functions. Future work is to extension our approach in this direction.

Verification-based Test Generation Techniques

7

Verification-based Test Generation

7.1 Introduction

Overview

Software testing the most popular approach for gaining confidence in the correct behavior of software and for software fault detection. The third part of this thesis is dedicated to test generation approaches and techniques which *extend* the formal verification and fault detection approach described in the previous parts. Technically, these test generation techniques are also *based* on the techniques of the previous chapters and therefore an integration of verification, deductive fault detection, and testing is achieved in one tool and method.

In this chapter we describe two approaches for verification-based test generation (VBT). Common to these approaches is that they start with a verification attempt, which generates a proof tree, in order to extract abstract test cases from the program. The approaches differ in the second step where the actual tests are generated. The first approach and technique was proposed in [Engel and Hähnle, 2007] where it was called VBT.[1] The technique generates executable JUnit tests directly within KeY. We have reimplemented and extended the technique to a large extend and describe in this chapter a new version of it. The second approach is a tool-chain approach that we have proposed in [Beckert and Gladisch, 2007]. We generalize the name VBT to include both approaches.

---

[1] In standard terminology [IEE, 1990] the term verification-based testing has a different meaning and is not connected to formal software verification.

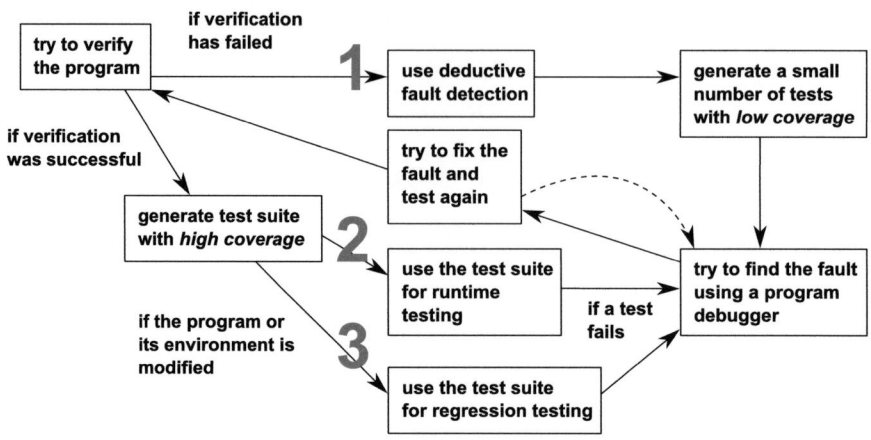

Fig. 7.1. Three use-cases of VBT

Motivation and Use-Cases of VBT

By using verification we can prove the correctness of a program with respect to a specification. On the other hand, software faults can be detected deductively based on a failed proof attempt. Hence, the question arises why testing should be integrated into verification and deductive fault detection. We regard three use-cases in which VBT complements verification and deductive fault detection. These are summarized in Figure 7.1.

The first use-case is finding software faults. Tests are helpful to find software faults because when a program is executed in its runtime environment, i.e. not symbolically, then a program debugger can be utilised. Program debuggers are powerful tools that enable the user to follow the program control flow at different levels of granularity and they enable the inspection of the program state. A strength of program debuggers is also that the user reads the source code as it is executed which is helpful for understanding it. When the deductive software fault detection approach (see Chapter 4) detects the existence of a software fault, then it additionally provides two kinds of information: a program execution trace which reveals the fault, and a counterexample which represents the initial state of the program revealing the fault. The representation is abstract and hardly readable by an inexperienced user. However, this information can be used to initialize a program in its runtime environment enabling to use a program debugger.

The second use-case of testing is to further increase the confidence in the correct behavior of a program even if verification of the program was successful. It is usually not practical to rigorously apply formal verification to all relevant components that are responsible for the behavior of the program. These components, such as the compiler, the hardware, and the software environment of the program, are, however, involved when the program is tested. Hence, testing complements verification where the latter has a principal deficiency. After all, proofs cannot substitute tests. A figurative example is that even if engineers have proved using mathematical models that an airplane should have the desired aerodynamic properties, passengers will not be seated in the airplane before it has undergone numerous test flights.

The third use-case is regression testing. Regression testing is used to ensure that modifications made to software, such as adding new features or changing existing features, do not worsen (regress) existing software features that should not change. As software evolves existing tests can be quickly repeated for regression testing. The construction of proofs on the other hand is more expensive and therefore it is reasonable to run a set of tests before proceeding to a verification attempt after the software has been modified.

Hence, in the first use-case a single test or a small number of focused tests is generated if the verification has failed. If the deductive fault detection attempt was successful, it is already known in advance that the test(s) must fail. A successful verification attempt on the other hand leads to the second and third use-case. Contrary to the first use-case, in the second and third use-cases a high code coverage by the tests is desired. A high coverage *can* also be achieved because in this case the program has been fully symbolically executed and a maximum of information about the program and case distinctions in the program is available.

Properties of VBT

Different software testing techniques exist for all kinds of software, for different sizes of software, for different phases of the software life cycle, and for testing different kinds of properties. It is therefore clear that there is no overall best testing technique. VBT can be used as a pure test generation tool which uses the underlying verification technology without the intention to verify a program. However, we regard VBT primarily as an extension of the verification and deductive fault detection approach for the use-cases shown in Figure 7.1. This is because the strengths and weaknesses of VBT are related to those of the underlying verification tool. VBT is best applicable to programs that could in principle be verified with the underlying verification technology. These programs are usually much smaller than those programs that are typically tested by traditional testing techniques. In contrast to traditional approaches, VBT can check more complex properties of programs that can be expressed in first-order logic and also the code coverage that can be achieved with VBT is higher.

Tests generated with VBT check whether the program violates its functional requirement specification. Generally, testing can also be used to detect other problems of a program such as high resource consumption or non-termination of the program. VBT, however, does not check these properties explicitly because they are not part of the requirement specification. The test result is independent of whether termination or non-termination of the program is required. If the user is interested in whether the program terminates they have to observe the testing process. The same applies to the resource consumption such as memory consumption and computation time.

The described VBT techniques generate unit tests. Unit testing plays a major role in the software development process and it is encouraged by different software development processes such as Extreme Programming (XP) [zEx]. A unit is a small testable part of an application which explores a particular aspect of the behavior of the unit. In the object-oriented paradigm a unit is a class. In the context of VBT we regard, however, a method as a unit. We chose the finer granularity of units due to the high complexity of formal verification, which is the basis of VBT, and the high complexity of the properties that are typically checked.

7.2 Related Work

Testing has been influenced in the last decade by formal methods. Prominent examples of such formal techniques are symbolic execution, theorem proving, satisfiability solving, and the usage of formal specifications and program annotations such as loop and class invariants. Formal testing techniques can achieve a high code coverage or they can generate a low number of tests that very likely exhibit software faults. Such techniques generate test data constraints which are first-order logic (FOL) formulas. These constraints are constructed from path conditions, specifications, and program annotation and describe program paths that are hard to be tested randomly.

The application of symbolic execution to test case generation has been proposed in the 1970s [King, 1974, 1976; Clarke, 1976]. This approach has gained much attraction in the last decade [Meudec, 2001; Zhang et al., 2004; Xie et al., 2005; Deng et al., 2006b]. Symbolic execution requires, however, full access to the source code or machine code in order to guarantee full structural code coverage. To overcome this problem symbolic execution has been combined with concrete execution [Sen et al., 2005; Cadar et al., 2008; Tillmann and de Halleux, 2008; Pasareanu et al., 2008]. The approach, which is called concolic execution or dynamic symbolic execution by different research groups, achieves a high code coverage. Concolic, respectively, dynamic symbolic execution is not used for software verification – except as an add-on to support verification [Vanoverberghe et al., 2008] – because it does not guarantee the exploration of all program states. However, in the context of verification, method contracts and loop invariants are usually available which allow solving the same problem as will be described in Section 7.4.2. Due to this different setting, in the following we regard test generation techniques which are based on verification tools.

Some verification tools have extensions for test case generation that we call, hereafter, VBT extensions. A VBT extension for Spec# [Barnett et al., 2005], respectively for the underlying verification engine Boogie [Barnett et al., 2006], has been developed in [Billeter, 2008]. The tool generates tests from counterexamples of verification conditions. It shares similar ideas with our approach such as the generation of test inputs using loop invariants. ESC/Java2 [Cok and Kiniry, 2004] is a static checker that can automatically prove properties that go beyond simple assertions. A VBT extension of ESC/Java2 is Check'n'Crash [Smaragdakis and Csallner, 2007]. It generates JUnit tests for assertions that could not be proved using ESC/Java2. In this way, false warnings featured by ESC/Java2 are filtered out. HOL-TestGen [Brucker and Wolff, 2007] is a test generation tool extending the theorem prover Isabelle/HOL [Wenzel et al., 2008] which is frequently used for program verification. HOL-TestGen uses a tableaux calculus for deriving tests from specifications. Bogor/Kiasan combines symbolic execution, model checking, theorem proving, and constraint solving to support design-by-contract reasoning of object-oriented software [Deng et al., 2006b]. Its extension that we categorize as VBT is KUnit [Deng et al., 2007].

179

The tool focuses on heap-intensive JAVA programs and uses a lazy initialization algorithm with backtracking. The algorithm is capable of exploring all execution paths up to a bound on the configurations of the heap. KUnit then generates test data for each path and creates JUnit test suites. VBT extensions have also been realized for various model checkers [Gargantini et al., 2003; Beyer et al., 2004; Visser et al., 2004]. Finally, the VBT extension of the KeY tool has been originally proposed in [Engel and Hähnle, 2007; Beckert and Gladisch, 2007] and was extended in later works [Gladisch, 2008a; Engel et al., 2008; Gladisch et al., 2010].

The VBT technique of KeY, hereafter just VBT, differs from other approaches in the formalism and in the way how techniques were realized. The technical features of the tools whose development is continued, including KeY, are continuously extended. Hence, we omit a comparison of these features. Important about VBT is its underlying theory and technology which is based on deductive fault detection. This allows us to give coverage guarantees when loop invariants and method contracts are used and to generate tests which are guaranteed to detect faults. Specific advantages of different techniques underlying VBT are described in the respective sections.

7.3 Overview of the VBT Approaches in KeY

In the following we describe two approaches for verification-based test generation (VBT). Common to these approaches is the first phase where they start with a verification attempt and extract abstract test cases from the generated proof tree. The approaches differ in the second phase where the actual tests are generated. Figure 7.2 shows an overview of the two phases as well as of the two approaches. Although the description of the approaches is JAVA-specific in the following sections, we belief that they can also be applied to other programming languages that follow similar ideas as JAVA. Table 7.1 contains a description of software engineering terms that are important in this chapter.

The input to KeY is a JAVA method with its requirement specification, hereafter method under test (MUT). As it is the case in the deductive fault detection approach (see Chapter 4), the VBT approaches start with the creation of a proof tree structure. The proof tree is used to derive different test cases. As described in Section 2.4.5, the branches of the proof tree mimic the execution of the program with symbolic val-

Term	Description
black-box testing	Testing that ignores the internal mechanism of a system or component and focuses solely on the outputs generated in response to selected inputs and execution conditions.
path condition	A formula that describes initial states of the MUT that lead to the execution of the specific program path.
(program) branch	A sequence of statements that may or may not be executed depending on a condition.
(program) path	A complete run, from the beginning to the end, through a given method or sequence of statements
test case	A set of test inputs, execution conditions, and expected results developed for a particular objective, such as to exercise a particular program path or branch.
(test) coverage	The degree to which a given test or set of tests executes a program or specification.
test data	Values or the assignment of values used to initialize a program for a test. A partial model represents test data and vice versa.
test data constraint	A formula that test data has to satisfy.
(test) oracle	Code that is executed after the execution of the MUT and that determines for the final state of the MUT whether it satisfies the requirement specification of the MUT.
(test) preamble	Code that is executed before the execution of the MUT and initializes the MUT with test data.
test suite	A set of test cases or a set of executable tests.
unit testing	Testing of individual software units or groups of related units.
white-box testing	Testing that takes into account the internal mechanism of a system or component.

Table 7.1. Software engineering terms relevant for verification-based testing. The descriptions differ slightly from the definitions in the Standard Glossary of Software Engineering Terms [IEE, 1990]. Words in braces are optional.

ues. Case distinctions in the program are reflected as branches of the proof tree; these may also be implicit distinctions like, e.g., raising of exceptions (see also Remark 2.46 on page 58). Soundness of the system ensures that all paths through the MUT are analyzed, except for parts where the user chooses to use abstraction (see Section 2.4.6). Thus, creating tests for proof branches that were created using bounded symbolic execution ensures full feasible bounded path coverage (see Def. 7.2) of the regarded program part of the MUT, i.e., all paths of the symbolically executed program parts will be tested. Creating tests for proof

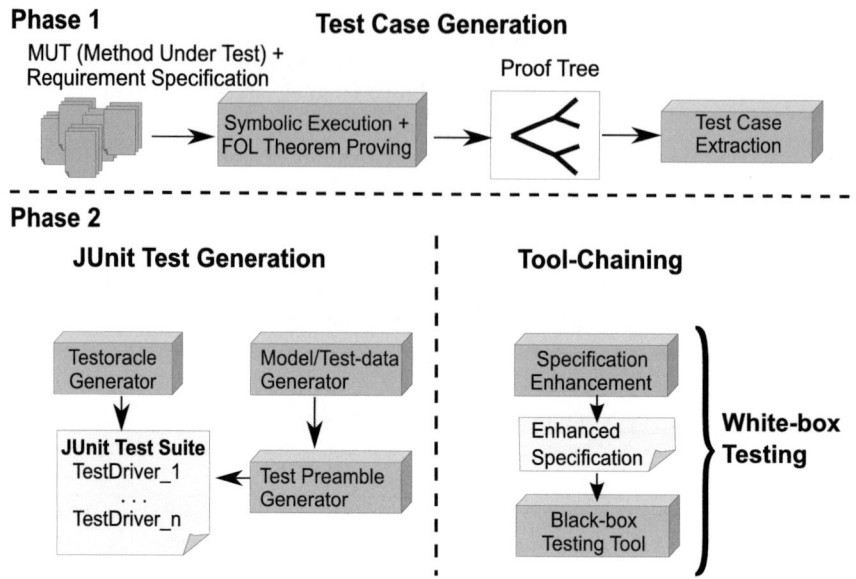

Fig. 7.2. Overview of two verification-based test generation approaches in KeY

branches that were created using abstraction, i.e. using contract rules, can ensure full feasible branch coverage (see Def. 7.3) of the regarded program part of the MUT, i.e., all program branches of the symbolically executed program parts may be tested depending on the properties of the abstraction, i.e. contracts. Each proof branch on which symbolic execution rules were applied contains a *path condition*. The path condition is a formula that describes initial states of the MUT that lead to the execution of the specific program path.

Definition 7.1. *If a path (see Table 7.1) cannot be executed because its path condition (see Table 7.1) is contradicting for all inputs, i.e. it is false, then the path, respectively the path condition, is called* infeasible. *Otherwise, the path, respectively the path condition, is* feasible. *A feasible or infeasible program branch (see Table 7.1) is defined analogously.*

Definition 7.2. *Let BP be the set of paths of a method or a sequence of statements P which are bound by the number of method invocations and loop iterations. A test suite T satisfies the* full feasible bounded path coverage *for P if every feasible path (see Def. 7.1) of BP is executed by at least one test of T.*

Definition 7.3. *Let BB be the set of branches of a method or a sequence of statements P. A test suite T satisfies the* full feasible branch coverage *for P if every feasible branch (see Def. 7.1) of BB is executed by at least one test of T.*

The path conditions as well as the precondition from the specification constitute test data constraints which represent the test cases. A test data constraint has to be satisfied in the pre-state of the MUT when executing a concrete test. The extraction of the test data constraints from the proof tree is described in Section 7.4. The test data constraints are then used in the second phase of both approaches.

JUnit Test Generation

This VBT approach generates executable JUnit[2] [Tahchiev et al., 2010] tests in the second phase (see Figure 7.2). JUnit is a popular test execution framework for JAVA which allows to execute a set of tests and generate test reports.

To create a concrete test which satisfies the test data constraint obtained from the first phase, a model generator is required. The challenge of model generation in the context of VBT is to generate models for quantified formulas that may stem from the requirement specification and contracts such as loop invariants. In Chapter 6 we have described a model generation technique that is suitable for this task.[3] Hence, also in the use-cases 2 and 3 shown in Figure 7.1, this VBT approach is technically based on deductive fault detection techniques. The model generator described in Chapter 6 represents models in form of updates. This is a welcome feature of the model generator because this representation is close to an imperative programming language which simplifies the generation of a test preamble.

The test preamble is a sequence of statements that initialize the program state in which the MUT is executed. The model which is generated by the model generator is therefore the input to the test preamble generator. The test preamble is the first part executed by each test driver (see Section 7.5.1).

---

[2] http://www.junit.org

[3] For the experimental results reported in this part of this thesis we have used the model generator described in [Engel and Hähnle, 2007; Engel, 2006] which is based on the theorem prover Simplify [Detlefs et al., 2005].

The test driver is a method which represents a test of the test suite. It prepares the initial state of the test, executes the MUT, and checks the final state after the execution of the MUT with a test oracle.

Tool-chaining

In the tool-chain approach the test data constraints obtained in the first phase are used to structurally enhance the requirement specification of the MUT. The enhanced specification is then used as input for black-box testing tools. If the black-box testing tool creates a test for each precondition of the enhanced specification, then the approach is effectively a white-box testing approach.[4] In this way, (1) the black-box testing method can use information about the program's structure that is contained in the specification, and (2) we get a separation of concerns and a clear interface between program analysis on the one hand and test-case generation and execution on the other hand.

The technique described in Chapter 6 should be used in order eliminate quantified formulas from the test data constraints. The generation of concrete test data satisfying the remaining formulas is left to the black-box testing tool.

7.4 Extraction of Test Cases from a Proof Tree

Verification-based test generation is a flexible technique with respect to the complexity of the test generation and the resulting quality of the tests. It supports a spectrum between the generation of random tests and tests that are guaranteed to reveal software faults. The quality of the tests depends on the extend of the proof tree construction and on the selection of test data constraints, i.e., formulas that have to be satisfied by test data. For instance, the simplest test is a random test that is generated if test data is derived from a proof tree which consists only of the root sequent. The most sophisticated kind of test which is a test that guarantees the detection of a software fault is derived from a falsifiable leaf of a validity preserving proof branch (see Chapter 4).

---

[4] If the black-box testing tool does not make use of the additional information in the enhanced specification, then the approach can also be considered as a white-box testing approach. In this case, however, the additional information is useless and structural coverage of the MUT is not ensured.

The branches of the proof tree represent different test cases. Any formula in the proof tree can be used as a test data constraint. However, depending on which formulas are chosen for the test data constraints different specification conditions, program branches, or paths are tested. The sequents in the proof tree express properties of the analyzed program. Hence, a test of a property of the program is a test of a formula in the proof tree. Sequents that contain parts of the MUT *typically* have the form (see Section 2.4.5, page 56)

$$\Gamma \Longrightarrow \mathcal{U}\langle p \rangle \phi, \Delta \tag{7.1}$$

where p is either the MUT, a part of the MUT, or it may be empty. The latter is the case if symbolic execution has terminated. The formula

$$\mathcal{U}\langle p \rangle \phi \tag{7.2}$$

expresses a property of the MUT that has to be satisfied (at least) in every state in which the remaining sub-sequent (i.e., subsets of the antecedent and succedent)

$$\Gamma \Longrightarrow \Delta \tag{7.3}$$

is not satisfied. Hence, in order to test if Formula (7.2) holds when the MUT is executed the MUT has to be executed in a state which satisfies the negation of sequent (7.3). Otherwise, the sequent 7.1 is trivially satisfied even if 7.2 is false. Thus negation of sequent (7.3), or equivalently the formula

$$\bigwedge \Gamma \wedge \neg \bigvee \Delta \tag{7.4}$$

is the test data constraint.

Recall from Section 2.4.5 that the update and the modal operator of Formula (7.2) represent a particular execution path of the MUT. The formulas in Γ and Δ contain the precondition of the requirement specification and the path condition that leads to this particular execution point of the MUT. Hence, for any path and for any branch of the MUT a test can be generated that executes the particular path or branch.

Assume we want to generate a test for the method m(). In order to derive a test for m() from a proof branch, VBT requires that a sequent of the form

$$\Gamma \Longrightarrow \mathcal{U}_0 \langle \mathtt{m()\,;} \rangle \phi, \Delta \tag{7.5}$$

185

occurs on the proof branch. This is a normal form of sequents which occur before and during symbolic execution (see Section 2.4.5). The sequent is important in order to determine the update $\mathcal{U}_0$ which has to be evaluated before the execution of m().

Let $(\mathcal{S}, \rho)$ be a Kripke structure (see Section 2.3.2) and let $s_0, s_1, s_2 \in \mathcal{S}$. The Sequent (7.5) expresses that if $\bigwedge \Gamma \wedge \neg \bigvee \Delta$ is true in s_0 and

$$s_1 = val_{s_0}(\mathcal{U}_0)(s_0)$$

then after the execution of m() in s_1, the state s_2 is reached with

$$\rho(s_1, \text{m}(), s_2)$$

in which $s_2 \vDash \phi$. Hence, s_1 (and not s_0) is the state in which the MUT has to be executed.

In the following we describe how to derive tests of different quality or precision.

7.4.1 Black-Box or Specification-based Test Cases

Black-box tests, or specification-based tests, are derived from a proof tree that is generated by using all calculus rules except for the symbolic execution rules. The remaining rules such as propositional rules and arithmetic rules operate on the precondition of the requirement specification. Applying the rules results in a proof tree with propositional and arithmetic case distinctions on the formulas in Γ and Δ. These formulas stem from the precondition of the requirement specification. The leaves of the proof tree have the form

$$\Gamma \Longrightarrow \mathcal{U}_0 \langle \text{m}() ; \rangle \phi, \Delta$$

Consider the following example.

—— JAVA + JML (7.1) ——————————————————

```
1  /*@ public normal_behavior
2    requires x>=0;  ensures  \result==x;
3  also
4    requires x<0;   ensures  \result==-x; @*/
5  int abs(x){...}
```

———————————————————————— JAVA + JML ——

KeY features the possibility to combine two pre- and postcondition pairs in one verification condition. The verification condition for the method `abs` is

$$\underbrace{(x \geqslant 0 \lor x < 0)}_{\Gamma} \rightarrow \{x' := x\}\langle\texttt{r=abs(x')}\rangle \underbrace{\left(\land \begin{array}{l} (x \geqslant 0 \rightarrow r \doteq x) \\ (x < 0 \rightarrow r \doteq -x) \end{array}\right)}_{\phi}$$

According to JML semantics, formal parameters that occur in the ensures clause are evaluated in the pre-state of the method. In this example the formal parameter is $x \in \mathrm{FSym}_{nr}$. In order to follow the JML semantics KeY replaces the formal parameter with a new symbol (here $x' \in \mathrm{FSym}_{nr}$). In this way the value of the formal parameter x is not changed by symbolic execution and it can be used in the postcondition to refer to the pre-state of the MUT. A combination of the preconditions in a conjunction $x \geqslant 0 \land x < 0$ would result also in a correct verification condition according to the JML semantics. However, the disjunction in the antecedent is needed for deriving the desired test cases as will become clear in the following.

The proof tree for this verification condition without using symbolic execution rules is:

$$\frac{\overbrace{x \geqslant 0}^{\Gamma_1} \Longrightarrow \{x' := x\}\langle\texttt{r=abs(x')}\rangle\phi \quad \overbrace{x < 0}^{\Gamma_2} \Longrightarrow \{x' := x\}\langle\texttt{r=abs(x')}\rangle\phi}{\dfrac{\boldsymbol{x \geqslant 0 \lor x < 0} \Longrightarrow \{x' := x\}\langle\texttt{r=abs(x')}\rangle\phi}{\Longrightarrow \boldsymbol{(x \geqslant 0 \lor x < 0)} \rightarrow \underbrace{\{x' := x\}}_{\mathcal{U}_0}\langle\texttt{r=abs(x')}\rangle\phi}}$$

$$(7.6)$$

The two branches represent test cases and are the result of the disjunction in the antecedent. The leaves of the branches contain the test data constraints which are $x \geqslant 0$ for the left branch and $x < 0$ for the right branch. After initializing x with a value that satisfies one constraint the effect of the update $\{x' := x\}$ has to be taken into account before testing if $\langle\texttt{r=abs(x')}\rangle\phi$ is satisfied.

7.4.2 White-box Test Cases

7.4.2.1 General Derivation of White-box Test Cases

White-box tests execute specific paths or branches of the MUT. Therefore the MUT is symbolically executed in order to obtain path conditions. The symbolic execution rules must ensure that case distinctions in the program are made explicit as case distinctions in the proof tree. For instance, the rule

$$\frac{\Rightarrow \{x := \text{if } x < 0 \text{ then } x \text{ else } -x\}\langle \pi \ \omega\rangle\phi}{\Rightarrow \langle \pi \ \texttt{if(x<0)\{x=-x;\}} \ \omega\rangle\phi}$$

which could be included in the calculus in addition to the `ifElseSplit` rule (see Figure 2.5, page 57) does not reflect the branches of the if-statement as branches in the proof tree. Hence, if a test case is derived from every branch of a proof tree and the rule above was used in the construction of the proof tree, then possibly only one of the branches of the if-statement will be covered by a test case. Therefore, simplification rules which do not reflect the structural information of the program in the proof tree must be omitted.

The path conditions obtained by symbolic execution are part of the test data constraints. Additionally the test data constraints contain the precondition of the requirement specification as in the specification-based testing approach, see Section 7.4.1 on page 186. Thus, the white-box test cases satisfy the precondition of the requirement specification.

In principle any formula in the proof tree can be used as a test data constraint. However, depending on which formulas are chosen for the test data constraints different paths are taken through the MUT or different conditions of the program or specification are satisfied. The test data constraints for white-box tests are derived from sequents of the form of Formula (7.1) (page 185), i.e.,

$$\Gamma \Rightarrow \mathcal{U}\langle p\rangle\phi, \Delta$$

where p is either a part of the MUT or p is empty. The test data constraint is given by the negation of (7.3), i.e.,

$$\bigwedge \Gamma \wedge \neg \bigvee \Delta$$

and ensures the execution of the program path that was also symbolically executed during proof construction. If p is empty, then the execution of the program path is completely determined by the test data constraint.

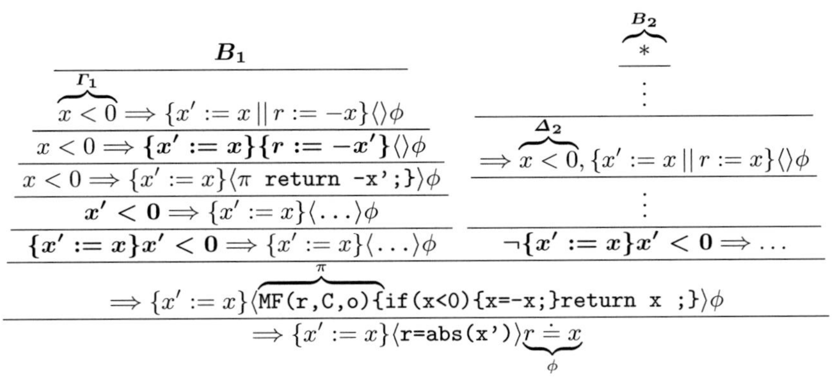

$$\cfrac{\cfrac{\cfrac{\cfrac{\cfrac{\overbrace{x < 0}^{\Gamma_1} \Rightarrow \{x' := x \,||\, r := -x\}\langle\rangle\phi}{x < 0 \Rightarrow \{x' := x\}\{r := -x'\}\langle\rangle\phi}}{x < 0 \Rightarrow \{x' := x\}\langle\pi \text{ return } -x'; \rangle\phi}}{x' < 0 \Rightarrow \{x' := x\}\langle\ldots\rangle\phi}}{\{x' := x\}x' < 0 \Rightarrow \{x' := x\}\langle\ldots\rangle\phi}}^{\;B_1}}{\Rightarrow \{x' := x\}\langle\overbrace{\text{MF}(\text{r,C,o})}\{\text{if(x<0)\{x=-x;\}return x ;\}}\rangle\phi}$$

$$\cfrac{\cfrac{\overbrace{\ast}^{B_2}}{\vdots}}{\cfrac{\Rightarrow \overbrace{x < 0}^{\Delta_2}, \{x' := x \,||\, r := x\}\langle\rangle\phi}{\vdots}}$$

$$\neg\{x' := x\}x' < 0 \Rightarrow \ldots$$

$$\Rightarrow \{x' := x\}\langle\text{r=abs(x')}\rangle\underbrace{r \doteq x}_{\phi}$$

Fig. 7.3. Proof tree for deriving white-box test cases

Consider the example in Listing 7.2.

— JAVA + JML (7.2) ————————————————————

```
1  /*@ public normal_behavior
2    requires true;  ensures \result ==x; //Fault in spec.
3  @*/
4  void abs(x){
5    if(x < 0){ x = -x;}
6    return x;
7  }
```

————————————————————————— JAVA + JML —

A verification attempt of the method `abs` in Listing 7.2 yields the proof tree with the branches B_1 and B_2 shown in Figure 7.3. The two branches of the proof tree represent test cases. The test data constraints are extracted from the last sequent on the branch which has the form of Formula (7.1). In Figure 7.3 these sequents are, for B_1

$$\overbrace{x < 0}^{\Gamma_1} \Rightarrow \{x' := x \,||\, r := -x\}\langle\rangle\phi$$

and for B_2

$$\Rightarrow \overbrace{x < 0}^{\Delta_2}, \{x' := x \,||\, r := x\}\langle\rangle\phi$$

The test data constraints in form of Formula (7.3) are given by Γ_1 and $\neg\Delta_2$, respectively. A test derived from the branch B_2 will succeed and

```
—— Java + JML (7.3) ——————        —— Java + JML (7.4) ——————
void foo1(int n){                   int i;
  int i=0;                          /*@ public normal_behavior
  /*@ loop_invariant 0<=i && i<=n;      requires i<=n; ensures i==n;
      modifies i;                       modifies i; @*/
  @*/                               void D(int n){
  while(i < n){                       while(i < n){ ... }
    if(i==10){ A();}                  }
    B();
    i++;                            void foo2(int n){
  }                                   D(n);
  if(i==20){ C(); }                   if(i==20){ C(); }
}                                   }
————————————— Java + JML ——       ————————————— Java + JML ——
```

Fig. 7.4. Examples of programs for which bounded symbolic execution may not achieve branch coverage

a test derived from the branch B_1 will detect the fault. For instance, $x \doteq -1$ satisfies the test data constraint of the branch B_1 and results in the return value 1 of the method **abs** which contradicts the requirement

$$\text{ensures } \backslash \text{result==x;}$$

7.4.2.2 Utilising Contracts for Full Feasible Branch Coverage

When finite unfolding of method calls and loops is used during symbolic execution, the user does not have to provide method contracts or loop invariants. This technique is also known as bounded symbolic execution. When using VBT as an extension to verification (see Figure 7.1, page 176), then method contracts and loop invariants are typically available. Furthermore, the proof tree generated by the verification attempt can be directly reused for test case derivation.

In [Gladisch, 2008a] we have shown that method contracts and loop invariants, hereafter contracts, can be used to create test cases that are likely to be missed by bounded symbolic execution. In some cases the latter requires an exhaustive inspection of all execution paths which is infeasible in the presence of complex methods and impossible in the presence of loops, because loops represent infinitely many paths.

Figure 7.4 shows examples of programs for which branch coverage is hard to be achieved using bounded symbolic execution. In order to execute A() (Listing 7.3) the loop body has to be entered at least 11 times and in order to execute C() it has to be executed exactly 20 times. In similar programs these numbers could be much larger or be the result of complex expressions requiring an exhaustive inspection of all paths in order to find the case where the branch conditions are satisfied. A similar situation is in Listing 7.4 where an exhaustive inspection of D() may be required to find a path such that after the execution of D() the branch condition $i \doteq 20$ holds.

When using the contract rules (see Section 2.4.6) during proof construction, test data constraints can be derived from the proof tree solving the described problem. If the contracts are strong enough, the test data constraints ensure the execution of desired feasible branches (a) after loops and method calls or (b) within loops. In case (a) the test data constraint is extracted from the third branch of the contract rule application. It is extracted in the same way as described before, i.e., a sequent of the form of Formula (7.1) (e.g., on page 185) has to be located in the proof tree from which the test data constraint of the form of Formula (7.3) is extracted. In case (b) the test data constraint is extracted from the second branch of the loop invariant rule, i.e., the branch constructed from Premiss 2 of the rule. On this branch a sequent of the form

$$\Gamma \Longrightarrow \mathcal{U}\mathcal{V}_M[b']I, \Delta \tag{7.7}$$

has to be located – in analogy to the Formula (7.1) on other branches – where b' is the loop body, part of the loop body, or it is empty. The test data constraint is given in this case by the formula

$$\bigwedge \Gamma \wedge \neg \bigvee \Delta \tag{7.8}$$

which is analogous to the Formula (7.3).

Strength of Contracts

Whether the contract is strong enough to ensure that the test data constraint has the desired properties can be checked in an obvious way, namely by formalizing and proving the desired property. Checking the strength of the contract is not part of the test data generation process. The strength property can be used to prove that full feasible branch coverage is achieved when using a particular contract.

For the program parts we use the notation that we have used also in Table 5.1. Let

$$pre \rightarrow \mathcal{U}[ABC]post$$

be the verification condition at the root of the proof tree, where B is the loop or method call, and A and C are other statements. Let σ be the contract of B, let ψ be the condition that has to be satisfied *immediately* after B in order to execute the desired branch in C, and let φ_σ be the test data constraint extracted from the proof tree according to the above description. The contract of B is strong enough, i.e., such that φ_σ ensures the satisfaction of ψ after the execution of AB, iff:

$$\vDash \varphi_\sigma \rightarrow \mathcal{U}[AB]\psi \qquad (7.9)$$

Condition 7.9 is a property of the contract because it is the only variable component in this statement.

Similarly, one can formalize the strength condition of a loop invariant for ensuring the execution of a branch within the loop. The condition in this case is

$$\vDash \varphi_\sigma \rightarrow \mathcal{U}\mathcal{V}_M[AB'B'']\psi \qquad (7.10)$$

where $\mathcal{V}_M$ is the anonymising update generated from the modifier set of σ (see Def. 2.52) and ψ is the condition that has to be satisfied at the beginning of an arbitrary loop iteration in order to executed the desired branch within the loop. The program part B' is the program part that is abstracted by the loop invariant, i.e., it is a prefix of loop iterations before the termination of the loop. The program part B'' is the part of the loop body before the branch condition in the loop is checked that leads to the desired branch within the loop. For instance, for the loop of Listing 7.3 (page 190), B' is a prefix of the form

```
if(i==10)A();B();i++;...;if(i==10)A();B();i++;     (7.11)
```

the branch condition for the branch `A()` is `i==10`, and B'' is empty. A generalization of B' for arbitrary loop iterations is possible. Further details can be found in [Gladisch, 2008a].

Example

Figure 7.5 shows a proof tree constructed from the method `foo1` of Listing 7.3. Branch B_1 is built from Premiss 1 of the `loopInv` rule (see Table 2.5) and the Branches $B_{2,1}$ and $B_{3,1}$ are build from Premisses 2 and 3 of the rule, respectively. The anonymising update $\mathcal{V}_M$ is derived

$$
\cfrac{\cfrac{\cfrac{B_{2,1}}{\mathcal{UV}_M(I \wedge i < n \wedge i \doteq 10) \Rightarrow \ldots}}{\vdots \qquad \vdots}}{\cfrac{\Rightarrow \cfrac{\mathcal{UV}_M(I \wedge i < n \rightarrow}{[\text{if(i==10)\{A();\}}\ldots]I)}}{\vdots}} \qquad \cfrac{\cfrac{\cfrac{B_{3,1}}{\mathcal{UV}_M(I \wedge i \geqslant n \wedge i \doteq 20) \Rightarrow \ldots}}{\vdots \qquad \vdots}}{\cfrac{\Rightarrow \cfrac{\mathcal{UV}_M(I \wedge i \geqslant n \rightarrow}{[\text{if(i==20)\{C();}\ldots]\phi)}}{\vdots}}
$$

$$
B_1 \quad \Rightarrow \underbrace{\{i := 0\}}_{\mathcal{U}}[\text{while(i<n)\{if(i==10)\{A();}\ldots\text{\}if(i==20)}\ldots]\phi
$$

$$
\vdots
$$

$$
\Rightarrow [\text{foo1(int n)}]\phi
$$

Fig. 7.5. Proof tree with test data constraints obtained by using the loop invariant rule

from the modifier set of the loop invariant and is given by $\mathcal{V}_M = \{i := i_{sk}\}$, where $i_{sk} \in \text{FSym}$ is a fresh symbol.

The test data constraints are derived from the leaves of the proof tree shown in Figure 7.5. The leaf of branch $B_{2,1}$ is the sequent

$$
\overbrace{\{i := 0\}}^{\mathcal{U}} \overbrace{\{i := i_{sk}\}}^{\mathcal{V}_M} \overbrace{(0 \leqslant i \wedge i \leqslant n}^{I} \wedge i < n \wedge i \doteq 10) \Rightarrow [\text{A();}\ldots]I
$$
$$
(7.12)
$$

According to Formulas (7.7) and (7.8) the test data constraint derived from this sequent is

$$
\overbrace{\{i := 0\}}^{\mathcal{U}} \overbrace{\{i := i_{sk}\}}^{\mathcal{V}_M} \overbrace{(0 \leqslant i \wedge i \leqslant n}^{I} \wedge i < n \wedge i \doteq 10) \qquad (7.13)
$$

which simplifies to

$$
(i_{sk} < n \wedge i_{sk} \doteq 10)
$$

and implies $n > 10$.

The strength condition (7.10) is provable in this case. For test generation it is not necessary to prove or to generate the strength condition. However, the fact that it is provable implies that if the test data constraint is satisfied, i.e. $n > 10$, then A() will be executed in Listing 7.3.

The test data constraint derived from $B_{3,1}$ is

$$
\overbrace{\{i := 0\}}^{\mathcal{U}} \overbrace{\{i := i_{sk}\}}^{\mathcal{V}_M} \overbrace{(0 \leqslant i \wedge i \leqslant n}^{I} \wedge i \geqslant n \wedge i \doteq 20)
$$

It simplifies to

$$(i_{sk} \doteq n \wedge i_{sk} \doteq 20)$$

which implies that if $n \doteq 20$, then C() will be executed in Listing 7.3. This is correct because the strength condition (7.9) is provable in this case as well.

Similarly test data constraints can be obtain in order to execute C() for Listing 7.4.

7.4.3 Test Cases with Fault Detection Guarantee

The branch B_2 of the proof tree shown in Figure 7.3 on page 189 does not close because the code in Listing 7.2 has a fault. The deductive fault detection approach described in Chapter 4 can detect the fault and provide an initial state of the MUT that reveals it. Such test cases are derived in the use-case 1 of Figure 7.1. Revealing the fault means that the postcondition will not be satisfied after the execution of the MUT. In principle a test oracle can be used in this case which returns false. We formalize this in the following theorem.

Theorem 7.4. *Let $S_0, \ldots, S_n$ be a branch of a proof tree where S_n has the form*

$$\Gamma_n \Longrightarrow \Delta_n$$

and S_0 has the form

$$\Gamma_0 \Longrightarrow \mathcal{U}_0 \langle p \rangle \phi, \Delta_0$$

If Algorithm 1 (see Chapter 4, page 86) has detected a fault on the branch $S_0, \ldots, S_n$, then any test satisfying the test data constraint

$$\bigwedge \Gamma_n \wedge \neg \bigvee \Delta_n \tag{7.14}$$

leads to an execution of p such that the postcondition ϕ is violated or p does not terminate.

Proof. If Algorithm 1 has detected a fault on the branch $S_0, \ldots, S_n$, this means that a) S_n has a counterexample, and b) the branch is validity preserving, i.e. $\vDash S_0 \rightarrow S_n$ (see Section 4.4.1, page 92). Validity preservation of the branch can also be expressed as $\vDash \neg S_n \rightarrow \neg S_0$. Formula (7.14) is the negation of S_n. Hence, every partial model $\mathcal{S}$ (see Definitions 2.6 and 2.19) of (7.14) is also a partial model of $\neg S_0$, respectively a counterexample of S_0. It cannot be that $\mathcal{S} \vDash \mathcal{U}_0 \langle p \rangle \phi$

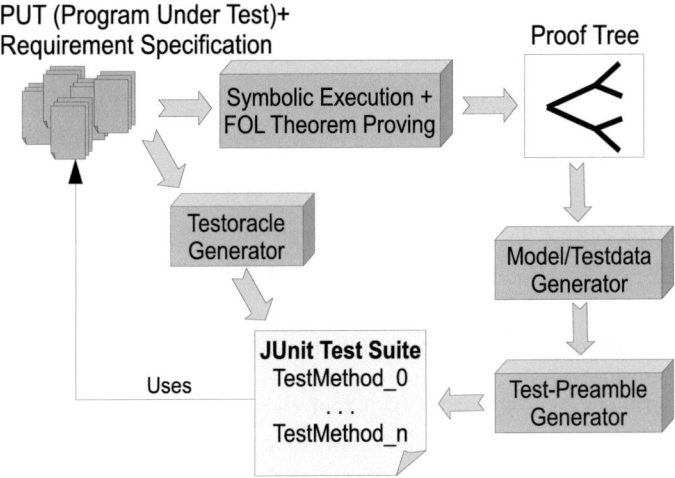

Fig. 7.6. Generation of executable JUnit tests

because then $\mathcal{S}$ would not be a counterexample of S_0 (see Def. 2.29). Hence, it is necessarily the case that $\mathcal{S} \not\models \mathcal{U}_0\langle p \rangle \phi$ which means that after the execution of p the postcondition ϕ is violated or p does not terminate (see also Def. 2.25 and Lemma 2.26 on page 42). ∎

7.5 Generation of Executable JUnit Tests

This section describes techniques for the generation of executable JUnit tests which are based on the test cases, or test data constraints, obtained in first phase (see Section 7.4). This approach is shown in Figure 7.6.

The original version of this VBT approach was developed by Engel [Engel, 2006]. From the time [Engel, 2006] was published KeY has evolved requiring changes to the original implementation as well as extensions for handling new features of KeY such as quantified updates and a different translation from JML specifications to verification conditions. In the following sub-sections we describe new techniques for the generation of JUnit tests that were developed by the author of this thesis, if not stated otherwise.

A JUnit test suite consists of a set of test drivers which execute the MUT. A test driver is a method with the following structure.

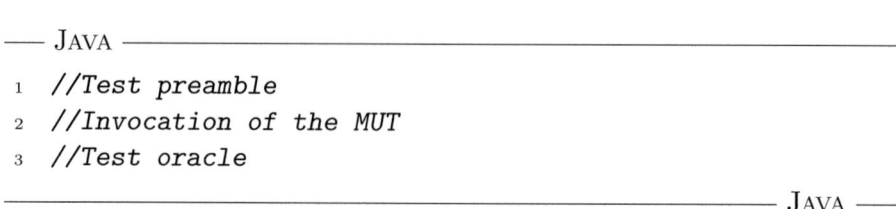

```java
1  //Test preamble
2  //Invocation of the MUT
3  //Test oracle
```

In the following we describe a test preamble generator and two test oracle generators. Hence, these sub-sections are technically oriented.

7.5.1 Test Preamble Generation

The test preamble is the part of a test driver that initializes the state in which the MUT is executed. It initializes the MUT with the respective test data of each branch at a time and ensures the execution of the program paths represented in the proof tree.

In Section 7.4 we have described how to obtain test data constraints which are the input to a model generator to generate test data. As described in Section 6.7 (page 168), the model generator presented in Chapter 6 can be used to generate test data. In this approach a models, respectively the assignment of test data to memory locations, is syntactically represented in form of updates. The task of the preamble generator is to convert the updates into a JAVA program. For this task the following problems have to be solved.

a) Function symbols have to be represented in the test driver.
b) Parallel and quantified updates have to be transformed into sequential programs.
c) Objects have to be created.
d) Read and write access to private and protected object fields must be enabled.

7.5.1.1 Representing Function Symbols in JAVA

An update assigns a value to a function for a specific argument value. If the update was generated by the calculus rule `assignment` (see Table 2.5), the location term is an assignable JAVA expression. Hence, in this case the function is a program variable, an object field, or an array.

Updates not generated by the `assignment` rule may assign values to functions that are not constructs declared in the program. A typical example of this situation is storing the value of an expression in the pre-state of the MUT in a temporary function in order to refer to it in the post-state of the MUT. For example, in Listings 7.1 and 7.2 of Section 7.4 (page 186) the temporary function x' is used to store the value of the formal parameter x in the pre-state of the MUT. In such cases, where a unary function symbol is used, the function symbol can be modelled by a program variable. In practice, however, also function symbols with arity greater than zero are relevant for test generation as shown in the following example.

— JAVA + JML (7.5) ————————————————————

```
1  Object[] a;
2  /*@ public normal_behavior
3     requires a!=null;
4     ensures (\forall int i;0<=i && i<=a.length();
5              (\exists int j;0<=j && j<=a.length();
6                      \old(a[i]) == a[j]   ) );
7     modifies a[*]; @*/
8  void sort(){...}
```

———————————————————————————— JAVA + JML —

Listing 7.5 specifies that after executing the method `sort()` the array `a` has the same elements as before the execution.[5] Hence, in order to make a comparison of the array in the pre-state and the post-state of the MUT, the old values of the array elements have to be stored. For this purpose KeY creates from Listing 7.5 a verification condition of the form 7.5 (page 185), i.e. $\Gamma \implies \mathcal{U}_0\langle \mathtt{m}();\rangle\phi, \Delta$, with the update $\mathcal{U}_0$ defined as

$$a^{Pre} := a \,||\, \mathtt{for}\ x_0, x_1;\ \mathtt{true};\ get^{Pre}(x_0, x_1) := x_0[x_1] \qquad (7.15)$$

where $a^{Pre}, get^{Pre} \in \mathrm{FSym}_{nr}$, $[] \in \mathrm{FSym}_r$ (see Def. 2.2, page 24), $x_0, x_1 \in \mathrm{VSym}$, and the typing of the symbols is (see Def. 2.2)

$$\alpha(a^{Pre}) = \alpha(a) = \mathtt{Object[]}$$
$$\alpha(get^{Pre}) = ((\mathtt{Object[]}, \mathtt{int}), \mathtt{Object})$$
$$\alpha(x_0) = \mathtt{Object[]}$$
$$\alpha(x_1) = \mathtt{int}$$

The function a^{Pre} stores the old reference to the array (object) and the function get^{Pre} stores the array elements of all arrays of type `Object[]`.

———————

[5] The multiplicity and sortedness of the array elements is not specified.

The expression \old(a[i]) in the postcondition of the specification is therefore translated to $get^{Pre}(a^{Pre}, i)$. Hence, function symbols with arity greater than zero have to be modelled in JAVA. ☐

A general way to represent a first-order logic function over a finite domain in JAVA is to use a hashmap. A function with multiple arguments can be represented as a hashmap with one argument that returns another hashmap with one argument. If the argument is of type int, also an array can be used to represent the function.

7.5.1.2 Transformation of Updates to a JAVA Program

As described in the beginning of Section 7.5.1, updates represent the assignment of test data to memory locations. In the previous sub-section we have described that updates are also used to store the old values of expressions in order to make them accessible after the execution of the MUT. Therefore, updates occurring before the MUT must be treated as a prefix program of the MUT. The resulting program should exhibit the same state change that is expressed by the update or an approximation of it. In some cases it is not possible or not desired to transform an update into an equivalent JAVA program. This is for instance the case if the update performs an infinite state change such as the update (7.15) on page 197.

The update language consists of five constructs (see Def. 2.16). Update applications can be reduced to the other constructs using Lemma 2.42. Throughout this section we define and explain the transformation function τ which transforms an update to another update or to JAVA statements. We do not define the transformation function strictly mathematically. This is because not all updates can be transformed into equivalent JAVA programs and there are also different possibilities and room for creativity how to realize the transformation.

Function and Sequential Updates

Function updates and sequential updates can be transformed trivially to a sequence of assignments in JAVA. However, not all updates have to be transformed to the program. If it is known that a function symbol cannot be accessed during the execution of the MUT or the test oracle, the update can be ignored. Hence, the transformation function τ for function updates and sequential updates is defined as follows.

Definition 7.5. *The transformation function* $\tau : Updates \rightarrow (Updates \cup Programs)$, *where* $Programs$ *denotes the set of sequences of* JAVA *statements, has the following properties.*

Let $(f(t_1, \ldots, t_n) := t), u_1, u_2 \in Updates$ *be function updates.*

- *The transformation* $\tau(f(t_1, \ldots, t_n) := t)$ *is defined as:*
    - *an empty statement, if* $f(t_1, \ldots, t_n)$ *does not represent any of the following: a program variable, an object field, the array access operator, a temporary symbol as described in Section 7.5.1.1, or a temporary symbol introduced by* τ *as described in this section;*
    - *otherwise, it is defined as a program* p *which*
        - *ensures that* $\langle p \rangle f(t_1, \ldots, t_n) \doteq t$ *holds and* t *is not changed,*
        - *uses the* JAVA *representation of* $f(t_1, \ldots, t_n)$ *and* t *as described in Section 7.5.1.1,*
        - *uses the techniques described in Section 7.5.1.4 to access the memory locations,*
        - *uses the techniques for object creation described in Section 7.5.1.3.*
- *The transformation* $\tau(u_1 \,;\, u_2)$ *yields the sequential program* $\tau(u_1)\,;\, \tau(u_2)$.

Parallel Updates

The transformation of parallel updates without quantified updates has been described in [Engel, 2006]. The approach is to transform a parallel update into a sequential update before it is transformed into a program. The approach requires that no sequential update occurs as a sub-update of the parallel update which can be achieved with Lemma (2.41). It ensures that the arguments of both, the location terms and the value terms of all function updates that occur below the parallel update, are evaluated in the pre-state of the update (see Def. 2.23).

For instance, consider the sequential update

$$f(a) := b\,;\, g(f(a)) := f(a) \tag{7.16}$$

Assume that s is the state in which the update is evaluated, then location term argument a and the value term b of the first update are evaluated in s. However, the location term argument and value term $f(a)$ are evaluated in the state $val_s((7.16))(s)$. In contrast, when the update (7.16) is replaced by the parallel update

$$f(a) := b \,||\, g(b) := b \tag{7.17}$$

the location term arguments and value terms are all evaluated in s.

The evaluation point of the location term arguments and the value terms has to be respected as the following example shows. The formula (let $P \in \text{PSym}$)

$$\{a := f(a) \,||\, f(a) := a\} P(a, f(a)) \tag{7.18}$$

is equivalent to

$$P(f(a), a)$$

If the parallel update in Formula (7.18) is replaced by a sequential update, the semantics of the formula is changed as shown by the following simplification steps

$$\{a := f(a) \,;\, f(a) := a\} P(a, f(a))$$
$$\equiv \{a := f(a) \,||\, f(\{a := f(a)\} a) := \{a := f(a)\} a\} \quad \text{(Lem. 2.41)}$$
$$\equiv \{a := f(a) \,||\, f(f(a)) := f(a)\} P(a, f(a))$$
$$\equiv P(f(a), f(a))$$

In order to transform a parallel update into a sequential update, the approach is to store the values of the location term arguments and the value terms in temporary function symbols. Continuing the example, the update of Formula (7.18) can be transformed into the following sequential update

$$a' := a \,;\, a := f(a') \,;\, f(a') := a'$$

which is equivalent to the update in (7.18) except for the modification of the temporary function $a' \in \text{FSym}_{nr}$.

A more general transformation of parallel updates to sequential updates is given in the following definition.

Definition 7.6. *Let* $u \in$ *Updates be in update normal form (see Def. 2.37):*

$$u = (\text{for } \bar{x}_1; \, \phi_1; \, f_1(\bar{t}_1) := s_1 \,||\, \ldots \,||\, \text{for } \bar{x}_n; \, \phi_n; \, f_n(\bar{t}_n) := s_n)$$

The transformation $\tau(u)$ *is defined as*

$$\tau(u_{prefix} \,;\, u')$$

where $u_{prefix} \in$ *Updates is defined as the sequential update*

$$(\texttt{for } \bar{x}_1;\ \phi_1;\ (\overline{t'}_1 := \bar{t}_1\,;\, s'_1 := s_1))\,;\,...\,;\,(\texttt{for } \bar{x}_1;\ \phi_1;\ (\overline{t'}_n := \bar{t}_n\,;\, s'_n := s_n))$$

and $u' \in$ *Updates is defined as the sequential update*

$$(\texttt{for } \bar{x}_1;\ \phi_1;\ f_1(\overline{t'}_1) := s'_1)\,;\,...\,;\,(\texttt{for } \bar{x}_n;\ \phi_n;\ f_n(\overline{t'}_n) := s'_n)$$

$\square$

In the definition the update u_{prefix} stores the values of the terms $\bar{t}_i$ and s_i with $1 \leqslant i \leqslant n$ in the pre-state of the update u. The values are stored in the constants $\overline{t'}_i$ and s'_i which are used in the update u'. The update u' is the sequential version of u which ensures that the arguments of the location term and the value term are not influenced by the sequence. This is because $\overline{t'}_i$ and s'_i cannot be modified by u'.

Quantified Updates

A quantified update of the form $(\texttt{for } x;\ \text{true};\ u)$ can be *informally* seen as an infinite composition of parallel updates of the form $u_{+\infty} \,||\, ... \,||\, u_{-\infty}$ where each sub-update has its own variable assignment for x. A quantified update of the form $(\texttt{for } x;\ \phi;\ u)$ allows a sub-update to be effective only if ϕ is true for the particular assignment of x. For instance, the quantified update

$$\texttt{for } x;\ 0 \leqslant x \leqslant 2;\ f(x) := x$$

is equivalent to the update

$$f(2) := 2 \,||\, f(1) := 1 \,||\, f(0) := 0$$

Hence, it seems reasonable to transform a quantified update into a loop statement which iterates over the values of x, and to use an if-statement to check whether ϕ is satisfied before executing the sub-update. Since loops are executed sequentially a conversion from the parallel composition to a sequential composition of updates is necessary. This conversion can be achieved with the approach followed at the beginning of Section 7.5.1.2 (see page 199). Based on this intuition we extend the transformation function τ for quantified updates as follows.

Definition 7.7. *Let* $\mathcal{K}_{\preceq}$ *be a Kripke structure. Let*

$$u = (\texttt{for } \bar{x};\ \phi;\ f(\bar{t}) := s)$$

The transformation $\tau(u)$ *is defined as*

$$\tau(\texttt{QUpToLoop}_{\preceq}(u_{prefix}); \texttt{QUpToLoop}_{\preceq}(u'))$$

where $u_{prefix} \in$ *Updates is defined as*

$$\texttt{for } \bar{x};\ \phi;\ (\overline{t'} := \bar{t};\ s' := s)$$

$u' \in$ *Updates is defined as*

$$\texttt{for } \bar{x};\ \phi;\ f(\overline{t'}) := s'$$

and `QUpToLoop`$_{\preceq}$ *represents a* JAVA *program in form of Algorithm 5. The sets* $dom_{x_i}^{\phi}$ *with* $1 \leqslant i \leqslant m$ *contain all values of the variables* x_i *for which* ϕ *is satisfiable.*

Algorithm 5 QUpToLoop$_{\preceq}(\mu)$

Require: $\mu \in$ *Updates* has the form (`for` $x_1, \ldots, x_m$; ϕ; u).
 1: **for all** $x_1 \in dom_{x_1}^{\phi}$ respecting the order relation $\preceq$ **do**

 2: $\quad \vdots$
 3: $\qquad$ **for all** $x_n \in dom_{x_m}^{\phi}$ respecting the order relation $\preceq$ **do**
 4: $\qquad\quad$ **if** ϕ **then**
 5: $\qquad\qquad \tau(u)$
 6: $\qquad\quad$ **end if**
 7: $\qquad$ **end for**

 8: $\quad \vdots$
 9: **end for**

□

In Definition 7.7 a general transformation is given which converts a quantified update with a function sub-update to a schema for a sequential program. Similarly as in Definition 7.6, the update u_{prefix} evaluates the terms $\bar{t}$ and s in the pre-state of the update u. The values are stored in the constants $\overline{t'}$ and s' allowing to break the parallelism of u. The update u' is the sequential version of u.

Algorithm 5 is a program schema. An implementation of a loop which iterates over all elements in $dom_{x_i}^{\phi}$ is, however, not practical or not possible in several cases. The problem of the transformation is the domain of the quantification.

One problem is that if the domain is infinite, Definition 7.7 may yield an infinite loop or a loop that iterates, e.g., over all JAVA integer values. This is for instance the case with the quantified variable x_1 in the update (7.15) which we have defined in Section 7.5.1.1 as

$$a^{Pre} := a \,||\, \texttt{for } x_0, x_1; \text{ true}; \; get^{Pre}(x_0, x_1) := x_0[x_1]$$

A practical transformation can be achieved if the formula ϕ restricts the domain of quantification to a finite set. This is for instance the case if ϕ specifies upper and lower bounds in case of quantification over the integer domain.

Another problem is to handle quantification over the domain of JAVA objects as it is, e.g., the case with the variable x_0 in the update (7.15). The problem is that it is not possible to determine and access all objects of the Java Virtual Machine. Furthermore, JAVA CARD DL uses constant domain semantics, which implies that the domain of quantification includes all created objects as well as objects that are not created yet. Accessing the latter kind of objects is not possible in JAVA.

Fortunately, quantified updates such as (7.15), which create a copy of memory locations for later use, can be handled in a special way. The functions which are assigned values by the update do not occur in the program but only in the postcondition of the MUT. Hence, it is possible to look-up which expressions need to be evaluated with respect to the pre-state of the MUT.

For instance, $\texttt{\textbackslash old(a[x])}$ is the only expression in Listing 7.5 that refers to the function $[] : \texttt{Object[]} \times \texttt{int} \rightarrow \texttt{Object}$ in the pre-state of the MUT. Using this information the update (7.15) can be transformed to

$$a^{Pre} := a \,||\, \texttt{for } x_0, x_1; \; \boldsymbol{x_0 \doteq a}; \; get^{Pre}(x_0, x_1) := x_0[x_1] \qquad (7.19)$$

Hence, quantification over all JAVA objects of type $\texttt{Object[]}$ is not required. From the postcondition of Listing 7.5 upper and lower bounds for the quantification of x_1 can be determined. The update (7.20) can be transformed to the parallel update

$$a^{Pre} := a \,||$$
$$\texttt{for } x_0, x_1; \; \underbrace{x_0 \doteq a \wedge 0 \leqslant x_1 \leqslant a.length}_{\phi}; \; get^{Pre}(x_0, x_1) := x_0[x_1]$$

$$(7.20)$$

This update can be transformed into a sequential program by using Definition 7.7.

What the example does is reducing the domains of quantification $dom_{x_0}^{\phi}$ and $dom_{x_1}^{\phi}$ to finite sets. The reduction of the quantification

203

domains implemented in KeY is technical and hence is not explained here any further. However, with these reductions quantified updates occurring in practice are transformed into a correct test preamble.

Finally, in cases where a sufficient reduction of a quantification domain is not possible, KeY performs instantiations of the quantified update with primitive values or object references that occur in the test data constraint $\bigwedge \Gamma \wedge \neg \bigvee \Delta$ (see Formula (7.3), page 185). This approach yields, however, only an approximation of the updates that does not guarantee soundness of the test driver, i.e., the initial state of the MUT may not satisfy the test data constraint.

7.5.1.3 Object Creation

Primitive values assigned by updates are represented as terms and can be trivially transformed into JAVA expressions. In contrast, a reference to a JAVA object of type A is an identifier in JAVA CARD DL which is retrieved by the injective function $\texttt{A::get} : \texttt{integer} \rightarrow A$ (see Def. 2.2). For instance, a partial interpretation of a program variable $o : A$ is represented in the output of the model generator as an update of the form $(o := \texttt{A::get}(t))$, where $t \in \mathrm{Trm}^{FOL}$. Simply transforming each such update into an assignment $\texttt{o=new A()};$ is not correct. This is because the two updates may assign the same reference to different program variables, e.g.,

$$o1 := \texttt{A::get}(t_1) \, ; o2 := \texttt{A::get}(t_2)$$

with $t_1 \equiv t_2$ but two calls of the **new** operator would result in two different objects, i.e. $\langle \texttt{o1=newA()};\texttt{o2=newA()}\rangle \neg o1 \doteq o2$. The solution proposed in [Engel, 2006] is to perform equivalence analysis of the value terms which ensures that the same object reference is used for all equivalent object identifier terms $\texttt{A::get}(t)$. We propose an alternative solution that is more technically oriented but is simpler to implement.

Definition 7.8. *Let $u \in$ Updates be a function update of the form*

$$o := \texttt{A::get}(t)$$

The transformation $\tau(o := t)$ is defined as

$$\texttt{A tmp = getObjectA(t)}; \tau(o := tmp)$$

where $\texttt{tmp}$ *is a new program variable of type A. The method* $\texttt{getObjectA}$ *is defined as*

--- JAVA ---

```
1  public static A getObjectA(int id){
2    if(hm.contains(id)){ return hm.get(id); }
3    else {hm.put(id, newObjA()); return getObjectA(id); }
4  }
```

--- JAVA ---

where `hm` *is a static hashmap which maps* `int` *to* `A`, *and* `newObjA()` *creates a new instance of class* `A`.

The method `getObjectA()` returns an instance of class `A` and ensures injectivity with respect to the parameter `id`.

Creating an instance of a class automatically is generally not a trivial task if the class has no public default constructor. The problem is that using a non-default constructor may require a recursive search procedure in order to initialize parameters of a non-default constructor with references to other objects. Therefore this task is abstracted by the method `newObjA()` in Definition 7.8. In [Engel, 2006] the problem was solved by creating a copy of the whole program under test and extending all class definitions with public default constructors. We use in contrast the OBJENESIS API [Walnes et al.] which solves this problem without the necessity to modify the original program and is used by the method `newObjA()`.

7.5.1.4 Read and Write Access to Private and Protected Object Fields

Enabling read and write access to *private* and *protected* object fields is a technical JAVA issue.[6] In [Engel, 2006] this problem is solved by creating a copy of the whole program under test and extending all class definitions with *get* and *set* methods for each private or protect field. These methods enable the desired read and write access. In addition each class is equipped with a public standard constructor (see Section 7.5.1.3). This approach is useful for testing programs in the JAVA dialects JAVA CARD or JAVA ME where JAVA's Reflection API is not available.

We have extended VBT to generate test drivers which access private and protected fields via JAVA's Reflection API. This approach has

---

[6] The terms *private* and *protected* refer to the JAVA modifiers `private` and `protected`, respectively.

several advantages that we describe in the following. For further information on JAVA's Reflection API we refer the reader to the available online reference.

An advantage of using the reflection API rather than extending the program under test (PUT) with *set* and *get* methods is that the PUT is not modified, and thus the original program is tested. Another advantage of our approach is that it allows to access memory locations that otherwise cannot be accessed when using *set* and *get* methods. This is for instance the case if the source code is not available or if it is not appropriate to modify the library classes. Such cases occur if the state of instances of library classes has to be initialized with test data.

Consider for instance the following code that may occur in the MUT.

—— JAVA (7.6) ————————————————————————————

```
1  Vector v;.
2  ..
3  if(v.get(1)==2){...}
```

————————————————————————————————— JAVA ——

The MUT contains a conditional statement on the outcome of a library method. The class `Vector` of the *Java Runtime Environment* (JRE) declares a protected array `elementData` which stores the elements of each instance of the class. The techniques of VBT described so far yield a model in which `elementData[1]` has to be initialized with the value 2. However, an assignment to `elementData[1]` in the test preamble cannot be created due to the visibility restrictions of the field. Extending the declaration of the class `Vector` with a suitable *set* would require to use a custom JRE which is especially not suitable in the use-case 2 of Figure 7.1.

7.5.2 Test Oracle Generation

In order to check if the MUT meets its specification a test oracle is executed after running the MUT. The test oracle evaluates the postcondition of the MUT in its post-state. Ideally the test oracle is a decision procedure for the postcondition in the post-state of the MUT. There are at least three principle limitations when generating a test oracle. The first is that first-order logic is semi-decidable and therefore not every postcondition can be transformed into an oracle deciding it. The second is the problem of handling postconditions that express properties of infinitely many memory locations, e.g. $\forall x . a[x] = 0$. Accessing infinitely many memory locations leads to a non-terminating program. The third is that not all objects of the JVM may be known to the test oracle which is required, e.g., to evaluate the formula $\exists a.a.length \doteq 1$.

Since the state of the JVM is determined by finitely many memory locations which store concrete values from finite sets the question arise what causes the above mentioned problems. Any formula that depends only on the memory locations and values of the JVM is decidable. The problem is that in the context of verification the user sometimes expresses properties for the sake of simpler specification that go beyond the JVM state. For instance, it is easier to specify (and possibly to verify) $\forall x.a[x] = 0$ rather than $\forall x.(0 \leq x \wedge x \leq a.length) \rightarrow a[x] = 0$. The oracle may also not be able to decide a postcondition in a concrete JVM state because theoretically the postcondition may contain some arbitrary FOL formula expressing a property that is not related to the state of the JVM. Hence, in practice the user has to understand the limitations of the test oracle generator and design the postcondition accordingly.

In the following we describe two techniques, respectively approached, for test oracle generation. For accessing object fields we assume that the techniques described in Section 7.5.1.4 are used.

7.5.2.1 Approach 1

A simple approach is to convert recursively each sub-formula of the postcondition into a method. Each of these methods evaluates one logical operator. For instance, the formula ϕ_0 defined as $\phi_1 \wedge \phi_2$ is converted into a method of the form:

—— JAVA ——
```
1  public static boolean subFormula0(...){
2    boolean b1 = subFormula1(...);
3    boolean b2 = subFormula2(...);
4    return b1 && b2;
5  }
```
————————————————————— JAVA ——

Obvious translations are performed for the other propositional operators. Quantification is restricted to the bounded integer domain and is handled with for-loops. In order to determine the lower and upper bounds for the quantified variable the implementation described in [Engel and Hähnle, 2007; Engel, 2006] restricts quantified formulas to one of the following two forms.

$$\forall x.((lower \leqslant x \wedge x \leqslant upper) \rightarrow \phi)$$

$$\exists x.((lower \leqslant x \wedge x \leqslant upper) \wedge \phi)$$

We have weakened this restriction. The matrix of the quantified formula is not restricted anymore to a certain syntactical form. Instead, by traversing the structure of the postcondition literals have to be found which determine the lower and upper bounds of the quantified variable. If several terms are found expressing lower and upper bounds, then the smallest interval is computed at runtime of the test oracle. This generalization has been developed in scope of the minor thesis [Bender, 2010].

7.5.2.2 Approach 2

In this approach the deductive fault detection techniques described in Part II of this thesis is used to implement a test oracle. The implementation of this approach is still in development. The test oracle is given as Algorithm 6.

Algorithm 6 testOracle$_\phi$()

1: p =stateToProg$_\phi$()
2: **return** tryToVerifyOrToFindABug$((\bigwedge \Gamma \wedge \neg \bigvee \Delta) \rightarrow \mathcal{U}\langle p\rangle\phi)$ (see Sec. 4.3.1)

The assumptions in the definition of Algorithm 6 are:

- $\phi \in$ *Formulae* is the postcondition of the requirement specification.
- $\Gamma \implies \mathcal{U}\langle\rangle\phi, \Delta$ is sequent from which the current test has been derived according to Section 7.4, i.e., the symbolic execution of the MUT has terminated and $\bigwedge \Gamma \wedge \neg \bigvee \Delta$ is the test data constraint.
- *stateToProg$_\phi$()* is a method returning a JAVA program which captures the values of memory locations that are relevant for ϕ.

When using the test oracle defined by Algorithm 6, VBT performs almost the same steps as the deductive fault detection approach does which is described in Chapter 4. The difference is that that the symbolic execution of the MUT is by-passed with the execution in its runtime-environment.

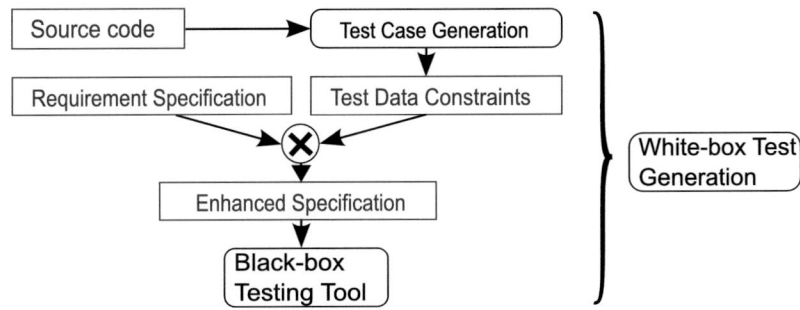

Fig. 7.7. White-box testing by combining structural specification enhancement and black-box testing

Algorithm 6 can be considered as a general test oracle allowing to prove complex first-order logic formulas. The method $stateToProg_\phi()$ translates the state of the JVM to a JAVA CARD DL state in order to evaluate the postcondition in KeY. If ϕ accesses either infinitely many memory locations or memory locations that cannot be accessed, these methods do not terminate or do not exist. A similar problem exists for the translation of quantified updates where the JAVA CARD DL state is translated into the JVM state (see Section 7.5.1.2, page 201).

The program p overrides the memory locations which are assigned in $\mathcal{U}$ with the actual values from the JVM. For instance, if in the initial state of the MUT $a \equiv 0$ and after the execution of the MUT $a \equiv 1$, then $\mathcal{U}\langle p\rangle\phi$ is given by $\{a := 0 \,||\, \ldots\}\langle \texttt{a=1} ; \ldots\rangle\phi$. Note that p must assign concrete values to the memory locations in order to be independent from $\mathcal{U}$. Otherwise the concatenation of $\mathcal{U}$ and $\langle p\rangle$ would describe the result of double execution of the MUT.

7.6 Tool-chain Approach for Test Generation

In Section 7.3 we have given an overview of two test generation approaches. Common to both approaches is the first phase where test cases are extracted from a proof tree (see Section 7.4). In this section we describe the second phase of the tool-chain approach which is an alternative to the JUnit test generation approach described in Section 7.5.

Verification and testing tools can benefit from each other when being combined. However, they do not offer interfaces providing information that could be used for the other task. The solution that we propose in this section is to use specifications that encode structural information of programs for interfacing (see Figure 7.7). The specifications are in between program analysis and deductive verification on one side and test-case generation on the other side. On both sides, there are tools that can produce specifications respectively take them as input for test-case generation. Tools that do not immediately offer the required interface can be extended with little effort. In the following we use the term requirement specification in order to distinguish the user-provided specification of desired semantic properties from generated specifications in our approach.

The test data constraints which are obtained as described in Section 7.4 are used in this approach in order to structurally enhance the requirement specification of the MUT. The structurally enhanced specification (hereafter, enhanced specification) is then used as input to a black-box testing tool (e.g. [Cheon et al., 2008; Parasoft; Kosmatov et al., 2004; Legeard et al., 2002]). Thus, (1) the black-box testing method can make use of information about the program's structure that is contained in the specification, and (2) we separate concerns and get a clear interface between program analysis on the one hand and test-case generation and execution on the other hand, which allows the combination of different tools. If the black-box testing tool generates a test for each test data constraint contained in the enhanced specification, then effectively it generates white-box tests.

7.6.1 Generation of the Enhanced Specification in JML

We have extended KeY with a utility for deriving the enhanced specification from a proof tree. The implementation follows the description in [Beckert and Gladisch, 2007] where we had a slightly different view on the approach than in Figure 7.7. Figure 7.8 shows the implemented approach which extracts a specification from the source code – also known as specification mining – and combines the extracted specification with the requirement specification. The extracted specification carries structural information of the MUT's source code. The resulting enhanced specification has the form shown in Listing 7.7 where *req* is the requirement specification and the other parts constitute the extracted specification.

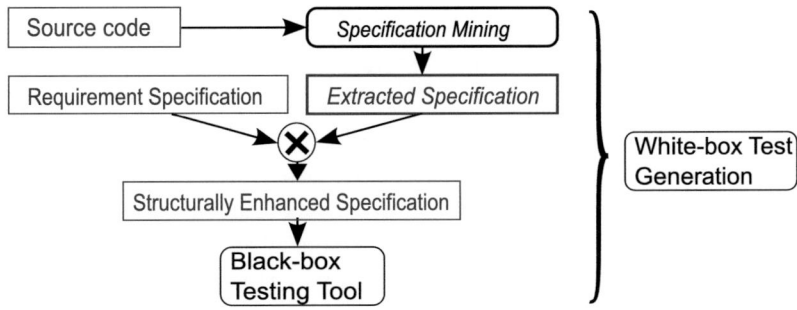

Fig. 7.8. White-box testing by combining specification mining and black-box testing

— JAVA + JML (7.7) ————————————————————

```
1  /*@ req
2  also
3    requires c₁;   ensures  e₁;
4  also
5    ...
6  also
7    requires cₙ;   ensures  eₙ;
8  *@/
```

———————————————————————————— JAVA + JML —

The JML expressions $c_1, \ldots, c_n$ are test data constraints according to the description of Section 7.4. The difference of the approach shown in Figure 7.8 with respect to the approach shown in Figure 7.7 is that in addition to the test data constraints also the postconditions $e_1, \ldots, e_n$ are generated – justifying the term *extracted specification*. These postconditions describe the post-state of the MUT that was computed by symbolic execution and must not be confused with the postcondition of the requirement specification provided by the user. If an extracted precondition is satisfied, the respective postconditions must be satisfied as well, otherwise the symbolic execution does not comply with the execution of the MUT in its runtime-environment. Hence, the extracted postconditions can be considered as a feature but they are not as important as the preconditions are. The postconditions can be set to **true** because the actual requirement is checked by the postcondition of the specification *req*. This insight has led us to the newer view

211

of the approach depicted in Figure 7.7. Nevertheless, we give a short description of the postcondition extraction technique.

The postconditions are computed from the update $\mathcal{U}$ that is in front of the DL formula that is in the focus of symbolic execution (see Section 7.4). In order to generate a meaningful postcondition, the symbolic execution of the MUT must have terminated, i.e., the program p in Formula (7.1) has to be empty. Otherwise, the update does not represent the final state of the MUT and in this case we simply chose the postcondition `true`.[7] We assume that the update is in normal form (see Def. 2.37) and it represents a final state of the MUT. Updates containing terms which cannot be evaluated in the postcondition at runtime are ignored or replaced by alternative equivalent terms. For instance, updates to (local) program variables and formal parameters are ignored.

A functional update of the form $t := s$ is transformed into a JML-expression of the form

$$\texttt{t==\textbackslash old(s)}$$

where `t` and `s` are JML-representations of the terms t and s respectively. Parallel updates with different top-level function symbols are translated into a conjunction of JML-equations. For instance, the update $a := 1 \,||\, b := 2$ is translated into the expression:

$$\texttt{a==1 \&\& b==2}$$

Parallel updates with the same top-level function symbol on the other hand are translated into a disjunction of JML-equations. For instance, the update $o.a := 1 \,||\, u.a := 2$ is translated into the JML expression

$$\texttt{o.a==1 || u.a==2}$$

In order to handle both cases, function updates with the same top-level function symbol are first grouped together and treated in a disjunction while groups of function updates with different top-level symbols are treated in a conjunction. For instance, the update $o.a := 1 \,||\, u.b := 2 \,||\, u.a := 3 \,||\, o.b := 4$ is translated into the JML expression

$$\texttt{(o.a==1 || u.a==3) \&\& (u.b==2 || o.b==4)}$$

Quantified updates did not exist at the time of the implementation and were therefore not treated.

---

[7] Note that an update represents state changes and it represents states in combination with the context formulas.

7.6.2 Example and Experiments

We have applied the approach shown in Figure 7.8 to several small programs. One of them is the method `sqrt` – the *running example* in this thesis – that we use as an example in the following.

Example

The first step of the approach is to generate a proof tree for the method `sqrt` and to extract test cases from it according to Section 7.4. . Section 4.3.2 describes the construction of a proof tree for the method `sqrt` using finite loop unwinding. In Figure 4.2 on page 91 we have shown the proof tree which has for instance the branch B_1 on which symbolic execution has terminated. The sequent containing the test data constraint and the final update on this branch is

$$x \geqslant 0, o \neq \texttt{null}, 0 \leqslant x, 1 > x \Longrightarrow$$
$$\{i := 1 \,||\, r := 1\}\langle\rangle(r^2 \leqslant x \wedge (r+1)^2 > x) \qquad (7.21)$$

According to Section 7.4 the test data constraint is in this case:

$$x \doteq 0 \wedge o \neq \texttt{null} \wedge 0 \leqslant x \wedge 1 > x \qquad (7.22)$$

In the second step the enhanced specification is generated and a black-box testing tool is applied. Continuing the example, the test data constraint (7.22) is translated into JML and is used as one precondition of the extracted specification (see Listing 7.7 on page 211). The postcondition extracted from the update in the sequent (7.21) is

$$r \doteq 1$$

where the function symbol r is translated into the JML expression `\result`. The function update $i := 1$ is ignored because it determines the values of a (local) program variable which cannot be evaluated in the postcondition at runtime. This technique is applied also to other branches of the proof tree.

For the extraction of the specification from the method `sqrt` we have performed several loop unwindings. KeY's output containing the enhanced specification is shown in Figure 7.9. Lines 3-5 show the requirement specification which is the same as in Figure 3.1. The extracted specification is found in the Lines 6-20. In most cases, i.e. in

213

—— JAVA + JML ————————————————————————

```
1   public class TestC extends C {
2     ... //Constructors and other methods
3     /*@ public normal_behavior
4       requires x>=0;
5       ensures \result * \result <= x && (\result+1) * (\result+1)>x;
6     also
7       requires true && x <= 15 && x >= 9 && !(this == null);
8       ensures \result == \old((int)(4));
9     also
10      requires true && x >= 16 && !(this == null);
11      ensures true ;
12    also
13      requires true && x <= 8 && x >= 4 && !(this == null);
14      ensures \result == \old((int)(3));
15    also
16      requires true && x <= 3 && x >= 1 && !(this == null);
17      ensures \result == \old((int)(2));
18    also
19      requires true && x == 0 && !(this == null);
20      ensures \result == \old((int)(1));
21    @*/
22    public int _test_sqrt(int x){ return sqrt(x); }
23  }
```

——————————————————————————————————— JAVA + JML ——

Fig. 7.9. Generated wrapper class with a structurally enhanced specification

Lines 8, 14, 17, and 20, a postcondition was generated because symbolic execution on the respective proof tree branches has terminated. In Line 11 the trivial postcondition true is used instead.

The enhanced specification does not specify the method sqrt directly, but instead, it specifies the wrapper method _test_sqrt (see Line 22). In this way the specification and source code file of the method sqrt do not have to be modified for the purpose of testing. The black-box tool is then applied to the wrapper method. If the black-box testing tool generates a test for each pre- and postcondition pair, then the structural code coverage of the MUT is achieved.

Experiments

We have applied this technique also to bigger programs. Figure 7.10 shows one of the smallest pre- and postcondition pairs extracted from

—— JML ——————————————————————————————————————

```
 1   requires true && this.root.value == value &&
 2     this.root.left.value <= -1 + value &&
 3     (\forall Node n;true;(n == null|| n.left == null ||
 4                           n.left.value <= -1 + n.value)) &&
 5     (\forall Node n;true;(n == null || n.left == null ||
 6                                   n.left.parent == n)) &&
 7     (this.root.right == null || false) &&
 8     (\forall Node n;true;(n == null|| n.right == null||
 9                           n.right.value >= 1 + n.value)) &&
10     (\forall Node n;true;(n == null || n.right == null ||
11                                   n.right.parent == n)) &&
12     !(this.root.right.value >= 1 + value) && !(this == null) &&
13     !(this.root == null);
14   ensures true;
```

——— JML ——

Fig. 7.10. Excerpt from a large structurally enhanced specification

a method of a binary search tree example. The whole enhanced specification was over 50 lines long. The size of the specification depends on the extent of the proof tree construction. This can be influenced, e.g., by the number of loop unwinding or the amount of quantifier instantiations. Generally such specifications are not suitable for reading but only for automatic processing.

In order to check if a black-box testing tool can handle the generated specifications we have used the black-box testing tool JET [Cheon et al., 2008]. It combines random test data generation with constraint solving. The tool was able to parse the enhanced specification and generate tests revealing faults that we have manually injected in different branches of the MUT. Unfortunately, it is not clear if a test was created for each pre- and postcondition pair of the enhanced specification. We assume, however, that it is easy to extend black-box testing tools with such coverage metrics. JML was developed by the formal verification community and therefore automatic JML black-box testing tools are rare. We have additionally used KeY as a black-box testing tool (see Sections 7.4 and 7.5) for the sake of demonstrating the feasibility of the approach. The generated enhanced specification was loaded back into KeY which has then generated the expected white-box tests without symbolic execution of the program.

Remark 7.9. If the MUT has a fault and the extracted postconditions is strong enough, e.g., it is not just true, then the extracted specification contains this fault as well. In principle, these faults can be detected by checking the consistency of the enhanced specification, because in case of a fault the extracted specification contradicts the requirement specification. However, the extracted specification may not reflect the behavior of the MUT completely and this approach would result in a purely deductive approach which would contradict our goal to test the MUT.

7.7 Experience with VBT and Conclusions

In this chapter we have described how test cases can be derived from a proof tree and we have described two approaches and techniques which use the test cases in order to generate executable tests.

The test generation capabilities are based on the creation of a proof tree for a formula expressing program correctness. Therefore it naturally extends the deductive software fault detection approach described in Part II of the thesis. The advantages and limitations of VBT are connected to the underlying verification technique. The typical size of programs that can be verified is much smaller than the typical size of industrial programs. However, VBT features different levels of program analysis resulting in a spectrum between black-box tests, white-box tests, and tests which are guaranteed to reveal software faults. The user can chose to what extent the program is symbolically executed and if they want to use method contracts and loop invariants or not. Hence, VBT can be adapted to the needs and skills of the user. The more precise the program analysis is the closer are the advantages and restrictions of VBT to verification and deductive software fault detection. Due to this relationship we have described three use-cases in which VBT is strong. Those use-cases extend or complement the verification and deductive fault detection process.

The VBT utility of the KeY tool which generates executable JUnit tests *out of the box* is frequently used by researchers of the KeY team and by others for teaching and research. Hence, the utility is used in practice. It has been original developed by Engel [Engel and Hähnle, 2007; Engel, 2006]. However, in this chapter we have described new techniques developed by the author of this thesis which differ from the original implementation. Each time the implementation is modified or extended it undergoes a set of regression tests. The regression tests consist of a set of different algorithms which served as a case study in [Engel and Hähnle, 2007; Engel, 2006]. Hence, the case study was repeated for the new version of the utility. VBT has been tested on algorithms such as operations on tree structures, sorting algorithms and other small algorithms, as well as on programs consisting of 10 to 20 JAVA classes. In most cases we have generated test cases using bounded symbolic execution without contracts. The result was that full feasible branch coverage was achieved for the mentioned algorithms when choosing a loop unwinding depth of 2 or 3. Scalability of bounded symbolic execution is limited because with a loop unwinding depth of 2 the symbolic execution did not terminate for programs consisting of 10 to 20 JAVA classes. Hence, in the latter case the coverage of the program parts that were not symbolically executed was not guaranteed. The results show that full feasible branch coverage and full feasible bounded path coverage can be achieved in practice. The coverage is achieved if the program branches and paths are represented in the proof tree of the underlying verification technique which usually requires to use method contracts and loop invariants. If method contracts and loop invariants are written for VBT, then the time and effort to achieve full feasible branch coverage is slightly lower than for verification, because in contrast to verification the correctness of the program does not have to be ensured.

The tool-chain approach uses specifications for interfacing the verification-based *test case* generation or specification mining tool with a black-box testing tool. In this way, (1) the black-box testing method can make use of information about the program's structure that is contained in the specification, and (2) we achieve a separation of concerns and a clear interface between program analysis on the one hand and test-case generation and execution on the other hand, which allows the combination of different tools. If the structurally enhanced specification encodes the path conditions of a program and the black-box testing tool generates a test for each pre- and postcondition pair of the specification, then effectively white-box tests are generated. The enhanced specification consists of pre- and post-conditions expressed in classical first-order logic. Since that is the basis for specification languages such as the JML, Spec#, OCL, or Z, simple syntactic changes are sufficient to generate the appropriate input for a particular testing tool. We have tested this approach with several small programs and the black-box testing tool JET [Cheon et al., 2008]. The experiments show that the extracted specification becomes very large and is unreadable for non-trivial programs. Nevertheless, JET was able to parse and evaluate the the enhanced specification quickly. We have additionally used KeY as the black-box testing tool to be sure that a test is generated for each pre- and postcondition pair of the extracted specification. In this way we have achieved the same coverage as with the out-of-the-box VBT approach.

Our experiments show that the two VBT approaches can generate executable test suites with a high test coverage if the MUT is fully symbolically executed or if contracts are provided which are sufficiently strong. If only bounded symbolic execution is used without contracts to generate test cases, then scalability of the approach is more limited and depends on speed and memory consumption of the verification tool to perform symbolic execution. The implementation of the two VBT approaches is not yet fully connected with the techniques described in Part II of this thesis because VBT was developed before that. Future work is therefore to improve this connection.

8

Generating Regression Unit Tests Using a Tool-Chain Approach

8.1 Introduction

In Chapter 7 we have described three use-cases in which unit testing complements verification and deductive fault detection (see Figure 7.1). One of them is regression testing and is the topic of this chapter. For this purpose we have enhanced the verification-based test generation approach (VBT) described in previous chapters with a tool-chain. To generalize our method in this chapter we refer by verification-based test generation techniques not only to the techniques described in Chapter 7 but also to other techniques that follow similar ideas. With VBT techniques we refer to general test generation techniques which derive tests in the context of verification and that achieve high code coverage. The underlying verification techniques can use symbolic execution and theorem proving but also techniques based on model checking, e.g. [Gargantini et al., 2003; Beyer et al., 2004; Visser et al., 2004], can be regarded as VBT techniques.

Motivation

Regression testing means to rerun a set of tests. The goal of regression testing is to check if the program under test (PUT) fulfills its requirements after the program or its environment has been changed. It is used during the software development process and during the maintenance phase. The maintenance phase is estimated to comprise at least 50% of the total software development expenses [van Vliet, 2000]. Regression tests usually consist of a set of unit tests. The advantage of using unit testing is that test selection and test prioritization techniques, e.g. [Graves et al., 1998; Chen et al., 2002; Harrold et al., 2001], can be used. These techniques select a subset of the unit tests to test only those units that are potentially affected by the software change. An important principle of unit testing is to test units in isolation. The regarded units in this chapter are JAVA classes. The behavior of classes, usually may depend on other classes – some of them may not even exist yet. *Mock objects* [Mackinnon et al., 2001] are often used to solve this problem. They expose the same behavior as the original classes for a subset of input situations. Replacing calls to the *other* classes by mock objects results in isolated unit tests.

Testing techniques are powerful for detecting software faults and for gaining some degree of confidence that the program under test (PUT) behaves correctly in its runtime environment. VBT techniques use information gained from a verification attempt. This enables the generation of targeted tests to reveal software faults or tests that exhibit a high code coverage. Thus, both verification and testing techniques can profit when being combined. Yet, we can even go a step further in combining both approaches. We found that more traditional testing techniques have complementary strengths to VBT techniques. One such technique is capture and replay (CaR), whose strengths are the generation of isolated unit tests [Pasternak et al., 2009; Saff et al., 2005] and regression test oracles [Pasternak et al., 2009; Xie, 2006; Elbaum et al., 2009].

Approach and Contributions

We propose an approach for the automatic generation of unit and regression tests in the context of verification. Our goal is to improve test suites that are generated by VBT tools and CaR tools in separation. The proposed approach maintains the high test coverage provided by VBT tools while at the same time it reduces the complexity of the tests through automatic generation of mock objects. Using mock objects facilitates the isolation of the unit under test. Some existing CaR tools enable to create mock objects. On the other hand, CaR tools do not provide means to achieve high code coverage, and can therefore benefit from being combined with coverage guaranteeing tools such as VBT tools. The advantage of using VBT tools is that the verification process can be used to ensure that only correct behavior is captured by the CaR tool.

Research related to regression testing often focuses on test selection and test prioritization techniques, e.g. [Graves et al., 1998; Harrold et al., 2001]. Our focus in this chapter is different. We exploit the *synergies* of combining VBT and CaR tools for unit regression testing. We identified that high code coverage and isolation are separate issues. They can be achieved independently using the two groups of techniques which have complementary strengths. Therefore we concluded that those groups of techniques are ideal candidates for the following tool-chain. The first phase produces, for a given system, unit tests with high code coverage. The second phase captures the various executions of the program, monitored by the output of the first phase. The output of the second phase is a set of unit tests with high coverage, which uses mock objects to test the units, in isolation.

The main contributions of this chapter are described in Sections 8.2 to 8.4. We identify what the complementary strengths of VBT and CaR techniques are (Section 8.2). In Section 8.3 we present a novel tool-chain approach for unit regression testing in the context of verification and unit regression testing in general. To the best of our knowledge, this tool-chain has not been considered with VBT tools so far. We have implemented a concrete tool-chain using KeY's verification-based test generator and the CaR tool GenUTest resulting in the tool-chain KeYGenU. By applying KeYGenU to the banking application described in Section 5.6 we provide a proof of concept of our approach (Section 8.4). The advantages and possible limitations of the approach are then discussed in Sections 8.3.2, 8.4.3, and 8.6. The other sections are related work (Section 8.5) and conclusions (Section 8.6).

This chapter is based on the paper [Gladisch et al., 2010] but it has been reduced to the contributions of the author of this thesis.

8.2 Complementary Strengths of the Regarded Techniques

In Section 8.1 we have described the complementary strengths of verification and testing in general. Both approaches should be combined in order to achieve reliable software and in order to optimize the verification and testing process. In this section we describe, by means of simple examples, advantages and disadvantages of CaR tools and coverage guaranteeing tools like VBT tools that are more specific to our tool-chain approach.

Regression Test Oracles

Code that checks whether the result of a test-run is as expected is called *test oracle* (see Section 7.5.2, page 206). A *regression-test oracle* checks if the result is the same as in a previous version of the tested software.

Suppose there exists a well functioning application P. Let *evalExam(int points, int id)* be one of the methods of P returning a boolean value.

—— JAVA (8.1) ————————————————————————

```
1  public class Exam{
2    boolean[] passed;
3    public boolean evalExam(int points, int id){
4      boolean res=false;
5      if(points > 50){
6        res=true;
7      }
8      passed[id] = res;
9      return res;
10  }}
```

———————————————————————————————————— JAVA ——

Suppose that P has no regression test oracles and that P has been changed. Regression testing should be performed to avoid regression faults. A CaR tool (e.g., [Pasternak et al., 2009; Elbaum et al., 2009]) can be used to create regression tests for the system. When executing evalExam(40,2), for example, the CaR tool captures the return value of this method which is false. It then creates a unit test that executes evalExam(40,2) and compares the result with the previously observed value false. If, at the course of changes, the user mistakenly changes Line 4 to res=true;, the generated test will detect the fault as the return value is true and it differs from the previously captured return value false.

Assume now that the user enters a mistake in Line 6 rather than in Line 4, by changing Line 6 to res=false;. Then the generated unit tests do not detect the fault, because the execution of this branch was not captured.

Code Coverage

Using a VBT tool on the very same program produces a unit test suite with a high code coverage, i.e., a test is generated for both execution paths through evalExam. In order to create meaningful tests using the VBT tool, the user has to provide a requirement specification for `evalExam`. In our example we use the following JML requirement specification:

— JAVA + JML (8.2) ————————————————————————

```
1  /*@ public normal_behavior
2      ensures \result==(points>50?true:false);@*/
3  public boolean evalExam(int points, int id){..}
```

————————————————————————————————— JAVA + JML —

Let us assume now that Line 4 has been changed to `res=true;` or that Line 6 has been changed to `res=false;`. In both cases the unit test suite generated by the VBT tool detects the fault.

By contrast, some CaR regression testing tools do not require writing a requirement specification, or even writing unit tests in advance, but there is a coverage problem with using CaR tools – unit tests are created only for the specific program run executed by the user or by a system test.

Testing in Isolation

Suppose the user changes the implementation of the method `evalExam()` by replacing the array `boolean[] passed` by a database management system. Line 8 is replaced by `passedDB.write(id,res);` that updates the database.

— JAVA (8.3) ————————————————————————————

```
1  public boolean evalExam(int points, int id){
2    boolean res=false;
3    if(points > 50){
4      res=true;
5    }
6    passedDB.write(id,res);
7    return res;
8  }
```

————————————————————————————————————— JAVA —

The strength of VBT tools is the generation of test inputs that ensure a high test coverage. The tests, however, are not isolated unit tests because the execution of `evalExam` leads to the execution of `write`.

Some existing CaR tools (e.g., [Saff et al., 2005; Pasternak et al., 2009]) can automatically create unit tests, using mock objects (see Section 8.3.1). This enables to perform unit testing in isolation, which in

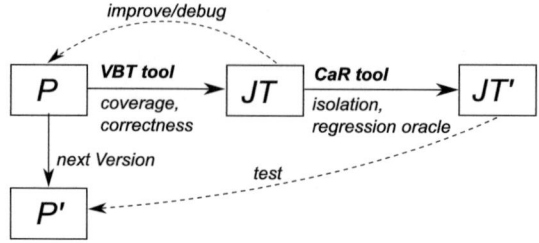

Fig. 8.1. The creation of a tool-chain and its application to unit regression testing

this case means that the generated unit test results in the execution of the method `evalExam` but not of `write`. Instead of calling the method `write` the generated mock object is activated which mimics a subset of input and output behavior of the database.

8.3 The Proposed Approach

We have analyzed the advantages and the problems of verification-based testing (VBT) tools and of capture and replay (CaR) tools separately. VBT tools support the verification process by helping to find software faults. They can generate test cases with high code coverage. These tools, however, usually generate neither mock objects nor regression test oracles that are based on previous program executions. CaR tools are strong at abstracting complicated program behavior and at automatically generating regression-test oracles. The CaR tools, however, can do this only for specific program runs, that have to be provided somehow. In contrast, VBT tools can generate program inputs for distinct program runs.

From this analysis it becomes clear that these kinds of tools should be combined into a tool-chain. Thus, the output of the VBT tool serves as input to the CaR tool, as shown in Figure 8.1. Our approach consists of two steps. In the first one the user tries to verify the program P using a verification tool that supports VBT. When a verification attempt fails, VBT is activated to generate a unit test suite JT for P. The so generated tests help in debugging P and the process is repeated until P is verifiable. When the verification succeeds the VBT tool is activated to generate a test suite JT that ensures coverage of the code of P. The generated test suite consists of one or more executable programs that are provided as input to the CaR tool. Thus, when JT is executed the execution of the code under test is captured. The CaR tool in turn creates another unit test suite – JT'. If the CaR tool replays the observed execution of each test, consequently the high code coverage of JT is preserved by JT'. Furthermore, JT' benefits from the improvements that are gained by using the CaR tool. Depending on the capabilities of the CaR tool this can be the isolation of units and the extension of tests with regression-test oracles. Hence the tool-chain employs the strengths of both kinds of tools involved. The test suite JT' can then be used to regression test P' that is the next development version of P.

8.3.1 Building a Tool-chain

Step I

The goal of this step is to ensure the correctness of the code and to generate the test suite JT that ensure a high execution coverage. We propose to use verification tools with their VBT extensions. Such tools are, e.g., KeY [Engel and Hähnle, 2007; Beckert and Gladisch, 2007], KUnit [Deng et al., 2007], Check'n'Crash [Smaragdakis and Csallner, 2007], the VBT extension of Spec# [Billeter, 2008], or extensions of model checkers [Gargantini et al., 2003; Beyer et al., 2004; Visser et al., 2004] (see Section 7.2). Some of these tools do not generate tests with a high coverage but rather they generate a small number of tests that are likely to reveal faults. Hence, in order to achieve a high coverage such tools have to be adjusted to generate tests also from path conditions of program branch which have been previously verified. One possibility to achieve that is to set the postcondition to false after the successful verification and then to run the VBT tool again.

Step II

The goal of the second step is to further improve the test suite JT using a CaR tool. When JT is executed, the CaR tool executes and captures each path through the method, generating JT', a test suite for the PUT with the same coverage provided by JT. Depending on the used CaR tool, JT' may be a unit test suite supporting isolation or it may be extended with regression-test oracles.

In [Saff et al., 2005], test factoring is described that turns system tests into isolated unit tests by creating mock objects. For the capturing phase a wrapper class is created that records the program behavior to a transcript, and the replay step uses a mock class that reads from the transcript. The approach addresses complications that arise from field access, callbacks, object passing across boundaries, arrays, native method calls, and class loaders. The generation of mock objects is also supported by KUnit. The approaches, however, have different properties because in the latter approach mock objects are created from specifications instead of from runtime executions.

Some VBT tools can generate test oracles from the specifications that are used in the verification process. Such oracles are suitable for regression testing. Yet, not all parts of the system that are executed by JT may be specified. Our approach can be even applied if no test oracles are generated for JT. In this case a CaR tool like Orstra [Xie, 2006] can be used. During the capturing phase, Orstra collects object states to create assertions for asserting behavior of the object states. It also creates assertion that check return values of public methods with non-void returns. The assertions are then checked when the system is modified. In [Elbaum et al., 2009], a CaR approach is presented that creates regression tests from system tests. Components of the exercised system that may influence the behavior of the targeted unit are captured. A test harness is created that establishes the pre-state of the unit that was encountered during system test execution. From that state, the unit is replayed and differences with the recorded unit poststate are detected.

GenUTest [Pasternak et al., 2009] is a CaR tool featuring both capabilities, i.e., the creation of isolated unit tests and the creation of regression-test oracles. It is described in Section 8.4.1.

8.3.2 Advantages and Limitations

We regard our approach from two perspectives. On the one hand, CaR tools can be used to further increase the quality of VBT. On the other hand, CaR tools can benefit from being combined with VBT tools. The VBT generated tests can be used to drive program's execution to ensure the coverage of the whole code. From this perspective our approach can be generalized by allowing general coverage ensuring tools for the first phase. However, for CaR tools, such as [Elbaum et al., 2009; Xie, 2006; Pasternak et al., 2009], it is important that during the capture phase only correct program behavior is observed – and this can be best ensured when a verification tool is used in the first phase.

The approach combines also the limitations of the involved tools. CaR-based regression testing tools can discover changes in the behavior

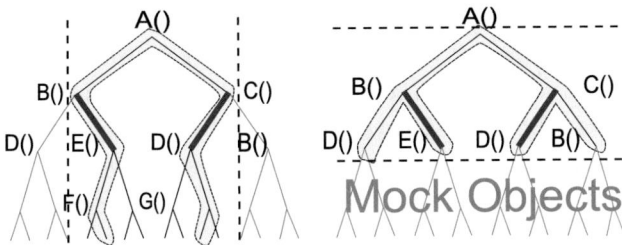

Fig. 8.2. The traditional test selection (left) versus our approach (right)

when a program is modified, but they can not distinguish between intentional and not intentional changes. Another problem occurs with CaR tools that generate mock entities. It is often unclear under what preconditions the behavior of a mock entity is valid when the mock entity is executed in a state not previously observed by the CaR tool. Some advantages and limitations are specific to the particular tools and techniques. So are also the choice of the test target and mock objects. We advise the reader to refer to the referenced publications.

Verification tools are typically applicable to much smaller programs than testing tools. Our approach targets therefore at quality assurance of small systems that are safety or security critical. Building a tool-chain adds complexity to the verification process. We expect, however, a payoff on the workload when the target system is modified and the quality of the software has to be maintained. Most VBT techniques are based on symbolic execution which is a challenging issue. Considering Listing 8.3 of Section 8.2, when symbolic execution reaches Line 8 the source code of `write()` may not be available or it may be too complicated for symbolic execution. Typically, in such situation method contracts that abstract the method call can be provided. Alternatively techniques such as [Tillmann and de Halleux, 2008] can be used that combine symbolic execution and runtime-execution.

Regression testing techniques such as [Harrold et al., 2001], for example, are often concerned with test selection and test prioritization. The goal is to reduce the execution time of the regression test suite and thus to save costs. Graves et al. [Graves et al., 1998] describe test selection techniques for given regression test suites. They reduce the scope of the PUT that is executed by selecting a subset of the test suite. Our approach provides an alternative partitioning of the PUT (Figure 8.2) that can reduce its tested scope and should be considered in combination with test selection techniques. Instead of reducing the number of tests, parts of the program are substituted by mock entities.

Graves et al. state that most regression test selection techniques are not designed to be safe [Graves et al., 1998]. Safe regression test selection techniques guarantee that the selected subset contains all test cases in the original test suite that can reveal regression faults [Graves et al., 1998]. By executing only the unit tests of classes that have been modified a safe and simple selection technique should be obtained. Regression faults that result from interactions between objects of different classes can be detected by unmocked execution where required.

8.4 KeYGenU

We have implemented a concrete tool-chain according to Figure 8.1, called KeYGenU and have applied it to several test cases. In this section we describe the tool GenUTest, and provide an example to demonstrate our ideas.

8.4.1 GenUTest

GenUTest is a prototype tool that generates unit tests [Pasternak et al., 2009]. The tool captures and logs inter-object interactions occurring during the execution of JAVA programs. The recorded interactions are then used to generate JUnit tests and mock-object like entities called mock aspects. These can be used independently by developers to test units in isolation. The comprehensiveness of the generated unit tests depends on the software execution. Software runs covering a high percentage generate in turn unit test with similar code coverage. Hence, GenUTest cannot guarantee a high coverage.

Figure 8.3 presents a high level view of GenUTest's architecture and highlights the steps in each of the three phases of GenUTest: the *capture phase*, the *generation phase*, and the *test phase*. In the capture phase the program is modified to include functionality to capture its execution. When the modified program executes, inter-object interactions are captured and logged. The interactions are captured by utilizing *AspectJ*[1], the most popular *Aspect-Oriented Programming* extension for the JAVA language. The generation phase utilizes the log to generate unit tests and *mock aspects*, mock-object like entities. In the

---

[1] http://www.eclipse.org/aspectj

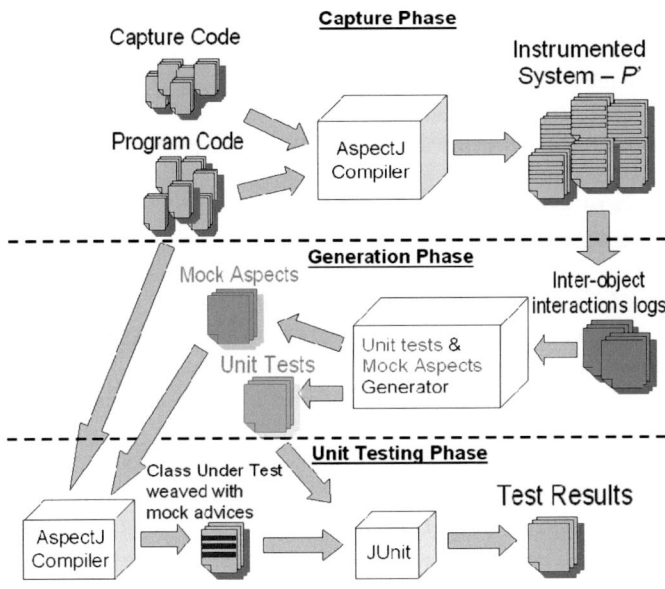

Fig. 8.3. Overview of capture and replay implemented in GenUTest [Pasternak et al., 2009]

test phase, the unit tests are used by the developer to test the code of the program.

8.4.2 A Detailed Example

For our experiments we have applied KeYGenU to the banking software described in Section 5.6. Figure 8.4 presents a part of the banking software that we use as an example to describe KeYGenU in detail.

The first step is to load the banking application into KeY and to select a method for symbolic execution; following the code excerpt in Figure 8.4, this is either `transfer()` or `registerSpendingRule()`. KeY generates a JUnit test suite from the obtained proof tree. It consists of a test method for every execution path of the method under test. Thus, the test suite provides a high test coverage. Figure 8.5 shows one of the generated test methods for testing the method `transfer()`. In Lines 2–4 variables are declared and assigned initial values; Lines 5–9 assign test data to variables and fields; in Line 12 the method under test is executed; and in Line 16 the test oracle, implemented as `subformula5()`, is evaluated.

```
1   /* Copyright (c) 2002 GEMPLUS group. */
2   package banking; import ...;
3   public class Transfers_src {
4    protected MyRuleVector rules=new MyRuleVector();
5    private AccountMan_src accman;
6    ... //field and method declarations
7   /*@ requires true;
8   modifies rules.size(), Rule.nbrules ;
9   ensures ((account <0 || spending_account <0)
10          && (threshold > 0 && period >= 0))==> \result==3;
11  ensures (threshold<=0 && period>=0 && account>=0
12                  && spending_account >=0)==> \result==5;
13  ensures (threshold>0 && period<0 && account>=0
14                  && spending_account>=0) ==> \result==6;
15  ...
16  signals (Exception e) false; @*/
17  public int registerSpendingRule(String date, int account,
18                int threshold, int spending_account, int period) {
19   if (account<0||spending_account<0)        return  3;
20   Account account1 = accman.getRef(account);
21   Account account2 = accman.getRef(spending_account);
22   if ((account1==null)||(account2==null)) return  3;
23   if (threshold <= 0)                       return  5;
24   if (period < 0)                           return  6;
25   Rule rule=new SpendingRule (date,account,
26                  threshold,spending_account,period,accman);
27   ...
28  }
29  /*@ requires true;
30      ensures (amount<=0 ==> \result==1); @*/
31  public int transfer(int from_account,int to_account, int amount){
32   Account fromAccount = accman.getRef(from_account);
33   Account toAccount = accman.getRef(to_account);
34   if(fromAccount!=null && toAccount!=null &&  amount > 0) {
35    if(amount < fromAccount.getBalanceamount()){
36       fromAccount.debit(amount);
37       toAccount.credit(amount);
38       return  0;
39    }else
40       return  1;
41   }
42   return  1;
43  } }//class declaration
```

Fig. 8.4. Excerpt from the banking case study

```
— Java —————————————————————————————————————————————
 1  public void testcode0 () {
 2  /** variable declarations **/
 3  int from_account=0; int to_account=0; int res=0; int _to_account=0;
 4  int _from_account=0; int _amount=0; int amount=0;
 5  Throwable exc=null; Transfers_src o=null;
 6
 7  /** test data initialization **/
 8  int testData0=2; int testData1=2;
 9  o = new Transfers_src();
10  o._setrulesMyRuleVector(new MyRuleVector());
11  o._setaccmanAccountMan_src(new AccountMan_src());
12  from_account=testData0; to_account=testData1; _amnt=amount;
13  _from_account=from_account; _to_account=to_account;exc=null;
14
15  /** method under test **/
16  try {
17    res=o.transfer(_from_account,_to_account,_amnt);
18  } catch (java.lang.Throwable e) { exc=e; }
19
20  /** test oracle **/
21  StringBuffer buffer=new StringBuffer();
22  boolean _oracleResult=subformula5(amount,exc,res,buffer);
23  assertTrue(buffer.toString(),_oracleResult);
24  }
— Java —
```

Fig. 8.5. JUnit test method generated by KeY

This test suite is the data that is exchanged from KeY to GenUTest. It is, however, a fully functioning test suite and should be executed before the continuation of the tool-chain, in order to automatically detect program faults with respect to the JML-specification. In particular, this step turned out to be important because KeY is very good at detecting implicit program branches caused by, e.g., NullPointerExceptions, but on the other hand GenUTest expects the executed code *not* to throw any exception during capturing phase. Thus, we have either extended the specifications, stating that certain fields are non-null, or we simply have removed from the test suite generated by KeY those test method that have detected exceptions.

```java
 1  @Test public void testtransfer1(){
 2    AccountMan_src AccountMan_src_11; MyRuleVector MyRuleVector_8;
 3    TestGeneric0 TestGeneric0_1; Transfers_src Transfers_src_4;
 4    int intRet;
 5
 6    setSection("TestGeneric0",1,2);
 7      TestGeneric0_1 = new TestGeneric0();
 8    setSection("Transfers_src",4,37);
 9      Transfers_src_4= new Transfers_src();
10    setSection("MyRuleVector",40,67);
11      MyRuleVector_8 = new MyRuleVector();
12    setSection("Transfers_src",68,73);
13      Transfers_src_4._setrulesMyRuleVector(MyRuleVector_8);
14    setSection("AccountMan_src",76,129);
15      AccountMan_src_11 = new AccountMan_src();
16    setSection("Transfers_src",132,137);
17      Transfers_src_4._setaccmanAccountMan_src(AccountMan_src_11);
18    setSection("Transfers_src",140,149);
19      intRetVal5 = Transfers_src_4.transfer(2,2,0);
20    assertEquals(intRet,1);
21  }
```

Fig. 8.6. JUnit test method generated by GenUTest

Capturing code of GenUTest is weaved-in into the KeY-generated test methods, such as in Figure 8.5, by running the test suite as an AspectJ application in the Eclipse IDE. After the capturing phase, GenUTest produces another JUnit test suite consisting of test methods like, e.g., in Figure 8.6, and mock aspects such as in Figure 8.7. As expected, the coverage of the KeYgenerated tests is preserved by the GenUTest-generated tests; for instance, changes to any of the return values of the method `registerSpendingRule()` or the method `transfer()` have been detected.

Figure 8.6 presents the test method generated by GenUTest. The method invocations that were observed during the capture phase are replayed in Lines 4-14. GenUTest tries to minimize this code using some static analysis. The calls to `setSection()` are important for choosing the correct mock aspect as explained below. In Line 14 the actual method under test is called and its return value is compared in Line

—— AspectJ ——————————————————————————

```
1   pointcut restriction(): !adviceexecution() &&
2     this(Transfers_src) && !target(Transfers_src);
3   Account around(int param1):call(banking.AccountMan_src.getRef(int))
4                               && args(param1) && restriction() {
5    MockAspectHandler.Section currentSection =
6     MockAspectHandler.getInstance().getClassSection("Transfers_src");
7    if (currentSection.start == 884 && currentSection.end == 905){
8      if (currentSection.statementCounter==1){
9        currentSection.statementCounter++;
10       Account Account_157 = new Account();
11       if(reflectionCompare(param1,1)!=0){ return proceed(param1); }
12       return Account_157;
13   }}.../* commented out case distinctions */...}
```
———————————————————————————— AspectJ ——

Fig. 8.7. Mock aspect generated by GenUTest for the method `getRef()`

15 with the value that was observed during capturing phase. Thus, a regression test is performed.

In our experiments the calls to the methods `getRef()`, `debit()`, `credit()`, and `getBalanceamount()` (see Figure 8.4) were replaced, as expected, by mock aspect invocations, because these methods belong to classes different from the current class `Transfers_src`. For instance, Lines 2-4 in Figure 8.7 match the call to `getRef()` and Lines 7-11 check which occurrence of `getRef` in the call tree is currently processed, as different invocations may yield different return values. Line 11 checks if the given parameter value of `getRef()` has been actually observed during the capturing phase by using the reflection API. If this is not the case, then the original code is invoked with the current parameter value via the AspectJ keyword `proceed`, as shown in Line 11. Otherwise, the previously recorded return value is returned in Line 12, and thus unit testing in isolation is performed.

8.4.3 A Short Evaluation

We have tested KeYGenU on several use cases. It has automatically generated isolated unit-regression tests for classes of a banking application. Using the KeY-generated tests we have found several faults in the application with respect to the provided JML-specification. This result confirms the observations made in [Burdy et al., 2003; du Bousquet et al., 2004] that the available specification was incomplete; e.g., many errors were caused by throwing `Null PointerException` s that should have been excluded by appropriate method preconditions. We have therefore either extended the specification or ignored these error-detecting test cases, as our focus was on regression testing. KeYGenU generated also unit tests for an old version of some software. Then, the unit tests have been executed with newer versions of the software. The discrepancies have been examined to determine if they uncover regression faults. GenUTest generated a test suite that was able to detect changes to any branch of the tested methods, confirming the high test coverage.

Regarding scalability, KeYGenU generates in some cases a huge amount of unit tests. One of the reasons is that GenUTest generates tests not only for the method under test but also for the test code generated by KeY. For instance, the KeY-generated test oracle uses the class `StringBuffer` in order to collect debugging information about the evaluation of the post condition. This in turn resulted in over a hundred tests for the class `StringBuffer`. Also the selection of program paths is not optimized yet. Symbolic execution may lead to too many unwindings of loops producing many tests – some of which may be redundant, i.e., there may be more than one test that exercises the class under test in the same manner. These can be removed using the techniques described in [Xie et al., 2004].

8.5 Related Work

In Section 8.3.1 we described tools representing VBT techniques [Engel et al., 2008; Deng et al., 2007; Smaragdakis and Csallner, 2007; Visser et al., 2004] as well as tools that represent CaR techniques [Pasternak et al., 2009; Saff et al., 2005; Xie, 2006; Elbaum et al., 2009]. In Section 8.3.2 we related our work to test selection and prioritization techniques [Graves et al., 1998; Harrold et al., 2001]. Furthermore, a recent work that also automatically generates regression unit-tests is DiffGen [Taneja and Xie, 2008]. In this approach the PUT is instrumented with additional branches and then a coverage-based test generation tool is used to detect regression faults. In contrast, the approach presented in [Godlin and Strichman, 2009] suggests to use a verification tool for proving an equivalence relation between two version of a program. These approaches differ from ours as they do not use CaR techniques. In [Xie, 2006] the usage of a coverage guaranteeing tool is considered in combination with the CaR tool Orstra. However, the approaches used in [Godlin and Strichman, 2009; Xie, 2006] do not consider the generation of isolated unit tests and they do not provide means to guarantee that during capture phase the observed program behavior is correct.

Besides creating an approach for regression unit testing, our goal was also to investigate the combination of dynamic (runtime execution based) and static (symbolic execution based) analysis tools. Ernst [Nimmer and Ernst, 2001] and Smaragdakis et al. [Smaragdakis and Csallner, 2007] discuss the synergies and differences between static and dynamic analysis. The strength of static analysis is data generality and precision of code coverage, whereas the strength of dynamic analysis is speed of program execution and handling of black-box behavior without providing abstractions. While in [Tillmann and de Halleux, 2008], for example, static and dynamic analysis are combined in a rather coherent way, we suggest a tool-chain approach whose strength is the simplicity of the interface between the tools and their independence. Another tool-chain approach where KeY is used to obtain high code coverage has been realized in [Beckert and Gladisch, 2007]. However, while in [Beckert and Gladisch, 2007] a JML-specification is exchanged between the tools, in the here presented approach a unit test suite is exchanged from the VBT tool to the CaR tool.

8.6 Conclusion and Future Work

We have described an approach for automatic generation of unit tests that can also be used for regression testing. We aim at achieving high coverage of the tested code while testing each unit in isolation. This is accomplished by creating a tool-chain that combines two tools, a verification-based testing (VBT) and a capture and replay (CaR) test generation tool. We first run a VBT tool to generate tests for each path in a given system. This achieves a high coverage of the code, as desired. These tests are then used as input to a CaR tool that turns the tests into truly isolated unit tests by creating mock-object like entities. The advantage of using VBT tools is that the verification process can be used to ensure that only correct behavior is captured by the CaR tool.

To examine our ideas we have implemented KeYGenU a concrete tool- chain consisting of the VBT tool KeY and the CaR tool GenUTest. The tests that we have executed provide a proof of concept. The integration of different tools may, however, cause some additional work. For example, in the case of KeYGenU the fact that both tools have been developed independently caused some difficulties. Running the tools in combination has revealed some faults in each of the tools that have been fixed and that helped to improve both tools. GenUTest creates tests only for methods that return a value and only the returned value is analyzed by the generated regression tests. A considerable improvement would be to handle also void methods, e.g., by analyzing the state of the object on which the method was invoked.

Verification tools, such as KeY, are typically applicable to much smaller programs than testing tools. The scalability of the approach is bound by the scalability of the particular VBT and CaR tools. Our approach targets therefore at quality assurance of small systems that are safety or security critical. Building the proposed tool-chain adds complexity to the verification process. The expected payoff on the workload is, however, when the target system is modified and the quality of the software has to be maintained.

9

Conclusions

State of the Art and Contributions

Deductive verification tools are primarily used to show the correctness of software but they are not specialized for software fault detection. The ability to detect software faults is important to increase the efficiency of software verification. We have shown how a verification tool can be specialized also for software fault detection. We have developed a common approach, theory, and methodology that combines verification, deductive software fault detection, and testing in a unified way. Such combinations existed only in the context of model checking or abstract interpretation but not for the here regarded family of verification techniques. The latter deal with more expressive formalisms and more complex verification goals.

The development of the approach has led us to the discovery of fundamental problems with quantifiers and contract rules that have not been solved before. We have developed novel techniques that handle these problems effectively. We have also shown that dynamic logic with updates and KeY's sequent calculus, which combines FOL theorem proving and symbolic execution, has many other applications than just software verification.

Testing and the usage of program debuggers helps in *finding* faults that were detected deductively, and testing increases the confidence in the correct behavior of software even if the software has been verified. We have developed several test generation technique based on verification and deductive fault detection that have different properties regarding test coverage, the ability to expose faults, and scalability. These techniques can generate specification-based tests, tests with full feasible bounded path coverage, tests with full feasible branch coverage, tests that are guaranteed to find faults, isolated unit tests, and regression tests. We have described the strengths and limitations of these techniques.

Researcher that work either in the field of, verification, model generation, or testing, are often not aware of the challenges in the other respective fields, and they are often not aware of the solutions that the other respective fields may offer. We have studied these fields and explored synergies between them. We hope to have contributed to a better understanding of the problems and possibilities when combining techniques from the different fields and help to bringing these fields and researchers together.

All these techniques have been implemented as prototypes in the KeY tool and their effectiveness or feasibility has been shown. The step from the prototypes to an industrial tool could not be done in the scope of this PhD thesis and remains future work.

In the following paragraphs we summarize the three parts of this thesis in more detail and describe future work.

Part I

This thesis describes novel techniques for extending formal software verification tools with fault detection capabilities. The underlying verification tool in focus of this thesis is the KeY tool which was described in Part I. The KeY tool has been developed during the last 10 year by research groups in Koblenz, Karlsruhe, and Gothenburg (Sweden). Its underlying formalism is Dynamic Logic with a sequent calculus enabling a Hoare-style verification approach. While the details of the presented techniques were specific for the KeY tool we belief that they can also be realized for other verification tools which follow similar paradigms. These tools verify programs on the source code level rather than an abstract representation of the program. Such tools are, for example, VCC [Cohen et al., 2009], Spec# [Barnett et al., 2005], Why/Krakatoa/Caduceus [Filliâtre and Marché, 2007], ESC/Java2 [Chalin et al., 2005], as well as the proof assistants PVS [Owre et al., 1996] and Isabelle/HOL [Wenzel et al., 2008] in some of their applications. Techniques used by such tools are typically symbolic execution or weakest precondition computation, and theorem proving.

Part II

When a program is correct with respect to its specification and annotations such as method contracts, class invariants, and loop invariants are strong enough, then verification tools can prove the correctness of the program usually automatically. The problem is getting to the point where all these conditions are satisfied. Programs and specifications usually have faults and annotations are often not strong enough to close a proof. Due to the semi-decidability of first-order logic it is often not known, if the construction of the proof should be continued or not. An unclosed proof structure does not necessarily mean that a problem exists because continuing the proof attempt may perhaps lead to a successful proof.

Applying the techniques described in Part II of this thesis can help to detect software faults and to interrupt proof attempts which cannot succeed. These techniques reuse information from the verification attempt to reduce the additional computational overhead. By using deduction to conclude the existence of faults also the underlying technology of the verification tools is reused. The result is a symbiosis of verification and fault detection.

In order to deduce the existence of a fault based on an open proof tree two conditions have to be checked: (1) an open proof branch has to be validity preserving and (2) the leaf of the proof branch must have a counterexample. Checking these conditions is hard because condition (1) requires the handling of program abstractions such as method contracts, class invariants, and loop invariants, and condition (2) requires the handling of first-order logic quantifiers. In some cases verification tools generate counterexamples when a verification attempt fails. However, a counterexample does not necessarily imply that the target program has a fault because the problem may be that inappropriate program abstractions were used. This problem is solved by checking the condition (1) for which we have developed a very efficient technique. During experiments with this technique we found that SMT solvers, which are typically used to generate counterexamples, are often not powerful enough to check condition (2). The problem is the handling of quantified formulas in the context of model generation. This is a long-studied problem for which we have developed a new technique that is powerful enough for our needs.

Despite the positive results of our model generation technique for quantified formulas this technique is not yet mature. Future work is to study the heuristics for update construction, increase the automation of the technique, and to extend the approach for handling recursively defined functions. For checking the condition (1) we have developed a very efficient special validity preservation condition. The construction of this condition depends on the heap model used by KeY. Future work is to adapt this technique also to other heap models such as in Boogie [Barnett et al., 2006], where the heap is represented by a function symbol.

Part III

Our approach does not only detect faults but it also provides different information such as a program input, a program execution trace, and an executable test helping the user to find the fault. The tests generated with our approach described in Part III of the thesis can be executed with a program debugger. Using a program debugger enables the user to follow the program execution that reveals a fault and to inspect the program states. The tests are not only important if the existence of a fault was deduced, they are important even if the program verification was successful. A figurative example is that even if engineers have proved that an airplane should have the desired aerodynamic properties, passengers will not be seated in the airplane before it has undergone numerous test flights. In practice it is often very hard or even not practical to apply a formal verification process completely to the program, the compiler, and its environment consisting of software and hardware. These components are, however, engaged when software testing is applied.

The tests generated by the verification-based test generation approach (VBT) benefit from the detailed information contained in a proof tree which is obtained by verification and deductive fault detection. Case distinctions in the program are reflected as branches of the proof tree; these may also be implicit distinctions such as raising of exceptions. The proof tree contains the path conditions of the program paths. Hence, tests derived from the proof tree exhibit a high coverage of the specification and the program code giving the user a higher confidence in the correct functioning of the program. Tests can also be derived from specific branches which are, e.g., guaranteed to contain a fault. We have reused an existing implementation of VBT and modified and extended it with additional techniques. The implementation generates executable JUnit test suites out-of-the-box and is used by research teams for research and teaching.

We have also developed approaches which combine verification and VBT with more traditional testing tools such as black-box testing tools and capture & replay (CaR) tools. The path conditions contained in the proof tree can be exported into a JML specification. Combining the so generated specification with a black-box testing tool, which ensures a certain specification coverage, results in white-box tests. One advantage of this approach is that a clear interface is established between program analysis on the one hand and test generation on the other hand. Another advantage is that both the verification tool and black-box tool can benefit from reusing each other technical capabilities. This is also the case when combining VBT tools with CaR tools. We have built a tool-chain consisting of KeY and the CaR tool GenUTest. The latter uses dynamic program analysis and can transform program runs into isolated unit tests with test oracles which compare old program executions with new ones. KeY on the other hand yields tests with high coverage and *correct execution* if the program is verified. The resulting tool-chain of KeY and GenUTest yields isolated unit tests with high coverage which are ideal for unit regression testing.

The approaches and techniques have been developed almost in the reverse order as presented in this thesis. Starting with approaches for test generation we found that more fundamental problems have to be solved leading to the techniques described in Part II of the thesis. Therefore the implementation of VBT uses a model generator based on Simplify [Detlefs et al., 2005] rather than the model generator developed in Chapter 6. Future work is therefore to apply the new model generator for test data generation. Another future work is to update VBT to handle a wider scope of specification language features used in the verification community. Finally, since the development of black-box testing tools and capture & replay tools is ongoing it would be interesting to build new tool-chains and examine their properties.

References

IEEE standard glossary of software engineering terminology. IEEE-STD 610.12-1990, 1990. (Cited on pages 175 and 181.)

Jean-Raymond Abrial. *The B-Book*. Cambridge University Press, 1996. (Cited on page 5.)

Jean-Raymond Abrial, Stephen A. Schuman, and Bertrand Meyer. A specification language. In *On the Construction of Programs*, pages 343–410. Cambridge University Press, 1980. (Cited on page 73.)

Wolfgang Ahrendt. *Deduktive Fehlersuche in Abstrakten Datentypen*. PhD thesis, Universität Karlsruhe, Fakultät für Informatik, 2001. (Cited on page 144.)

Wolfgang Ahrendt, Andreas Roth, and Ralf Sasse. Automatic validation of transformation rules for Java verification against a rewriting semantics. In Geoff Sutcliffe and Andrei Voronkov, editors, *Proceedings, 12th International Conference on Logic for Programming, Artificial Intelligence and Reasoning, Montego Bay, Jamaica*, volume 3835 of *LNCS*, pages 412–426. Springer, Dec 2005. (Cited on pages 44 and 47.)

Ernst Althaus, Evgeny Kruglov, and Christoph Weidenbach. Superposition modulo linear arithmetic sup(la). In Silvio Ghilardi and Roberto Sebastiani, editors, *Proceedings, Frontiers of Combining Systems, 7th International Symposium, FroCoS 2009, Trento, Italy*, volume 5749 of *LNCS*, pages 84–99. Springer, 2009. (Cited on page 144.)

Thomas Ball and Sriram K. Rajamani. Automatically validating temporal safety properties of interfaces. In *SPIN 2001, Workshop on Model Checking of Software*, volume 2057 of *LNCS*, pages 103–122. Springer, 2001. (Cited on page 136.)

Michael Barnett, Robert DeLine, Manuel Fähndrich, Bart Jacobs, K. Rustan M. Leino, Wolfram Schulte, and Herman Venter. The Spec# programming system: Challenges and directions. In *Verified Software: Theories, Tools, Experiments (VSTTE 2005)*, volume 4171 of *LNCS*, pages 144–152. Springer, 2005. (Cited on pages II, 5, 137, 179, and 238.)

Michael Barnett, Bor-Yuh Evan Chang, Robert DeLine, Bart Jacobs 0002, and K. Rustan M. Leino. Boogie: A modular reusable verifier for object-oriented programs. In Frank S. de Boer, Marcello M. Bonsangue, Susanne Graf, and Willem P. de Roever, editors, *Formal Methods for Components and Objects, 4th International Symposium (FMCO 2005)*, volume 4111 of *LNCS*, pages 364–387. Springer, 2006. (Cited on pages 68, 179, and 240.)

Mike Barnett. The Spec# programming system: An overview. In Gilles Barthe, Lilian Burdy, Marieke Huisman, Jean-Louis Lanet, and Traian Muntean, editors, *Proceedings, Construction and Analysis of Safe, Secure, and Interoperable Smart Devices (CASSIS)*, volume 3362 of *LNCS*, pages 27–48. Springer, 2004. (Cited on page 73.)

Clark Barrett and Cesare Tinelli. CVC3. In Werner Damm and Holger Hermanns, editors, *Proceedings, Computer Aided Verification, 19th International Conference, CAV 2007*, volume 4590 of *LNCS*, pages 298–302. Springer, 2007. (Cited on pages 6, 8, 11, 98, 140, and 143.)

Peter Baumgartner, Alexander Fuchs, and Cesare Tinelli. Implementing the model evolution calculus. *International Journal on Artificial Intelligence Tools*, 15(1):21–52, 2006. (Cited on page 144.)

Bernhard Beckert. A dynamic logic for the formal verification of Java Card programs. In I. Attali and T. Jensen, editors, *Java on Smart Cards: Programming and Security. Revised Papers, Java Card 2000, International Workshop, Cannes, France*, volume 2041 of *LNCS*, pages 6–24. Springer, 2001. (Cited on page 34.)

Bernhard Beckert and Christoph Gladisch. White-box testing by combining deduction-based specification extraction and black-box testing. In Yuri Gurevich and Bertrand Meyer, editors, *Proceedings, Tests and Proofs, First International Conference, TAP 2007, Zurich, Switzerland*, volume 4454 of *LNCS*, pages 207–216. Springer, 2007. (Cited on pages V, 13, 14, 16, 18, 110, 175, 180, 210, 225, and 235.)

Bernhard Beckert and Vladimir Klebanov. Must program verification systems and calculi be verified? In *Proceedings, 3rd International Verification Workshop (VERIFY), Workshop at Federated*

Logic Conferences (FLoC), Seattle, USA, pages 34–41, 2006. (Cited on pages 44 and 47.)

Bernhard Beckert and André Platzer. Dynamic logic with non-rigid functions: A basis for object-oriented program verification. In U. Furbach and N. Shankar, editors, *Proceedings, International Joint Conference on Automated Reasoning, IJCAR, Seattle, USA*, volume 4130 of *LNCS*, pages 266–280. Springer, 2006. (Cited on pages 47, 93, and 94.)

Bernhard Beckert, Reiner Hähnle, and Peter H. Schmitt, editors. *Verification of Object-Oriented Software: The KeY Approach*, volume 4334 of *LNCS*. Springer, 2007. (Cited on pages II, 5, 9, 21, and 22.)

Markus Bender. Generating efficient test oracles from specifications. Minor thesis, Universität Koblenz-Landau, Institute of Computer Science, August 2010. (Cited on page 208.)

Frédéric Benhamou and Frédéric Goualard. Universally quantified interval constraints. In Rina Dechter, editor, *Principles and Practice of Constraint Programming - CP 2000, 6th International Conference, Singapore*, volume 1894 of *LNCS*, pages 67–82. Springer, 2000. (Cited on page 144.)

Dirk Beyer, Adam J. Chlipala, Thomas A. Henzinger, Ranjit Jhala, and Rupak Majumdar. Generating tests from counterexamples. In *Proceedings, 26th Annual International Conference on Software Engineering, ICSE 2004*. IEEE Computer Society Press, 2004. (Cited on pages 180, 219, and 225.)

Jürg Billeter. Counterexample execution. Master project report, ETH Zürich, Department of Computer Science, August 2008. (Cited on pages 179 and 225.)

Jasmin Christian Blanchette. Relational analysis of (co)inductive predicates, (co)algebraic datatypes, and (co)recursive functions. In Gordon Fraser and Angelo Gargantini, editors, *Proceedings, Tests and Proofs, 4th International Conference, TAP 2010, Málaga, Spain*, volume 6143 of *LNCS*, pages 117–134. Springer, 2010. (Cited on page 144.)

Egon Börger and Robert F. Stärk. *Abstract State Machines. A Method for High-Level System Design and Analysis*. Springer, 2003. (Cited on page 5.)

Aaron R. Bradley, Zohar Manna, and Henny B. Sipma. What's decidable about arrays? In E. Allen Emerson and Kedar S. Namjoshi, editors, *Proceedings, Verification, Model Checking, and Abstract Inter-*

pretation, 7th International Conference, VMCAI 2006, Charleston, SC, USA, volume 3855, pages 427–442. Springer, 2006. (Cited on pages 8 and 143.)

Achim D. Brucker and Burkhart Wolff. Test-sequence generation with HOL-TestGen with an application to firewall testing. In Yuri Gurevich and Bertrand Meyer, editors, *Tests and Proofs, First International Conference, TAP 2007, Zurich, Switzerland*, volume 4454 of *LNCS*, pages 149–168. Springer, 2007. (Cited on page 179.)

Richard Bubel, Reiner Hähnle, and Benjamin Weiss. Abstract interpretation of symbolic execution with explicit state updates. In Frank de Boer, Marcello M. Bonsangue, and Eric Madelaine, editors, *Post Conf. Proc. 6th International Symposium on Formal Methods for Components and Objects, FMCO*, volume 5751 of *LNCS*, pages 247–277. Springer-Verlag, 2009. (Cited on pages 7 and 110.)

Lilian Burdy, Antoine Requet, and Jean-Louis Lanet. Java applet correctness: A developer-oriented approach. In Keijiro Araki, Stefania Gnesi, and Dino Mandrioli, editors, *FME 2003: Formal Methods, International Symposium of Formal Methods Europe, Pisa, Italy*, volume 2805 of *LNCS*, pages 422–439. Springer, 2003. (Cited on pages 133 and 234.)

Cristian Cadar, Vijay Ganesh, Peter M. Pawlowski, David L. Dill, and Dawson R. Engler. EXE: Automatically generating inputs of death. *ACM Trans. Inf. Syst. Secur.*, 12(2):10:1–10:38, 2008. (Cited on pages 9 and 179.)

Patrice Chalin, Joseph R. Kiniry, Gary T. Leavens, and Erik Poll. Beyond assertions: Advanced specification and verification with JML and ESC/Java2. In Frank S. de Boer, Marcello M. Bonsangue, Susanne Graf, and Willem P. de Roever, editors, *Formal Methods for Components and Objects, 4th International Symposium, FMCO 2005, Amsterdam, The Netherlands*, volume 4111 of *LNCS*, pages 342–363. Springer, 2005. (Cited on pages II, 5, 73, and 238.)

Yanping Chen, Robert L. Probert, and D. Paul Sims. Specification-based regression test selection with risk analysis. In Darlene A. Stewart and J. Howard Johnson, editors, *Proceedings of the 2002 conference of the Centre for Advanced Studies on Collaborative Research (CASCON)*, pages 175 – 182. IBM Press, 2002. (Cited on page 219.)

Zhiqun Chen. *Java Card Technology for Smart Cards: Architecture and Programmer's Guide*. Java Series. Addison-Wesley, 2000. (Cited on page 21.)

Yoonsik Cheon, Antonio Cortes, Gary T. Leavens, and Martine Ceberio. Integrating random testing with constraints for improved efficiency and diversity. In *Proceedings of the Twentieth International Conference on Software Engineering & Knowledge Engineering (SEKE'2008), San Francisco, CA, USA*, pages 861–866. Knowledge Systems Institute Graduate School, 2008. (Cited on pages 210, 215, and 218.)

Koen Claessen and Hans Svensson. Finding counter examples in induction proofs. In Bernhard Beckert and Reiner Hähnle, editors, *Proceedings, Tests and Proofs, Second International Conference, TAP 2008, Prato, Italy*, volume 4966 of *LNCS*, pages 48–65. Springer, 2008. (Cited on pages 108, 136, and 137.)

Edmund M. Clarke, Orna Grumberg, Somesh Jha, Yuan Lu, and Helmut Veith. Counterexample-guided abstraction refinement. In *Proceedings, Computer Aided Verification, 12th International Conference, CAV 2000, Chicago, IL, USA,*, volume 1855 of *LNCS*, pages 154–169. Springer, 2000. (Cited on pages 7 and 139.)

L. A. Clarke. A system to generate test data and symbolically execute programs. *IEEE Trans. Softw. Eng.*, 2:215–222, May 1976. ISSN 0098-5589. (Cited on pages 9 and 179.)

Ernie Cohen, Markus Dahlweid, Mark A. Hillebrand, Dirk Leinenbach, Michal Moskal, Thomas Santen, Wolfram Schulte, and Stephan Tobies. VCC: A practical system for verifying concurrent C. In Stefan Berghofer, Tobias Nipkow, Christian Urban, and Makarius Wenzel, editors, *Proceedings, Theorem Proving in Higher Order Logics, 22nd International Conference, TPHOLs 2009, Munich, Germany*, volume 5674 of *LNCS*, pages 23–42. Springer, 2009. (Cited on pages II, 5, 73, and 238.)

David R. Cok and Joseph Kiniry. ESC/Java2: Uniting ESC/Java and JML. In Gilles Barthe, Lilian Burdy, Marieke Huisman, Jean-Louis Lanet, and Traian Muntean, editors, *Proceedings, Construction and Analysis of Safe, Secure, and Interoperable Smart Devices, International Workshop, CASSIS 2004, Marseille, France*, volume 3362 of *LNCS*, pages 108–128. Springer, 2004. (Cited on page 179.)

P. Cousot and R. Cousot. Abstract interpretation frameworks. *Journal of Logic and Computation*, 2(4):511–547, August 1992. (Cited on page 7.)

Leonardo Mendonça de Moura and Nikolaj Bjørner. Efficient E-Matching for SMT solvers. In Frank Pfenning, editor, *Proceedings, Automated Deduction - CADE-21, 21st International Conference on Automated Deduction, Bremen, Germany*, volume 4603 of *LNCS*, pages 183–198. Springer, 2007. (Cited on page 143.)

Leonardo Mendonça de Moura and Nikolaj Bjørner. Z3: An efficient SMT solver. In C. R. Ramakrishnan and Jakob Rehof, editors, *Tools and Algorithms for the Construction and Analysis of Systems, 14th International Conference, TACAS 2008, Held as Part of the Joint European Conferences on Theory and Practice of Software, ETAPS 2008, Budapest, Hungary*, volume 4963 of *LNCS*, pages 337–340. Springer, 2008. (Cited on pages III, 6, 8, 11, 98, 140, and 143.)

David Déharbe and Silvio Ranise. Satisfiability solving for software verification. *STTT*, 11(3):255–260, 2009. (Cited on page 140.)

Xianghua Deng, Jooyong Lee, and Robby. Bogor/Kiasan: A k-bounded symbolic execution for checking strong heap properties of open systems. In *Proceedings, 21st IEEE/ACM International Conference on Automated Software Engineering (ASE 2006), Tokyo, Japan*, pages 157–166. IEEE Computer Society, 2006a. (Cited on page 137.)

Xianghua Deng, Robby, and John Hatcliff. Kiasan: A verification and test-case generation framework for Java based on symbolic execution. In *Proceedings, Leveraging Applications of Formal Methods, Second International Symposium, ISoLA 2006, Paphos, Cyprus*, pages 137–137. IEEE Computer Society, 2006b. (Cited on pages 9 and 179.)

Xianghua Deng, Robby, and John Hatcliff. Kiasan/KUnit: Automatic test case generation and analysis feedback for open object-oriented systems. In *TAICPART-MUTATION '07: Proceedings of the Testing: Academic and Industrial Conference Practice and Research Techniques - MUTATION*, pages 3–12, Washington, DC, USA, 2007. IEEE Computer Society. (Cited on pages 179, 225, and 234.)

David Detlefs, Greg Nelson, and James B. Saxe. Simplify: a theorem prover for program checking. *J. ACM*, 52(3):365–473, 2005. (Cited on pages 5, 8, 143, 183, and 241.)

E. W. Dijkstra. *A Discipline of Programming*. Prentice-Hall, Englewood Cliffs, NJ, 1976. (Cited on pages III and 33.)

Lydie du Bousquet, Yves Ledru, Olivier Maury, Catherine Oriat, and Jean-Louis Lanet. Case study in JML-based software validation. In *19th IEEE International Conference on Automated Software Engi-*

neering, ASE 2004, Linz, Austria, pages 294–297. IEEE Computer Society, 2004. (Cited on pages 133 and 234.)

Bruno Dutertre and Leonardo de Moura. The Yices SMT solver. Technical report, Computer Science Laboratory, SRI International, 2006a. `http://yices.csl.sri.com/tool-paper.pdf`. Visited December 2010. (Cited on pages 6, 8, 11, 98, 140, and 143.)

Bruno Dutertre and Leonardo Mendonça de Moura. A fast linear-arithmetic solver for DPLL(T). In Thomas Ball and Robert B. Jones, editors, *Proceedings, Computer Aided Verification, 18th International Conference, CAV 2006, Seattle, WA, USA*, volume 4144 of *LNCS*, pages 81–94. Springer, 2006b. (Cited on pages 140 and 143.)

Sebastian G. Elbaum, Hui Nee Chin, Matthew B. Dwyer, and Matthew Jorde. Carving and replaying differential unit test cases from system test cases. *IEEE Trans. Software Eng.*, 35(1):29–45, 2009. (Cited on pages 220, 222, 226, and 234.)

Margaret A. Ellis and Bjarne Stroustrup. *The Annotated C++ Reference Manual*. Addison-Wesley, 1990. (Cited on page 73.)

Christian Engel. Verification based test case generation. Master's thesis, University of Karlsruhe, Institut für Theoretische Informatik, 2006. (Cited on pages 183, 195, 199, 204, 205, 207, 216, and 217.)

Christian Engel and Reiner Hähnle. Generating unit tests from formal proofs. In Yuri Gurevich and Bertrand Meyer, editors, *Proceedings, Tests and Proofs, First International Conference, TAP 2007, Zurich, Switzerland*, volume 4454 of *LNCS*, pages 169–188. Springer, 2007. (Cited on pages 13, 175, 180, 183, 207, 216, 217, and 225.)

Christian Engel, Christoph Gladisch, Vladimir Klebanov, and Philipp Rümmer. Integrating verification and testing of object-oriented software. In Bernhard Beckert and Reiner Hähnle, editors, *Proceedings, Tests and Proofs, Second International Conference, TAP 2008, Prato, Italy*, volume 4966 of *LNCS*, pages 182–191. Springer, 2008. (Cited on pages V, 14, 18, 180, and 234.)

Jean-Christophe Filliâtre and Claude Marché. The Why/Krakatoa/-Caduceus platform for deductive program verification. In Werner Damm and Holger Hermanns, editors, *Proceedings, Computer Aided Verification, 19th International Conference, CAV 2007, Berlin, Germany,*, volume 4590 of *LNCS*, pages 173–177. Springer, 2007. (Cited on pages II, 5, 137, and 238.)

Angelo Gargantini, Elvinia Riccobene, and Salvatore Rinzivillo. Using SPIN to generate testsfrom asm specifications. In Egon Börger,

Angelo Gargantini, and Elvinia Riccobene, editors, *Proceedings, Abstract State Machines, Advances in Theory and Practice, 10th International Workshop, ASM 2003, Taormina, Italy*, volume 2589 of *LNCS*, pages 263–277. Springer, 2003. (Cited on pages 180, 219, and 225.)

Yeting Ge and Leonardo Mendonça de Moura. Complete instantiation for quantified formulas in satisfiabiliby modulo theories. In Ahmed Bouajjani and Oded Maler, editors, *Proceedings, Computer Aided Verification, 21st International Conference, CAV 2009, Grenoble, France*, volume 5643 of *LNCS*, pages 306–320. Springer, 2009. (Cited on pages 8 and 143.)

Yeting Ge, Clark W. Barrett, and Cesare Tinelli. Solving quantified verification conditions using satisfiability modulo theories. *Ann. Math. Artif. Intell.*, 55(1-2):101–122, 2009. (Cited on page 140.)

Ian P. Gent, Peter Nightingale, and Kostas Stergiou. QCSP-Solve: A solver for quantified constraint satisfaction problems. In Leslie Pack Kaelbling and Alessandro Saffiotti, editors, *Proceedings of the Nineteenth International Joint Conference on Artificial Intelligence, Edinburgh, Scotland, UK (IJCAI 2005)*, pages 138–143. Professional Book Center, 2005. (Cited on page 144.)

Silvio Ghilardi. Quantifier elimination and provers integration. *Electr. Notes Theor. Comput. Sci.*, 86(1):22–34, 2003. (Cited on pages 8 and 145.)

Martin Giese. Incremental closure of free variable tableaux. In Rajeev Goré, Alexander Leitsch, and Tobias Nipkow, editors, *Proceedings, Automated Reasoning, First International Joint Conference, IJCAR 2001, Siena, Italy*, volume 2083 of *LNCS*, pages 545–560. Springer, 2001. (Cited on pages 143 and 148.)

Christoph Gladisch. Verification-based test case generation for full feasible branch coverage. In Antonio Cerone and Stefan Gruner, editors, *Proceedings, Sixth IEEE International Conference on Software Engineering and Formal Methods, SEFM 2008, Cape Town, South Africa*, pages 159–168. IEEE Computer Society, 2008a. (Cited on pages V, 13, 14, 17, 104, 136, 180, 190, and 192.)

Christoph Gladisch. Could we have chosen a better loop invariant or method contract? In Catherine Dubois, editor, *Proceedings, Tests and Proofs, Third International Conference, TAP 2009, Zurich, Switzerland*, volume 5668 of *LNCS*, pages 74–89. Springer, 2009. (Cited on pages V, 13, 17, and 104.)

Christoph Gladisch. *Extending KeY for the Verification of C Programs.* VDM Verlag Dr. Mueller e.K., 2008b. (Cited on page 18.)

Christoph Gladisch. Test data generation for programs with quantified first-order logic specifications. In Alexandre Petrenko, Adenilso da Silva Simão, and José Carlos Maldonado, editors, *Proceedings, Testing Software and Systems - 22nd IFIP WG 6.1 International Conference, ICTSS 2010, Natal, Brazil,* volume 6435 of *LNCS,* pages 158–173. Springer, 2010a. (Cited on pages V, 11, 17, and 142.)

Christoph Gladisch. Satisfiability solving and model generation for quantified first-order logic formulas. In Bernhard Beckert and Claude Marché, editors, *Conf. Post. Proc., Formal Verification of Object-Oriented Software International Conference, FoVeOOS 2010, Paris, France,* volume 6528 of *LNCS.* Springer, 2010b. (Cited on pages V, 11, 17, and 142.)

Christoph Gladisch. How C differs from Java for symbolic program execution. In Hendrik Tews, editor, Proceedings, C/C++ Verification Workshop, Oxford, United Kingdom, Technical Report ICIS-R07015, Radboud University Nijmegen, Juli 2007. (Cited on page 18.)

Christoph Gladisch. Verification-based test case generation with loop invariants and method specifications. In Bernhard Beckert und Reiner Hähnle, editors, Tests and Proofs: Papers Presented at the Second International Conference, TAP 2008, Prato, Italy, Reports of the Faculty of Informatics 5/2008, University of Koblenz-Landau, April 2008c. (Cited on page 18.)

Christoph Gladisch, Shmuel Tyszberowicz, Bernhard Beckert, and Amiram Yehudai. Generating regression unit tests using a combination of verification and capture & replay. In Gordon Fraser and Angelo Gargantini, editors, *Proceedings, Tests and Proofs, 4th International Conference, TAP 2010, Málaga, Spain,* volume 6143 of *LNCS,* pages 61–76. Springer, 2010. (Cited on pages V, 16, 17, 180, and 221.)

Benny Godlin and Ofer Strichman. Regression verification: Proving the equivalence of similar programs. In Ahmed Bouajjani and Oded Maler, editors, *Proceedings, Computer Aided Verification, 21st International Conference, CAV 2009, Grenoble, France,* volume 5643 of *LNCS,* pages 63–68. Springer, 2009. (Cited on pages 234 and 235.)

James Gosling, Bill Joy, and Guy Steele. *The Java Language Specification.* Addison-Wesley, 1996. (Cited on page 37.)

Susanne Graf and Hassen Saïdi. Construction of abstract state graphs with PVS. In Orna Grumberg, editor, *Computer Aided Verification, 9th International Conference, CAV '97, Haifa, Israel*, volume 1254 of *LNCS*, pages 72–83. Springer, 1997. (Cited on page 7.)

Todd L. Graves, Mary Jean Harrold, Jung-Min Kim, Adam A. Porter, and Gregg Rothermel. An empirical study of regression test selection techniques. In *Proceedings of the 20th international conference on Software engineering, ICSE 1998, Kyoto, Japan*, pages 188–197. ACM, 1998. (Cited on pages 219, 220, 227, 228, and 234.)

Bhargav S. Gulavani, Thomas A. Henzinger, Yamini Kannan, Aditya V. Nori, and Sriram K. Rajamani. SYNERGY: a new algorithm for property checking. In Michal Young and Premkumar T. Devanbu, editors, *Proceedings of the 14th ACM SIGSOFT International Symposium on Foundations of Software Engineering, FSE 2005, Portland, Oregon, USA*, pages 117–127. ACM, 2006. (Cited on page 136.)

John V. Guttag, James J. Horning, and Jeannette M. Wing. The Larch family of specification languages. *IEEE Software*, 2(5):24–36, 1985. (Cited on page 73.)

David Harel. Dynamic logic. In D. Gabbay and F. Guenthner, editors, *Handbook of Philosophical Logic*, volume II: Extensions of Classical Logic, chapter 10, pages 497–604. Reidel, Dordrecht, 1984. (Cited on pages II, 9, 21, 33, 34, 93, and 94.)

David Harel, Dexter Kozen, and Jerzy Tiuryn. *Dynamic Logic*. The MIT Press, London, England, 2000. (Cited on page 21.)

Mary Jean Harrold, James A. Jones, Tongyu Li, Donglin Liang, Alessandro Orso, Maikel Pennings, Saurabh Sinha, S. Alexander Spoon, and Ashish Gujarathi. Regression test selection for Java software. In *Proceedings of the 2001 ACM SIGPLAN Conference on Object-Oriented Programming Systems, Languages and Applications, OOPSLA 2001, Tampa, Florida*, pages 312–326. ACM, 2001. (Cited on pages 219, 220, 227, and 234.)

Thomas A. Henzinger, Ranjit Jhala, Rupak Majumdar, and Grégoire Sutre. Lazy abstraction. *SIGPLAN Not.*, 37:58–70, January 2002. ISSN 0362-1340. (Cited on page 136.)

C. A. R. Hoare. An axiomatic basis for computer programming. *Commun. ACM*, 12(10):576–580, October 1969. (Cited on pages II, 3, and 34.)

Matthias Horbach and Christoph Weidenbach. Deciding the inductive validity of for all there exists* queries. In Erich Grädel and Reinhard

Kahle, editors, *Proceedings, Computer Science Logic, 23rd international Workshop, CSL 2009, 18th Annual Conference of the EACSL, Coimbra, Portugal,*, volume 5771 of *LNCS*, pages 332–347. Springer, 2009a. (Cited on page 144.)

Matthias Horbach and Christoph Weidenbach. Decidability results for saturation-based model building. In Renate A. Schmidt, editor, *Proceedigns Automated Deduction - CADE-22, 22nd International Conference on Automated Deduction, Montreal, Canada*, volume 5663 of *LNCS*, pages 404–420. Springer, 2009b. (Cited on page 144.)

Daniel Jackson. Alloy: a lightweight object modelling notation. *ACM Trans. Softw. Eng. Methodol.*, 11(2):256–290, 2002. (Cited on page 5.)

KeY-Home. KeY project homepage. At `http://www.key-project.org/`. (Cited on pages 2 and 5.)

James C. King. A new approach to program testing. In Clemens Hackl, editor, *IBM Symposium: Programming Methodology*, volume 23 of *LNCS*, pages 278–290. Springer, 1974. (Cited on pages 9 and 179.)

James C. King. Symbolic execution and program testing. *Communications of the ACM*, 19(7):385–394, 1976. (Cited on pages II, 9, 47, 56, and 179.)

Joseph R. Kiniry, Alan E. Morkan, and Barry Denby. Soundness and completeness warnings in ESC/Java2. In *Proc. Fifth Int. Workshop Specification and Verification of Component-Based Systems*, pages pp. 19–24, 2006. (Cited on page 143.)

Gerwin Klein, June Andronick, Kevin Elphinstone, Gernot Heiser, David Cock, Philip Derrin, Dhammika Elkaduwe, Kai Engelhardt, Rafal Kolanski, Michael Norrish, Thomas Sewell, Harvey Tuch, and Simon Winwood. seL4: Formal verification of an OS kernel. *Communications of the ACM*, 53(6):107–115, Jun 2010. (Cited on page 6.)

Nikolai Kosmatov, Bruno Legeard, Fabien Peureux, and Mark Utting. Boundary coverage criteria for test generation from formal models. In *Proceedings, Software Reliability Engineering, Saint-Melo, France*, pages 139–150. IEEE Computer Society, 2004. (Cited on page 210.)

G. Leavens and Y. Cheon. Design by contract with JML, 2006. `http://www.eecs.ucf.edu/~leavens/JML//jmldbc.pdf`. Visited December 2010. (Cited on page 73.)

Gary T. Leavens, Erik Poll, Curtis Clifton, Yoonsik Cheon, Clyde Ruby, David Cok, Peter Müller, Joseph Kiniry, Patrice Chalin, and

Daniel M. Zimmerman. *JML Reference Manual. Draft Revision 1.200*, September 2009. (Cited on page 73.)

David Lee and Mihalis Yannakakis. Online minimization of transition systems (extended abstract). In *Proceedings of the twenty-fourth annual ACM symposium on Theory of computing, STOC '92*, pages 264–274. ACM, 1992. (Cited on page 136.)

Bruno Legeard, Fabien Peureux, and Mark Utting. Automated boundary testing from Z and B. In Lars-Henrik Eriksson and Peter A. Lindsay, editors, *Proceedings, FME 2002: Formal Methods - Getting IT Right, International Symposium of Formal Methods Europe, Copenhagen, Denmark*, volume 2391 of *LNCS*, pages 21–40. Springer, 2002. (Cited on page 210.)

Dirk Leinenbach and Thomas Santen. Verifying the Microsoft Hyper-V Hypervisor with VCC. In Ana Cavalcanti and Dennis Dams, editors, *Proceedings, FM 2009: Formal Methods, Second World Congress, Eindhoven, The Netherlands*, volume 5850 of *LNCS*, pages 806–809. Springer, 2009. (Cited on page 6.)

K. Rustan M. Leino and Francesco Logozzo. Loop invariants on demand. In Kwangkeun Yi, editor, *Proceedings, Programming Languages and Systems, Third Asian Symposium, APLAS 2005, Tsukuba, Japan*, volume 3780 of *LNCS*, pages 119–134. Springer, 2005. (Cited on page 136.)

T. Mackinnon, S. Freeman, and P. Craig. Endo-testing: unit testing with mock objects. In *Extreme Programming Examined*, pages 287–301. Addison-Wesley, 2001. ISBN 0-201-71040-4. (Cited on page 220.)

Christophe Meudec. ATGen: automatic test data generation using constraint logic programming and symbolic execution. *Softw. Test., Verif. Reliab.*, 11(2):81–96, 2001. (Cited on pages 9 and 179.)

Bertrand Meyer. Design by contract: Making object-oriented programs that work. In *Proceedings, TOOLS 1997: 25th International Conference on Technology of Object-Oriented Languages and Systems, Melbourne, Australia*, page 360. IEEE Computer Society, 1997. (Cited on pages II, 3, and 73.)

Bertrand Meyer. *Eiffel: The Language*. Prentice-Hall, 1991. (Cited on page 73.)

Michał Moskal. *Satisfiability Modulo Software*. PhD thesis, University of Wrocław, 2009. (Cited on page 143.)

Michal Moskal, Jakub Lopuszanski, and Joseph R. Kiniry. E-matching for fun and profit. *Electr. Notes Theor. Comput. Sci.*, 198(2):19–35, 2008. (Cited on pages 98, 140, and 143.)

Peter Müller. *Modular Specification and Verification of Object-Oriented Programs*. PhD thesis, FernUniversität Hagen, 2002. (Cited on page 74.)

Robert Nieuwenhuis, Albert Oliveras, Enric Rodríguez-Carbonell, and Albert Rubio. Challenges in satisfiability modulo theories. In Franz Baader, editor, *Term Rewriting and Applications, 18th International Conference, RTA 2007, Paris, France*, volume 4533 of *LNCS*, pages 2–18. Springer, 2007. (Cited on pages 98 and 140.)

Jeremy W. Nimmer and Michael D. Ernst. Static verification of dynamically detected program invariants: Integrating Daikon and ESC/Java. *Electr. Notes Theor. Comput. Sci.*, 55(2):255–276, 2001. (Cited on page 235.)

S. Owre, S. Rajan, J.M. Rushby, N. Shankar, and M.K. Srivas. PVS: Combining specification, proof checking, and model checking. In Rajeev Alur and Thomas A. Henzinger, editors, *Proceedings, Computer Aided Verification, 8th International Conference, CAV '96, New Brunswick, NJ, USA*, volume 1102 of *LNCS*, pages 411–414. Springer, 1996. (Cited on pages II, 5, and 238.)

Parasoft. JTest. `http://www.parasoft.com/jtest`. Visited December 2010. (Cited on page 210.)

Corina S. Pasareanu, Peter C. Mehlitz, David H. Bushnell, Karen Gundy-Burlet, Michael R. Lowry, Suzette Person, and Mark Pape. Combining unit-level symbolic execution and system-level concrete execution for testing NASA software. In Barbara G. Ryder and Andreas Zeller, editors, *Proceedings of the ACM/SIGSOFT International Symposium on Software Testing and Analysis, ISSTA 2008, Seattle, WA, USA*, pages 15–26. ACM, 2008. (Cited on pages 9 and 179.)

B. Pasternak, S. Tyszberowicz, and A. Yehudai. GenUTest: a unit test and mock aspect generation tool. *Journal on Software Tools for Technology Transfer (STTT)*, 11(4):273–290, 2009. (Cited on pages V, 220, 222, 223, 226, 228, 229, and 234.)

Wolfgang Paul. Towards a worldwide verification technology. In Bertrand Meyer and Jim Woodcock, editors, *Proceedings, Verified Software: Theories, Tools, Experiments, First IFIP TC 2/WG*

2.3 Conference, VSTTE 2005, Zurich, Switzerland, volume 4171 of *LNCS*, pages 19–25. Springer, 2005. (Cited on page 6.)

André Platzer. An object-oriented dynamic logic with updates. Master's thesis, University of Karlsruhe, Institut für Theoretische Informatik, September 2004. (Cited on pages 47, 93, and 94.)

Caferra Ricardo, Leitsch Alexander, and Peltier Nicolas. *Automated Model Building*, volume 31 of *Applied Logic Series*. Springer, 2004. (Cited on page 144.)

Philipp Rümmer. A sequent calculus for integer arithmetic with counterexample generation. In Bernhard Beckert, editor, *Proceedings of 4th International Verification Workshop in connection with CADE-21, VERIFY'07, Bremen, Germany*, volume 259 of *CEUR Workshop Proceedings*. CEUR-WS.org, 2007. (Cited on pages 44, 60, 92, 96, and 118.)

Philipp Rümmer. *Calculi for Program Incorrectness and Arithmetic*. PhD thesis, Chalmers University of Technology and Göteborg University, Department of Computer Science and Engineering, 2008. (Cited on pages 44, 53, 55, 60, and 135.)

Philipp Rümmer and Muhammad Ali Shah. Proving programs incorrect using a sequent calculus for Java dynamic logic. In Yuri Gurevich and Bertrand Meyer, editors, *Proceedings, Tests and Proofs, First International Conference, TAP 2007, Zurich, Switzerland*, volume 4454 of *LNCS*, pages 41–60. Springer, 2007. (Cited on pages 136 and 143.)

David Saff, Shay Artzi, Jeff H. Perkins, and Michael D. Ernst. Automatic test factoring for Java. In David F. Redmiles, Thomas Ellman, and Andrea Zisman, editors, *Proceedings, 20th IEEE/ACM International Conference on Automated Software Engineering, ASE 2005, Long Beach, CA, USA*, pages 114–123. ACM, 2005. (Cited on pages 220, 223, 225, and 234.)

Wolfram Schulte, X Songtao, Jan Smans, and Frank Piessens. A glimpse of a verifying C compiler (extended abstract). In *C/C++ Verification Workshop*, 2007. (Cited on page 137.)

Koushik Sen, Darko Marinov, and Gul Agha. CUTE: a concolic unit testing engine for C. In Michel Wermelinger and Harald Gall, editors, *Proceedings of the 10th European Software Engineering Conference held jointly with 13th ACM SIGSOFT International Symposium on Foundations of Software Engineering, 2005, Lisbon, Portugal (ESEC/SIGSOFT FSE)*, pages 263–272. ACM, 2005. (Cited on pages 9 and 179.)

Yannis Smaragdakis and Christoph Csallner. Combining static and dynamic reasoning for bug detection. In Yuri Gurevich and Bertrand Meyer, editors, *Proceedings, Tests and Proofs, First International Conference, TAP 2007, Zurich, Switzerland*, volume 4454 of *LNCS*, pages 1–16. Springer, 2007. (Cited on pages 179, 225, 234, and 235.)

Michael J. Spivey. *The Z notation : a reference manual (2nd Edition)*. Prentice Hall, 1992. (Cited on pages 5 and 73.)

Norihisa Suzuki and David Jefferson. Verification decidability of Presburger array programs. *J. ACM*, 27(1):191–205, 1980. (Cited on page 81.)

Petar Tahchiev, Felipe Leme, Vincent Massol, and Gary Gregory. *JUnit in Action, Second Edition*. Manning Publications Co., 2010. (Cited on page 183.)

Kunal Taneja and Tao Xie. DiffGen: Automated regression unit-test generation. In *Proceedings, 23rd IEEE/ACM International Conference on Automated Software Engineering, ASE 2008, L'Aquila, Italy*. IEEE Computer Society, 2008. (Cited on page 234.)

Nikolai Tillmann and Jonathan de Halleux. Pex-white box test generation for .NET. In Bernhard Beckert and Reiner Hähnle, editors, *Proceedings, Tests and Proofs, Second International Conference, TAP 2008, Prato, Italy*, volume 4966 of *LNCS*, pages 134–153. Springer, 2008. (Cited on pages 9, 179, 227, and 235.)

Isabel Tonin. Verifying the mondex case study - the KeY approach. Technical Report ISSN: 1432-7864, Fakultät für Informatik (Fak. f. Informatik) Institut für Theoretische Informatik (ITI), 2007. (Cited on page 6.)

Kerry Trentelman. Proving correctness of JavaCard DL taclets using Bali. In B. Aichernig and B. Beckert, editors, *Proceedings, Third IEEE International Conference on Software Engineering and Formal Methods, SEFM 2005, Koblenz, Germany*. IEEE Computer Society, 2005. (Cited on pages 44 and 47.)

H. van Vliet. *Software Engineering: Principles and Practice (2nd ed.)*. John Wiley & Sons, Inc., 2000. ISBN 0-471-97508-7. (Cited on page 219.)

Dries Vanoverberghe, Nikolaj Bjørner, Jonathan de Halleux, Wolfram Schulte, and Nikolai Tillmann. Using dynamic symbolic execution to improve deductive verification. In Klaus Havelund, Rupak Majumdar, and Jens Palsberg, editors, *Proceedings, Model Checking Software, 15th International SPIN Workshop, Los Angeles, CA,*

USA, volume 5156 of *LNCS*, pages 9–25. Springer, 2008. (Cited on page 179.)

Willem Visser, Corina S. Pasareanu, and Sarfraz Khurshid. Test input generation with Java PathFinder. In George S. Avrunin and Gregg Rothermel, editors, *Proceedings of the ACM/SIGSOFT International Symposium on Software Testing and Analysis, ISSTA 2004, Boston, Massachusetts, USA*, pages 97–107. ACM, 2004. (Cited on pages 180, 219, 225, and 234.)

Joe Walnes, Henri Tremblay, and Leonardo Mesquita. Objenesis. `http://objenesis.googlecode.com/svn/docs/index.html`. Visited December 2010. (Cited on page 205.)

Benjamin Weiß. Predicate abstraction in a program logic calculus. In Michael Leuschel and Heike Wehrheim, editors, *Proceedings, Integrated Formal Methods, 7th International Conference, IFM 2009, Düsseldorf, Germany*, volume 5423 of *LNCS*, pages 136–150. Springer, 2009. (Cited on pages 7 and 110.)

Makarius Wenzel, Lawrence C. Paulson, and Tobias Nipkow. The Isabelle Framework. In Otmane Aït Mohamed, César Muñoz, and Sofiène Tahar, editors, *Proceedings, Theorem Proving in Higher Order Logics, 21st International Conference, TPHOLs 2008, Montreal, Canada*, volume 5170 of *LNCS*, pages 33–38. Springer, 2008. (Cited on pages II, 5, 179, and 238.)

T. Xie, D. Marinov, and D. Notkin. Rostra: A framework for detecting redundant object-oriented unit tests. In *Proceedings, 19th IEEE International Conference on Automated Software Engineering, ASE 2004, Linz, Austria*, pages 196–205. IEEE Computer Society, 2004. (Cited on page 234.)

Tao Xie. Augmenting automatically generated unit-test suites with regression oracle checking. In Dave Thomas, editor, *Proceedings, ECOOP 2006 - Object-Oriented Programming, 20th European Conference, Nantes, France*, volume 4067 of *LNCS*, pages 380–403. Springer, 2006. (Cited on pages 220, 226, 234, and 235.)

Tao Xie, Darko Marinov, Wolfram Schulte, and David Notkin. Symstra: A framework for generating object-oriented unit tests using symbolic execution. In *Proceedings, Tools and Algorithms for the Construction and Analysis of Systems (TACAS), Edinburgh, UK*, volume 3440 of *LNCS*, pages 365–381. Springer, 2005. (Cited on pages 9 and 179.)

zEx. Extreme Programming. `http://www.extremeprogramming.org`. Visited December 2010. (Cited on page 178.)

Jian Zhang and Hantao Zhang. Extending finite model searching with congruence closure computation. In Bruno Buchberger and John A. Campbell, editors, *Proceedings, Artificial Intelligence and Symbolic Computation, 7th International Conference, AISC 2004, Linz, Austria*, volume 3249 of *LNCS*, pages 94–102. Springer, 2004. (Cited on page 144.)

Jian Zhang, Chen Xu, and Xiaoliang Wang. Path-oriented test data generation using symbolic execution and constraint solving techniques. In *Proceedings, 2nd International Conference on Software Engineering and Formal Methods, SEFM 2004, Beijing, China*, pages 242–250. IEEE Computer Society, 2004. (Cited on pages 9 and 179.)

Index

Numbers of pages on which notions are defined are typeset in bold face; if a whole section is dedicated to discussing a notion or concept, the page numbers of that section are typeset in italics.